SO SHORT
A TIME

Books by BARBARA GELB

SO SHORT A TIME

O'NEILL *(with Arthur Gelb)*

SO SHORT A TIME

A Biography of John Reed
and Louise Bryant

BARBARA GELB

W · W · NORTON & COMPANY · INC ·

NEW YORK

FIRST EDITION

Library of Congress Cataloging in Publication Data
Gelb, Barbara.
    So short a time.
    1. Reed, John, 1887–1920.   2. Bryant, Louise,
1890–1936.   I. Title.
HX84.R4G4   070'.92'4   [B]   73–6630
ISBN 0–393–07478–1

1 2 3 4 5 6 7 8 9 0

For Arthur
and Michael and Peter
with love

SO SHORT
A TIME

Chapter One

LOUISE BRYANT TRULLINGER greeted her twenty-eighth birthday on December 5, 1915, in silent dismay. The day was cold and cloudy, typical of the long Oregon winter. But it was the fact of her age, not the weather, that distressed her. Louise had an obsessive image of herself as a romantic heroine. She had always believed she was destined for a life of worldly glamor. And she was sure that her talents and personal endowments were equal to this goal. To reach it while still young was central to the dream. Girlish looking as she was, she had no trouble in concealing her true age; not even her husband knew it. Nevertheless, she felt that time was pressing her. She was unaware that within two weeks she would be poised for an adventure that would transform her life. Within two years she would be the wife of a celebrated journalist and the lover of the man who would be America's greatest playwright. She would be on her way as a journalist herself, and be in Russia at the moment it shook the world.

To Louise's acquaintances in the Portland of 1915, it seemed she had a good life. They would not have understood or sympathized with her compulsion to press on to something bigger.

She had been married for six years to a handsome, intelligent, successful man. She was slender and small-boned with vividly pretty Irish features—reddish-brown hair, a pert nose, mischievous mouth, and blue-gray eyes

9

set widely apart in a heart-shaped face. Childless by choice, she was free to pursue her interest in art, politics, and writing. She had collected a small group of friends from Portland's artists, writers, and political activists, who shared her advanced views.

The Portland in which she lived was, for its day, a fairly cosmopolitan city, hospitable to culture and tolerant of liberal political ideas (provided they were only ideas). The city's climate was invigorating and its scenery spectacular, and Louise, sensitive to nature, was highly appreciative of Portland's mountain, forest, and river views.

If Louise had been in love with her husband, her life in Portland would probably have seemed as stimulating and enjoyable at twenty-eight as it had at twenty-two, and her dream of a bigger life might have faded. But she no longer loved her husband.

The man she had married, Paul Trullinger, was thirty-four, blond-haired, blue-eyed, with a long, aristocratic nose, and a small moustache. He belonged to a solid, middle-class family and he pursued a solid, middle-class career, but he was not the complete conformist. Although he had allowed his family to dissuade him from taking up painting as a career (an uncle, John Trullinger, had never achieved more than second-rate success as an artist), Paul painted as a hobby. In addition, he collected art, jewelry, and antique furniture. As a further gesture of separation from his conventional family, he altered the pronunciation of his name from "*Trull*-inger" to "*Troo*-linger."

He earned his living as a dentist, having associated himself with a leading Portland practitioner named John Chance, and practiced successfully, but with minimum enthusiasm for the profession or for fellow dentists.

Paul shared Louise's interest in literature, though not theater. And he had to be a little more circumspect in his choice of friends than Louise, for it was the socially prominent residents of Portland Heights and the West Hills who formed the backbone of his practice. Even so, Paul rarely took the trouble to veil his ideas on controversial subjects, laughing off the snubs he sometimes drew from those of his patients he saw socially. For Paul regarded himself as a free thinker and something of a bohemian and quietly endorsed Louise's radical political views and espousal of the suffrage cause. When he and Louise first met, he was making his unconventional home on a houseboat in the Wilamette River. Louise, also living on a houseboat, was his neighbor.

Now he and Louise lived more conventionally in a modest shingle and clapboard house in a good neighborhood. It had a pleasant garden, was surrounded by large firs, overlooked the Wilamette, and on clear days had a view of snow-capped Mount Tabor. There was a railroad spur about fifty yards behind the house used for an electric commuter train between Portland and nearby communities. To Louise, whose stepfather had been a railroad man, the proximity of the spur was nostalgic rather than disturbing.

Louise had grown up in a small frontier town in Nevada, where her family had led a rough and spartan existence. While she was apt to romanticize her early family life, she was sincerely disinterested in material comfort. The house on Riverwood Road provided her with more luxury than she required. Louise, with Paul's approval, held a job as the society editor of a newspaper called the *Spectator;* she rented a small studio in downtown Portland, where she could work at her creative writing— mostly poetry; and she had an occasional love affair, which Paul, true to his image as a free thinker, accommodatingly pretended not to notice. Lacking a passionate or

11

jealous disposition, he believed that infidelity, if discreet, was permissible in a wife, as well as a husband.

Louise, understandably, did not get on very well with Paul's conservative relatives and family friends. The women, particularly, resented her freedom. The most charitable of them thought her, at best, flighty. But it was not only the women who mistrusted her. One of Paul's close friends, a newspaperman named Dean Collins, thought Paul had made an unfortunate marriage. Although, like most men, he found Louise attractive, he considered her obsessively self-centered. "She was a girl who would use anybody and anything to further her own ambition," Collins once said.

Bored with Paul's complaisance, finding little satisfaction in casual affairs with other men, Louise tried to convince herself that politics and poetry could fill her life. But her poems went unpublished and her political forays —mostly stumping in small, midwestern towns for the cause of womens' suffrage—merely confirmed her growing sense that she was living in a backwater, that her life was insufferably provincial and circumscribed.

Some of her Portland friends had lived in New York and still made occasional visits east, and they spoke of the artistic and political ferment taking place in Greenwich Village. They described the rebellious young midwesterners and New Englanders who were flocking to the Village and finding outlets for their talents and ideas with avant garde theater groups such as the Washington Square Players, and Socialist publications like the *Masses*. In Greenwich Village rents were cheap, marriage was regarded as an arbitrary convention, and women with careers were the rule rather than the exception.

The vest-pocket bohemia of Portland, dominated by the Portland Art Association and the Little Club, appeared pallid as Louise listened to descriptions of Greenwich Village from her friends, Carl and Helen Walters. Carl Walters was a well-known landscape painter, lithographer, and ceramic artist, who had visited colleagues in the Village. Louise admired him, but wondered at his willingness to live in Portland out of touch with the mainstream of life and art, when many of his friends and acquaintances were thriving in the Village. Her own longing for New York grew.

Louise, at twenty-eight, made up her mind that she had to leave Portland. Aside from discontent with her marriage and her milieu, Louise's concern about her age amounted to something close to panic. Her husband believed her to have been still in her teens when he married her. She had dropped only three years from her true age in 1915 (she was gradually to drop more) and claimed to be twenty-five. It was an unnecessary, if innocent deceit, in view of her youthful appearance, but it held a kind of magical significance for her. Twenty-five, she felt, was still young enough to start a new life.

It was instinctive with Louise to use a man to help her achieve an objective. Never obviously flirtatious, but always feminine, Louise treated the men she liked with a candor that appealed to their intellect. She had absolute confidence in her ability to attract a man, and the man she wanted at this particular moment happened to have become accessible. He had arrived in Portland, heralded by the local press, the day before her birthday.

Louise acted more on impulse than on calculation. What she wanted was a temporary friend and protector, someone to take her away from the Portland she had not the courage to leave on her own, someone to introduce her to Greenwich Village.

The man she selected was John Reed. Reed, who

lived in Greenwich Village, was visiting his mother in his native Portland. Louise asked the Walters, who were friends of Reed, to introduce them at a small dinner party, and they readily agreed.

Louise had set her sights audaciously high. Although only twenty-eight himself, Reed was a figure of international stature and had been pursued on two continents by women considerably more glamorous than Louise.

Reed was the *enfant terrible* of American journalism. Two years before, at twenty-six, he had established his reputation with a stunning series of dispatches about the Mexican War. His own daring and quixotic participation in the conflict, as much as the vivid copy he filed, were responsible for the high regard in which he was held. He was not only the brilliant young journalist, but the brave and reckless adventurer who had managed to make friends with the Mexican guerilla leader, Pancho Villa. Now he was back from covering the war in Eastern Europe. Between assignments, Reed had had time to become a champion of the labor movement in the East. To some of his admirers, this evidence of his courage and willingness to take personal risks was even more impressive than his reportorial talent. And the gossip about his love affair with a wealthy, older woman, who was still pursuing him, had reached as far as Portland.

Reed was a Harvard man. He was on intimate terms with diplomats, labor leaders, writers, and artists. And, in spite of his predatory mistress, he was still unmarried.

All this was a matter of more or less public information, and Louise, as an aspiring journalist and active radical, had followed Reed's career with more than casual interest. For her meeting with Reed, she armed herself with such additional bits of personal detail as his handful of Portland friends could supply: He was emotional and recklessly generous. He had a quick eye for a pretty girl. He was easily touched by a hard luck story. He was always unhappy and restless in Portland; deeply fond of his widowed mother, he nevertheless found it difficult to be with her, for their viewpoints clashed on almost every subject. He had nothing in common with those friends of his mother he was obliged, out of filial duty, to see.

That he was as vulnerable as Louise could have wished is evident from Reed's own words, written to a friend in New York the day after he arrived in Portland: "I have been here one day. It is awful beyond words. Mother is so kind, so loving, so absolutely helpless from my point of view. I don't feel as if I could talk to a single person here. . . . I wish I were home!"

Reed's discontent vanished a few days later. The Walters had set the date for their dinner party, but Louise did not have to wait until then to meet Reed. They were introduced by a mutual acquaintance at one of the artists' meeting places where Louise often dropped in. Reed was instantly attracted.

Louise, for her part, was thrilled to find Reed as personable as he was celebrated. Six feet tall, curly-haired, green-eyed, with a generous mouth and pugnacious chin, he could look by turns the raffish adventurer and the melancholy poet. A flamboyant, uninhibited, often witty conversationalist, he had a candid opinion about everything and his throbbing enthusiasm for his pet subjects was irresistible. Examined in retrospect, his ideas sometimes seemed grandiose, undigested, or simplistic; but Louise, even if she had had the maturity to criticize them, was not disposed to do so. She had gained Reed's attention and awakened his sympathy. Her fantasy had become fact.

Louise told Reed of her ambition to write, of her ad-

15

miration for the causes close to his heart. They discussed the war in Europe, the imminence of prohibition, President Wilson's marriage, and his reception of a petition for women's suffrage signed by one million women (Louise among them).

Reed, unsophisticated about women in spite of his previous involvements, could hardly contain his joyful surprise that Louise was not only beautiful, but intellectual. By comparison with many of the self-involved, narcissistic women of Reed's circle, Louise seemed refreshingly extroverted. They met again a day later, this time by arrangement. They exchanged more ideas and confidences, and Louise hinted at the unhappiness of her marriage. Reed accompanied her to her studio, where, diffidently, she showed him her unpublished poetry. Reed, too, wrote poetry, and he thought hers fine. She listened to the speech he would make on December 19 to the Civic League. She thought it fine.

Within a few days they were lovers. Louise's studio was their meeting place. Reed, in the joyous spontaneity of his new passion, made rough and playful love to Louise—at times, to her delight, leaving marks on her body.

She fussed over him in a burst of maternal solicitude that was not characteristic of her. Reed, whose health had never been robust, caught cold; she fed him hot milk and honey. Enchanted, Reed characterized her ministrations as "chivalrous." Louise demurred. Chivalry, she pointed out, was disinterested courtesy, and her feelings for Reed were not at all disinterested. Reed talked to her of his future hopes and plans, of the truly fine work he hoped to do. Moodily striking one of the romantic poses he sometimes assumed, he told her, "I've reached the limit of my fighting strength; one more battle will bust me."

When, finally, Reed and Louise arrived at the Walters's house for the dinner at which they were to have been introduced, Carl and Helen guessed that they were already in love. Though they made a public show of being only casually acquainted, Louise later confessed to Helen that she and Reed were having a love affair.

Reed, airily dismissing the fact that Louise was encumbered with a husband, took what he regarded as the honorable course, and asked Louise to come with him to New York. A divorce from Paul could be arranged later, but that was just a detail. He and Louise were committed to each other. Triumphantly, he wrote to the friend to whom, two weeks earlier, he had complained of the dreariness of his Portland visit: "I think I've found Her at last. She's wild, brave and straight—and graceful and lovely to look at. In this spiritual vacuum, this unfertilized soil, she has grown (how, I can't imagine) into an artist. She is coming to New York to get a job—with me, I hope. I think she's the first person I ever loved without reservation."

Louise, if not yet as deeply in love as Reed, was excited enough about her conquest and the promise of a new life to believe herself equally committed.

But eager as she was to establish herself quickly in New York, she could not bring herself to take the leap without a bit of soul searching. Her conscience began to nag over the about-to-be-abandoned Paul. She decided, reluctantly, to let Reed return to New York by himself after Christmas, when his stay with his mother ended. She would then explain things to Paul and join Reed a few days later.

She sought out a friend and companion-in-arms in the suffrage movement, Sara Bard Field—not so much to have the older woman's advice, as to receive reassurance and justification. Sara Field had herself left her husband to elope with another man.

As a prominent suffragist, Sara Field made frequent lecture tours in the Midwest, and was sometimes joined by Louise when the cause brought her to Portland and neighboring towns. At the moment of Louise's crisis, Sara Field happened to be staying at Portland's famous luxury hotel, the Multnomah, whose name out-of-towners found impossible to pronounce, and whose beds were furnished with eiderdown pillows. A woman of fiery political convictions, she was also a passionate romanticist and sentimentalist. Her friendships, as well as her oratory, tended to swim in bathos. Louise was "her very own little girl" and her spirit gave Sara Field "the sense of wings." Their intimate conversations dealt with "things of Beauty and of Longing." Years later, her flair for the florid undiminished, she wrote to Louise recalling her visit:

"I think of your coming to me at the Multnomah with the tremulous, wistful story of your love for Jack, of your heart-ache over all it would mean to the other Boy who loved you, of your insatiable need to feel your wings against the world! How I understood and responded. Had I not trod the same path, so bitter yet so luring that no suffering could make one turn back?"

Bolstered by Sara Field's rhetoric, Louise kissed Reed goodbye at the Portland railroad station on December 29. Reed had not shaken off his cold in spite of Louise's ministrations, and she cautioned him to stay away from open windows on the train. She hated to see him ill, she said, for she wanted everything in the world to be nice for him. They had agreed that Louise would take the next

18

three days to tidy her affairs and that she would leave Portland by train on January 2 for the four-day journey, joining Reed in New York on the sixth. She made her way home through the frosty afternoon, stopping off for a wistful look at her studio. The Irish janitor, who called her "Rosie," because she reminded him of "Sweet Rosie O'Grady," greeted her.

"Rosie, you look like a little gray bird, but I think lately you are a kinda wild little gray bird," he said.

"Gray birds are really like all other little birds," Louise archly replied. "Sometimes they seem wild when they are only happy, just as they sing because they have the grace of loving much."

"Well, I guess you love that big fellah, Rosie," the janitor said.

Louise found it difficult to sleep that night, and with dawn breaking, she sat down to write Reed a letter, first stoking her little bedroom stove until its sides glowed. "I think it is the only warm thing left in Portland," she wrote. "This evening when I came home the streets were all slippery with ice and now when the first light of day is coming through my window the world seems quite frozen. This is all as it should be—silly old town—it had your glowing presence here for weeks without appreciating it—now a capricious old winter has turned it to ice as soon as you are gone.

"I cannot explain why I write this. I know I have to talk with you—in my thoughts—and because the night is so empty without you. Wonderful man—I know there isn't another soul anywhere so free and so exquisite and so strong! Dear imitator of elephant's and camel's and giraffe's kisses, I have just looked at my brand. It is quite black! I can't write anymore. I want you too much—all of a sudden—dear. Goodnight."

Chapter Two

LOUISE'S LETTER reached Reed at his apartment at 42 Washington Square a day after his return to New York. Reed was impatient to see Louise and eager to show her off to his friends, but he was also frantically busy with anti-war activities. A sworn pacifist, he was always ready to fight—with words. He and his friends deplored the pro-war sentiment that was sweeping America, and maintained that the national Preparedness for War with Germany was being misdirected. Reed was also in the vanguard of the labor movement. Until now he had found little or no difficulty in selling his ideas to magazines. They were happy to print what Reed wanted to say. His pro-labor sentiments were accepted in intellectual circles. And he could still denounce the injustice of the war—it was, as yet, a European war—with relative impunity. But with his accusations against American capitalism and America's national heroes, in the face of America's possible involvement in the war, he was beginning to tread dangerous ground.

Reed was approaching the most important decision of his life. He did not yet see clearly that he would soon be forced to choose between journalism and propaganda, but he did sense that his personal commitment was subtly shifting emphasis.

Always inclined toward introspection, Reed recognized his own volatility. "Some men seem to get their direction early, to grow naturally and with little change to the thing they are to be," he wrote in a personal memoir not long after he met Louise.

"I have no idea what I shall be or do one month from now. Whenever I have tried to become some one thing, I have failed; it is only by drifting with the wind that I have found myself, and plunged joyously into a new role. I have discovered that I am only happy when I'm working hard at something I like. I never stuck long at anything I didn't like, and now I couldn't if I wanted to."

Reed's undisciplined nature was, at once, his most appealing characteristic and his most serious defect. He was born into and grew up in a milieu always sharply divided between conformity and rebellion. His maternal grandfather was a pioneer turned tycoon; his grandmother was a spoiled, willful, determined nonconformist whose wealth and charm enabled her to have her cake and eat it. His mother was a conventional matron, his father a businessman turned visionary.

From early childhood Reed had the choice of two family traditions to follow: wealthy respectability or hazardous nonconformity. Throughout most of his childhood and all during his adult life, Reed invariably chose not to conform.

Prolonged seizures of illness and physical weakness forced Reed, as a boy, to spend much time with his own thoughts and made him timid in his contacts with children of his own age. Defensiveness was the cause of his first rebellion.

"The beginning of my remembered life," he once wrote, "was a turmoil of imaginings—formless perceptions of beauty, which broke forth in voluminous verses, sensations of fear, of tenderness, of pain. Then came a period of intense emotion, in which I endowed certain girls with

21

the attributes of Guinevere, and had a vision of Galahad and the Sangrael in the sky over the school football field. I felt sure I was going to be a great poet and novelist."

There was much in his environment to feed this vision. He was born John Silas Reed, nicknamed Jack, on October 20, 1887, in Portland. It was a city that had been carved out of the Oregon forests only forty-two years earlier. His birth took place in the home of his maternal grandmother, an impressive estate called Cedar Hills, that had a view of snow-topped mountains to the east and north.

Reed remembered Cedar Hills as "a lordly gray mansion modelled on a French chateau, with its immense park, its formal gardens, lawns, stables, green-houses and glass grape arbor, the tame deer among the trees."

His grandfather, Henry Green, who had died two years before John Reed's birth, had sailed around the Horn in 1853, landing in Astoria on the Oregon coast and moving on, three years later, to Portland. Having arrived about ten years after the original pioneer builders of that city—the men who had already founded the steamship lines, laid down the railroad track, and opened the banks —he quickly took over what was left in the way of industrial power. By the late 1860s Green and his brother, John, were in control of Portland's gaslight, waterworks, and ironworks. After his death in 1885, Green's widow, Charlotte, continued to live at Cedar Hills in the grand manner. Impatient with what she regarded as the narrow-mindedness and extreme social conservatism of Portland in the 1880s, Charlotte contrived to hold on to her position of social prominence, while flouting convention in her manner of dress and the selection of friends when it pleased her. Periodically, when Portland's stuffiness oppressed her, she traveled abroad.

Her daughter, Margaret, one of four children, was married soon after Henry Green's death to a young businessman from the East recently settled in Portland named Charles Jerome Reed. Margaret and C.J., as he was always called, were more sober-minded than Charlotte, more decorous, and more conscious of their social obligations to the community. They were warmly welcomed into the circle of Portland's elite.

C.J.'s business enterprises were prosperous enough to maintain the Reeds in a household in downtown Portland that included a nursemaid for Jack and his younger brother, Harry, and several house servants. Reed retained an impression of his "gay young mother and father" surrounded by "a crowd of gay young people." But the gaiety was within the conventions of Portland's stringent propriety. Margaret was intolerant of any breach; she once rebuked a nursemaid for allowing her little Jack to be kissed by a girl from a neighborhood a cut below her own.

Reed, too young to be aware of this snobbery, continued to live in an insulated, fairy-tale world, abetted by the household's backstairs lore furnished by the servants who were predominantly Chinese. "They brought ghosts and superstitions into the house," he remembered, "and the tang of bloody feuds among themselves, strange idols and foods and drink, strange customs and ceremonies." They inspired him with a longing to visit the Orient that he never outgrew.

One of Reed's childhood heroes, who planted an early seed of wanderlust in his mind, was an uncle, Ray Green, who, like Charlotte, rebelled against the conventional mold. The stories he told when he returned from trips abroad seemed to Reed to be the quintessence of romance. "He played at coffee-planting in Central Amer-

23

ica," Reed recalled, "mixed in revolutions and sometimes blew in, tanned and bearded and speaking 'spigotty' like a mestizo. Once the tale ran that he had helped to lead a revolution that captured Guatemala for a few brief days, and was made Secretary of State; the first thing he did was to appropriate the funds of the National Treasury to give a grand state ball, and then he declared war on the German Empire—because he had flunked his German course in college! Later he went out to the Philippines as a volunteer in the Spanish War—and the tale of how he was made King of Guam is still told with shouts of mirth by the veterans of the Second Oregon."

In his periods of semi-invalidism, Reed inevitably fed his imagination on books. He read indiscriminately, devouring *Lorna Doone,* the works of Mark Twain and Bill Ney and Webster's Unabridged Dictionary with equal ardor. But his favorite reading was history, particularly medieval history. At the age of nine, he made up his mind to be a writer, and began a comic history of the United States.

In the same year his parents placed him and his brother in the Portland Academy, a private day school. Reed was eager to learn at first, but soon found himself bored with formal education. Rebelling deliberately for the first time, he slid through his studies, not bothering to earn more than passing grades in any but a few subjects that briefly stimulated him—elementary chemistry. English poetry, and composition. He was sophisticated enough to be offended by the shallowness of his teachers, whom he later characterized as "men and women whose chief qualification is that they can plough steadily through a dull round of dates, acts, half-truths and rules for style, without questioning, without interpreting, and without seeing how ridiculously unlike the world their teachings are." Reed continued to derive his education from reading outside school hours, racing through anything he could get hold of, from the sensational and popular Marie Corelli, to Scott, Stevenson, and Sir Thomas Mallory.

Because of his physical weakness and small stature—he started growing late—he was unable to hold his own among his schoolmates and other boys of the neighborhood. The only sport at which he was competent—at which, in fact, he excelled—was swimming. In his eleventh year, the focal point of his illness became a weak kidney. There seemed no cure for the condition, and for the next six years he suffered recurrent attacks of pain that kept him bedridden for periods of a week or more at a time. Frightened of rough physical contact of any kind, he miserably faced the fact that he was a coward. "I would sneak out over the back fence to avoid boys who were 'laying' for me," he later recalled. "Sometimes I fought, when I couldn't help myself, and sometimes even won; but I preferred to be called a coward rather than fight. I hated pain. My imagination conjured up horrible things that would happen to me, and I simply ran away.

"One time, when I was on the editorial board of the school paper, a boy I was afraid of warned me not to publish a joking paragraph I had written about him—and I didn't."

Treated with a mixture of contempt and grudging tolerance by the other boys, Reed defensively intellectualized his cowardice by flouting the rigid codes of honor and conduct that governed his contemporaries. He flaunted the fact that he could not be neatly labeled as either brave or altogether cowardly, either manly or sissified, either ashamed or unashamed.

His bravado carried him through his first sixteen

25

years, but not happily. His father sent him, at 16, to a small, rather clannish boarding school in New Jersey, called Morristown, to prepare him for Harvard. C.J., dissatisfied with his own formal education, had long before selected Harvard for both of his sons. Reed's kidney condition had abruptly ceased to trouble him in his sixteenth year. He had grown tall, and his parents' friends complimented them on his good looks. Happier and more hopeful than he had felt during most of his childhood, Reed went East eagerly and was not disappointed.

"Boarding school, I think, meant more to me than anything in my boyhood," Reed later wrote. "Among these strange boys I came as a stranger, and I soon found out they were willing to accept me at my own value. I was in fine health. The ordered life of the community interested me, I was impressed by its traditional customs and dignities, school patriotism, and the sense of a long-settled and established civilization, so different from the raw, pretentious West."

Reed's verses and stories were published in the school paper. He played football and ran the quarter-mile successfully. He had a fight or two and held his own. He joined his friends in the usual schoolboy escapades of sneaking out of his dorm at night to look for adventure in the town. And, as he put it, "with the school social butterflies, I 'fussed' girls in the town, and was not laughed at." Busy, happy, with lots of friends, he expanded into self-confidence. Without really trying, he had found himself.

Harvard, which he entered in the fall of 1906, was a shock. During his first year there he very nearly lost himself again. He became painfully conscious that he knew hardly a soul in the university and that it was not as easy to pick friends from among the more than 700 members of the freshman class as it had been at boarding school, which had a student body of only sixty.

"For the first three months it seemed to me," he later said, "as if every one of the 700 had friends but me. I was thrilled with the immensity of Harvard, its infinite opportunities, its august history and traditions—but desperately lonely.

"Fellows passed me in the Yard, shouting gaily to one another. I saw parties off to Boston Saturday night, whooping and yelling on the back platform of the street car, and they passed hilariously singing under my window in the early dawn. Athletes and musicians and writers and statesmen were emerging from the ranks of the class. The Freshman clubs were forming. And I was out of it all."

Reed nearly made the freshman rowing crew, only to be dropped from the squad just before its first race. He acquired a nodding acquaintance with numerous classmates, but when they became involved in various extracurricular activities that he found himself either unable or unwilling to join, they dropped him. One classmate with whom he hit it off agreed to room with him in his sophomore year, then abruptly backed out.

Reed could not seem to find his niche, did not know how to conform to his classmates' idea of "the right sort." And, having been snubbed, he in turn became the snubber. He had acquired one intimate friend, a Jewish boy.

"He was a shy, rather melancholy person," Reed recalled. "We were always together, we two outsiders. I became irritated and morbid about it—it seemed I would never be part of the rich splendor of college life with him around—so I drew away from him. . . . It hurt him very much, and it taught me better. Since then he has forgiven it, and done wonderful things for me, and we are friends."

Reed's second year at Harvard was better. He was elected an editor of two college newspapers and began acquiring friends among his classmates; several already showed signs of future distinction. Two of his new friends were Robert Hallowell and Walter Lippmann, who, soon after graduation, helped to launch *The New Republic*. Hallowell, who was from Denver, also distinguished himself as a painter. (His portrait of Reed, one of his best known works, is hung at Harvard.) Lippmann, two years Reed's junior, was the indulged, only child of a prosperous New York City clothing manufacturer. Unlike Reed, Lippmann had been a brilliant student before he entered Harvard. But, like Reed, he had a penchant for writing and became a contributor to various Harvard literary magazines.

The social leaders who filled the clubs no longer seemed attractive to Reed. When he was blackballed for the job of assistant manager of the varsity crew, he bore the insult stoically.

"During my freshman year I used to *pray* to be liked," he recalled, "to have friends, to be popular with the crowd. Now I *had* friends, plenty of them; and I have found that when I am working hard at something I love, friends come without my trying and stay; and fear goes, and that sense of being lost which is so horrible."

Having arrived at this discovery, Reed could come to terms with Harvard. He was never accepted by the university's aristocrats; but he worked on the newspapers, was elected president of the Cosmopolitan Club, which had a student membership representing forty-three nationalities, became manager of the Musical Club, captain of the water polo team, and active in numerous other un-

dergraduate activities. He began to see the college aristocrats for what they were. "The more I met," he recalled,
"the more their cold cruel stupidity repelled me. I began
to pity them for their lack of imagination and the narrow-
ness of their glittering lives—clubs, athletics' society."

He also began to appreciate the extraordinary institution of which he now felt himself to be a part. Reed
found Harvard, under President Charles W. Eliot,
"unique." "Individualism," he later wrote, "was carried to
the point where a man who came for a good time could
get through and graduate without having learned anything; but on the other hand, anyone could find there
anything he wanted from all the world's stores of learning.

"The undergraduates were practically free from control; they could live pretty much where they pleased and
do as they pleased—so long as they attended lectures."

Reed identified, among his classmates, "poets, philoso-
phers and cranks." He joined in talk fests that startled
him by their daring and intellectual insurgency, but he
soon found himself contributing outlandish ideas of his
own. ("Heresy," he later noted, "has always been a Harvard and a New England tradition.")

With his new friends, he criticized the faculty for not
understanding how to educate young men; he attacked
the sacred institution of inter-collegiate athletics, sneered
at undergraduate clubs "so holy that no one dared mention their names."

The disparity in life styles of the undergraduates
amazed Reed. "Some men came with allowances of fifteen
thousand dollars a year pocket money, with automobiles,
and servants, living in gorgeous suites in palatial apartment houses; others in the same class starved in attic
bed-rooms."

Reed himself did not starve, but he lived very modestly. His father was having difficulty finding the money for his education and for that of his brother, who followed him to Harvard. Reversing the middle-class, middle-aged tendency to move toward the right, C.J. Reed in the early 1900s had become involved in reform politics. When widespread land frauds and other political corruption were discovered in Oregon at the beginning of the century, Theodore Roosevelt appointed a Portland lawyer, Francis J. Heney, as his special investigator and Heney, in turn, enlisted C.J. Reed as United States Marshal. Many prominent Oregonians were exposed in the course of the investigation, and C.J. was regarded as a traitor to his class. Ostracized by much of Portland's business and social community, he was reduced to living on not much more than his salary as Marshal.

C.J. was distressed that he could not support his sons in the style and comfort he wanted for them, but he would not withdraw from his newfound political commitment. One of the rewards of his stand was the friendship of Lincoln Steffens, the leading muckraking journalist of his day.

Steffens was the son of an Illinois pioneer, who had crossed the plains by covered wagon to California in 1862. Liberally raised and educated in California and Europe, he started on a career of journalism in New York at the age of twenty-six. In 1902, when he was thirty-six, Steffens switched from newspaper reporting and editing to magazine writing, establishing a reputation as an exposer of political corruption at all levels of government. Rarely vindictive, Steffens brought a kind of benign, philosophical detachment to his exposés that earned him the respect of many of the most powerful men of his time and even the friendship of some of the very men whose activities he exposed.

Reed, far from resenting his father's reduced circumstances, was proud of C.J. He later described him as "a great fighter, one of the first of the little band of political insurgents who were afterwards, as the Progressive Party, to give expression to the new social conscience of the American middle class.

"His terrible slashing wit, his fine scorn of stupidity and cowardice and littleness, made him many enemies, who never dared attack him to his face, but fought him secretly, and were glad when he died."

At the beginning of his junior year, Reed was able to benefit from his father's friendship with Lincoln Steffens. Reed had become editor of one of the college publications and he wrote to Steffens asking for advice on the philosophy of journalism. Steffens was delighted to help C.J.'s son. Steffens was a born proselytizer with a proselytizer's vanity. He relished having young disciples sit at his feet.

"The way to go at your job," Steffens wrote Reed, "is to sit down together, you and your crowd, and together perceive what the *Harvard Monthly* should be. I think its function is to express Harvard, and all that Harvard stands for in the world—to the world. That's a large order, and I submit it in all its might, not because I think you can achieve it in one year, but because with that end in view, you will begin to clear your minds. . . .

"Magazine editors commonly err [by trying] to 'make' a magazine. They think up what will be a good article or story; then they set about getting some writer to write it up. Some of that has to be done, of course, and sometimes a writer will do pretty well with an order like

31

that. But we all hate it. We all do our best work when we are permitted to write that which it is in our minds and hearts to tell. . . . As an editor I found . . . it was hard very often to make the man understand that what I wanted was what he cared most to say. But when the right man once got that into his head something good came out of it. . . .

"Everybody [who can write] has some pet thought or theme or feeling. When you have found out what it is, consider whether it would be suitable for the Monthly, and if it is—order it. And anything is suitable for the Monthly that is interesting to the world; and each editor is to regard himself as the whole world: whatever will interest him involuntarily (not as an editor, but as a human being) will interest the rest of us human beings. . . . It's all a matter of expression, which is journalism and which may be literature—if the writer is striving not to make a work of art, but simply to tell his story for you and me and the man on the street."

Toward the end of his college career, Reed encountered "Copey." As it was for scores of other undergraduates, the experience for Reed was memorable. Charles Townsend Copeland was an English teacher and a legend. He became a strong influence on Reed, as he did on several generations of writers.

Under the pretense, as Reed put it, of teaching English composition—the course was listed as English 12, and it was not easy to be accepted for it—Copeland stimulated Reed to "find color and strength and beauty in books and in the world, and to express it again." In Copey, Reed found not only an inspiring instructor, but a friend in whom he could confide his dreams.

Reed was interested in, though he did not join, the Socialist Club, whose significance he did not fully understand until after he had left Harvard. Walter Lippmann was its president. The Socialist Club represented what Reed, still only an incipient political rebel, was about to embrace as a way of life. His eyes were newly opened to the concept of politics and economics, not as subjects for dry, theoretical study, but as "live forces acting on the world."

Reed was greatly impressed with Lippmann's ability to activate his ideas and he watched as the club began exerting an influence not only on the university, but on the community. The club drew up a platform for the Socialist Party in the city elections. It had social legislation introduced in the Massachusetts Legislature. It helped inspire the Harvard Men's League for Women's Suffrage. Its members wrote muckraking articles in the college papers, challenging such practices as Harvard's underpaying its housekeeping staff. Reed saw the effects of the club's influence all around him at Harvard, and rejoiced in the company of a steadily increasing band of activists.

"All over the place radicals sprang up," he recalled, "in music, painting, poetry, the theater. It made me and many others realize that there was something going on in the dull outside world more thrilling than college activities, and turned our attention to the writings of men like H.G. Wells and Graham Wallas, wrenching us away from the Oscar Wildeian dilletantism which had possessed undergraduate literateurs for generations."

In the summer of 1910, after graduating from Harvard, Reed, with his father's approval, took a year off to wander about Europe. He reluctantly accepted the hundred dollars his father pressed on him, but he was determined to earn his own keep whenever possible during his year abroad. To C.J. even a hundred dollars was now a sacrifice. Having refused that year to contribute to the

Republican campaign, C.J. had been dismissed from his job as Marshal by President Taft. C.J. had run for Congress and lost by a slim margin—mainly, Reed believed, because he took the time to go East to see his son graduate, instead of staying in Oregon to campaign.

With a college friend, Waldo Peirce, who planned to study painting in Paris, Reed signed on a cattle ship sailing from Boston. Peirce came from a rich and influential Maine family. He was characterized by a mutual friend as "the one man who was more daring, more irresponsible, more adventurous than John Reed."

They separated in Liverpool and Reed tramped across England alone, picking up work on farms and sleeping in haylofts. He toured northern France on foot, was joined by Peirce for a wild automobile trip through Touraine, and went on alone into Spain. He spent the winter in Paris, where he found a number of his Harvard friends, and took walking excursions into the country. On one of them he met a woman named Marguerite Filon, the niece of a celebrated French scholar. Reed, then twenty-four, in love with the world and optimistic about his future, asked her to marry him, promising he would send for her as soon as he had established himself at home.

Chapter Three

IN MANY WAYS the first twenty-four years of Louise Bryant's life ran parallel to Jack Reed's. Like Reed, Louise grew up in the West, influenced by the pioneer tradition. College-educated (by no means an automatic procedure for a young woman of the early 1900s), she developed a youthful interest in literature, journalism, and radical politics. And like Reed, her view of life was romantic and filled with dreams of adventure.

But because her background was less privileged than Reed's and because she was a woman, she had to fight harder than Reed to achieve the lifestyle she wanted. Louise's youth was precarious and sometimes grim, and she never outgrew her childhood need to escape into make-believe. She always tended to substitute romantic inventions for drab facts, and few of her friends knew the truth about her early life and background. To different friends at different times, she confided that her grandfather had been the younger son or an Irish lord, that she was related to Oscar Wilde and that her father had been an Irish officer in the British army. She was vague about details, rarely speaking of her mother. None of her friends recalled ever hearing her make more than a casual and ambiguous mention of the life she had lived before coming to Portland in 1909.

Louise was born Anna Louise Mohan on December 5, 1887, in San Francisco. (Nine years later, all trace of her family's existence was wiped out along with hundreds of thousands of other records destroyed by the great earthquake and fire. Louise was not the only one who later took advantage of this. The absence of documentation became a source of frustration to San Francisco immigration authorities, who had difficulty enforcing the quotas on Chinese; smuggled-in immigrants could claim that their legal entry papers had been burned, knowing it was impossible to disprove this.)

Louise's father, Hugh J. Mohan, was born in Minersville, Pennsylvania. As a youth, he worked in the coal mines of that town. He had a strong drive for self-improvement. After first learning the machinist's trade, he educated himself sufficiently to be appointed as a school teacher in Pottsville, Pennsylvania. From teaching he went on to become a reporter, and in his twenties he attended college in upstate New York. For the next ten years, until Louise's birth (when he was thirty-nine) he divided his time between politics, Irish-American lodge activities, and newspaper work, which took him on frequent trips across the country. His politics were strongly pro-labor, his personality was convivial, and he became a popular orator and toastmaster, achieving a small niche in national Democratic affairs. At one point he held a minor office in the United States Treasury in Washington.

In 1878 politics and journalism brought him to San Francisco, where he worked as a reporter on the *Chronicle* and made speeches against Chinese immigration. He stayed in California for several years, shifting back and forth between Sacramento and San Francisco, and holding jobs on the *San Francisco Mail* and the *San Francisco Daily Globe*. Presumably, he married Louise's mother sometime during this period. Their first child was a boy named Louis Parnell, and two years later Anna Louise

36

was born. Mohan appears to have vanished from San Francisco and probably from the lives of his wife and children soon after. The history of the Mohan family is a blank for the next seven years.

Louise's mother, according to an acquaintance of Louise, was of Spanish origin; her given name was Louisa. A college friend of Louise, who met the mother, recalled her only as "a very plain, unremarkable woman."

This unremarkable woman, with Anna Louise, aged seven, and Louis Parnell, aged nine, reappeared in the public records of 1892, apparently having made her way east across California to a stop not far inside the border of Nevada. She was now Louisa Mohan Bryant. She had married a railroad conductor named Sheridan Bryant on June 12, 1892.

Louise's stepfather was a farmer's son who had grown up on the banks of the Truckee River at a time when Indians still roamed the plains of Nevada. He settled his wife and stepchildren in Wadsworth, a railroad division point of the Southern Pacific, about thirty miles east of Reno.

Louise attended school in Wadsworth until she was sixteen. Her school records listed her stepfather as her guardian, and she used his name. (Although she continued to use the name Bryant, she never changed her name legally.) That year, 1904, the entire town of Wadsworth was relocated to a spot closer to, and just east of, Reno, the Southern Pacific having decided to change its division point. Bryant, along with the other residents of Wadsworth, was sold a lot by the railroad company at the new location for one dollar; his house was placed on a flatcar and moved to the new town, which, after considerable deliberation, was named Sparks.

Louise transferred to the University High School in

Reno in the fall of 1904 for the final year of her secondary education. Her grades were not distinguished, but this did not deter her from entering the University of Nevada in Reno the following September. She spent two years there, taking such subjects as rhetoric and public speaking, in addition to the required courses in history, English, and science. Her marks, as in high school, were only average. One of her classmates remembered Louise as being clever, though not studious. Another recalled being struck by her outspoken opposition to sororities; though invited to join, she firmly declined. After two years in Reno, Louise obeyed an urge to expand her horizons northward. At the end of her sophomore year she applied for a transfer to the University of Oregon, in Eugene, and was accepted as a major in Literature, Science, and the Arts.

There was no noticeable improvement in her scholarship at the University of Oregon. Like Reed, she was less interested in the academic life than she was in the extracurricular activities on campus. A thirty-page paper she wrote at the end of her junior year, when she was twenty, was typical of her slapdash approach to higher education. Its subject was the Modoc Indian War that took place on the border of Oregon and California in 1872. It was introduced by a map of the battle territory, in which she carelessly labeled the Oregon region as California and the California region as Oregon. The battles, however, were described with relish and substantiated with voluminous footnotes, and the paper left no doubt as to whose side its author was on.

"The Modocs inflicted defeat after defeat [on U.S. Army troops] and were not captured until treachery had played its maleficent part," she summed up, adding, "Insignificant people as they were, in their brief hour, they managed to stamp themselves on the pages of history."

But there was little evidence at the University of Oregon that Louise was a burgeoning individualist. She had even had a change of heart about sororities, and became a founding member of Chi Omega. She also made at least a token concession to formal religion by wearing a small gold cross on a chain around her neck. And she was something of a social butterfly. According to one of her schoolmates, a professor was in love with her. According to another, she broke the heart of a fellow student. According to both, she was "beautiful, intelligent and popular." The yearbook for her class described her lyrically, if ungrammatically, as being "such a creature as would quench the zeal of all professors; make proselytes of all who she but bid follow."

Dean Collins, the Portland newspaperman who later became a friend of Paul Trullinger, met Louise for the first time at the University of Oregon, where he was studying for his master's degree. According to him, Louise was piqued that he did not melt before her charms. He was told by some of her friends that she had characterized him as conceited because he passed her on the campus without speaking. Collins was startled at the change in Louise when he met her several years later as Trullinger's bohemian wife. "At the University," he recalled, "she was a Chi Omega, a girlish figure, a co-ed, regarding social customs as the word of God."

Louise was graduated in January 1909 at twenty-one. Unlike Reed, she did not take a year off to travel. Sheridan and Louisa Bryant were raising a family of younger children in Sparks and had no money to spare. Louise had to support herself, and she decided to stay in the Northwest. She did not arrive in Portland until the summer of 1909, and there are conflicting versions of how she spent the six months after her graduation. According to one friend, she held a teaching job in the Puget Sound area, but quit because she felt isolated and lonely. According to another, she took a job in a canning factory in Seattle, as a sort of sociological experiment. This brief exposure to the grim working conditions and pitifully low wages that prevailed in factories at the time, she told a friend, aroused her social conscience. This second version of how she spent the six months has the ring of truth; she had left college as an unworldly, conventional girl and arrived in Portland as a determined social rebel. Like a number of other young, middle-class men and women of that period, who became reformers and political activists, Louise felt that a middle-class existence was a fringe existence and not a real life. All of these young people shared an anxiety that life would pass them by unless they could shake loose from conformity.

Louise did not immediately seek out the radical or bohemian clique in Portland. Instead, she picked up her former friendships with several Chi Omega girls who had returned to Portland and taken their places in the social life of the city. With their help she obtained a job as society reporter for a weekly tabloid called the *Spectator*. The work entailed covering a monotonous round of sorority functions, luncheons, weddings, teas, and dances, and Louise's reportage was largely restricted to lists of names. Her escape from all this dreary gentility was to make her home on a houseboat on the Wilamette where Reed, as a boy, had learned to swim.

The houseboat colony had sprung up in 1905, and by 1909 it numbered among its residents several prominent professional and business men, including doctors and bankers. The boats were moored both on the east and west banks of a wide part of the river, about three miles north of the downtown section of Portland. While some of the houseboats were elaborate, two-story affairs that cost as much as $10,000, most were single-storied, with two small bedrooms, a small kitchen with a wood stove, and a sitting room, costing between $900 and $1,200. They were built on log floats and many had rounded, banana-shaped roofs.

Most of the houseboats were owned by those who lived in them but Louise rented hers. Aside from the pleasure of being waterborne, houseboating afforded the sort of picturesque informality Louise enjoyed. Housekeeping was simple; when she wanted to prepare a hot meal, Louise could collect driftwood at the river bank to stoke her stove. It was almost impossible not to meet her neighbors and it would have been hard for Paul Trullinger, who was one of them, to overlook her. It did not take Louise long to captivate the handsome young dentist. They were married on November 13 in Oregon City in the home of an Episcopal clergyman, the Reverend T. F. Brown. Louise gave her name on the marriage license as "Anna Louise Mohan."

Louise moved out of her houseboat and into Paul's, where they continued to live until 1912, when they moved to an apartment. Probably because of Paul's enthusiasm for art, and her own boredom with society reporting, Louise began sketching. Paul, who spent hours at his own easel, encouraged his bride soon after their marriage to rent a little studio for herself in downtown Portland. Louise kept the studio when, later, she switched from painting to poetry.

Both Trullingers held a liberal view of marriage that was unusual for a place like Portland, although it was becoming very much a way of life in New York's Greenwich Village. There was disapproving gossip among their

41

friends—particularly Paul's. When Louise sat for a portrait by Paul's uncle, gossip had it that she was posing in the nude. (The portrait—or, at any rate *a* portrait of Louise—was later exhibited locally, and turned out to be a fully clothed, formal pose, complete with parasol and picture hat.)

A cousin of Paul's, Mrs. Linley Crichton, was one of those who took a dim view of Paul's wife. "Louise was a very erratic person," Mrs. Crichton recalled. "She jumped into a project with much enthusiasm, but soon tired of it and dropped it flat—just as she later dropped Paul. She treated her men, her friends, and her activities with equal abandon." Mrs. Crichton said, however, that Louise could, when she wished, be "as charming as Cleopatra herself."

Another Portland woman, Nina Faubion, once expressed the view, in print, that Louise was "a brain picker," and was attractive to a man like Reed "only because she was different."

Dean Collins, himself not a dispassionate observer, because of his friendship for Trullinger, recalled that Louise "always brought out the worst possible reactions in a woman." This seems to have been true, however, only of certain women; Helen Walters, Sara Field, and a number of other women who lived more in the world of politics and the arts, regarded Louise with admiration and affection.

While convinced that Louise's intellectual pretensions and radicalism were motivated largely by a wish to be "different," and while he disapproved of her "amorality," Collins conceded that Louise was "extremely attractive to men."

During the years when the Trullingers' unconventional marriage seemed, even to Paul's friends, to be working, Paul and Louise often appeared together at the artists' gathering places in downtown Portland, attended concerts and art exhibits and occasionally the theater. They played bridge at the houses of their conventional friends, like Mrs. Crichton, and their conversation, on these occasions, was more apt to be domestic than global. Louise rarely discussed her newspaper job, her poetry, or any journalistic ambitions. But she did speak often of her affection for cats; she owned several.

Her fondness for animals was something that struck many of her friends, Carl Walters recalled a cold, snowy day when Louise, crossing a bridge in a carriage, found herself behind a heavy wagon being pulled by a team of tired horses. The driver was beating the horses and Louise angrily jumped down from her carriage, cursed the driver, threatened to report him to the police, and herself led the horses gently across the bridge. "She couldn't stand to see animals mistreated," Walters said. "And when she got excited about something, she didn't always use language proper to a lady."

The Trullingers changed residences several times, as Paul became more successful, finally moving, in 1914, to the house on Riverwood Road, which they bought brand new. It was not long after they established themselves at this address—with a family of cats—that their marriage began to go sour.

Chapter Four

DURING THE FOUR YEARS that Louise tried to make a life for herself in Portland, Reed shot to fame. Without a compulsive need to prove himself and establish a reputation, Reed simply let his zest for life propel him into the most dramatic arenas of his time. Instinctively, he found himself in the thick of battle—whether it was war, politics, or the labor struggle. And his enthusiasm, as much as his native flair for journalism, combined to form him into a dazzlingly persuasive reporter.

He had no real plan for his future when he returned to America from his year abroad. His engagement to Marguerite Filon he brought home like a romantic souvenir, to be sighed over wistfully from time to time. He knew he had to earn a living and eventually send for his fiancée. New York seemed a logical place to begin his career, but what that career was to be, he had only the vaguest notion. He began his life in New York by joining the Harvard Club and paying a call on Lincoln Steffens.

"When John Reed came, big and growing, handsome outside and beautiful inside, when that boy came to New York, it seemed to me that I had never seen anything so near to pure joy," Steffens wrote. "No ray of sunshine, no drop of foam, no young animal, bird or fish, and no star, was as happy as that boy was. If only we could keep him so, we might have a poet at last who would see and sing nothing but joy."

Reed told Steffens what he had seen and done in Europe, and Steffens asked Reed what he wanted to do now. Reed said he didn't know, except that he wanted to write.

"Steffens looked at me with that lovely smile," Reed recalled, "and answered, 'You can do anything you want to.'" Reed welcomed Steffens as his new mentor, with the same eager trustfulness he had given Copey at Harvard. Steffens got him a job as an assistant editor on the *American Magazine*, where he had formerly worked himself. The *American* still leaned heavily on muckraking articles at that time, though it was beginning to emphasize popular biographical articles and fiction. While Reed's work consisted mostly of reading manuscripts and correcting proofs, he occasionally wrote for the recently introduced "Department of Interesting People." One of his first contributions was an article on Copey that appeared in the *American* in November 1911, when Reed had just turned twenty-four.

Reed's journalistic style was a bit strained in this early effort. Describing a typical Saturday night gathering at Copey's home in a Harvard dormitory, Reed wrote, "There are athletes, editors of college papers, Socialists, atheists, gentlemen, social stars and the lesser orbs whose light is hid under the college bushel."

But Reed, even at the start of his journalistic career, could abandon such phrases as "lesser orbs" and swing into the kind of spontaneous, enthusiastic description that later became his hallmark—a style of personal journalism that had immediacy and intimacy, that put his readers on the scene, compelling them to share (if not always to approve) Reed's own passionate involvement with his subject. When he wrote cleanly and simply, as he soon realized, he was at his best. Going on with his description of the Copeland environment, he wrote:

45

"It is a wonderful room, lined from floor to low ceiling with books. The broad mantel and the little wall space are covered up with signed pictures of great people that you read about and all the long generation of boys whose friend he has been. Over the door is a horseshoe and a bunch of rowan berries. The only light is from the fire, perhaps a candle on the mantelpiece, and the reading light to the left of the fire, where sits the little man, interminably smoking an infamous brand of cigarettes. Everybody talks of the thing nearest his heart; everybody finds himself alert, quick, almost brilliant."

In another article the following month, describing a Christmas handout in the Bowery by a Tammany Hall politician, Reed was already writing more vividly. His subject this time was even closer to his heart than the venerated Copey—the poor and downtrodden victims of what Reed was beginning to characterize as the wicked capitalist system.

"They began to gather—the diners—at half-past six in the morning. It was clear and keenly cold. I came upon them about half-past ten—a thousand bent and haggard creatures in a single line that stretched five restless blocks along the Bowery. Flowed by the holiday crowd; some sodden and old, drifting, and seeming lost because the work that occupied their fingers and soothed their brains had stopped; some dull and old, who worked not; but mostly youth, hard-faced and young-faced, animated, happily filthy of tongue, harshly singing; touched as by the bizarre slip of a painter's brush, with some garish bit of color. A peddler stood on the corner with a trayful of brooches—imitations of precious stones, such as the dark, foreign sweat-shop girls love to clasp at their throats. He cried monotonously, 'Come git your genuyne Brazil di'monds'—A cop tried to bully Nicolo the bootblack into believing that his license was void; after he had gone, Nicolo told me cynically, 'He try-a graft da Chreestamus presunt.'

"There was on the frosty air a smell of fetid little Jewish shoe-cellars. Bowery dust and bad tobacco, stale beer and cheap coffee, and the foulness of men who have slept in Lower East Side lodging-houses.

"Vile little merry tales crept along the line, laughter spurted up like a fountain or a bursting drain, oaths crackled. The line writhed like a snake, rolling from one foot to another to keep both warm. The high-built, hideous Elevated filled the street with irregular thunder; and sunlight, checkering through rods and girders and ties, splashed the dreary faded heads and shoulders of Tim Sullivan's dinner guests with cruel contrasts. 'Merry Christmas to you, Shorty, you drunken loafer!' cried a man in the line to one who passed. The other came back to him with balled fists and a mean jaw, 'G'wan, I'll kick the head off you—and a happy New Year . . .'

"And then a man fell out of the line—slumped on the pavement and went frigid, with red foam on his lips. The ghastly crew behind him didn't wait until he was taken out before they surged forward to close up the line. They stepped over and on his body. After all, they had been waiting four hours."

During the three years Reed worked on the *American* he often took his problems, both professional and personal, to Steffens.

"Being with Steffens is to me like flashes of clear light," Reed noted. "It is as if I see him, and myself, and the world, with new eyes. I tell him what I see and think and it comes back to me beautiful, full of meaning. He does not judge nor advise—he simply makes everything clear. There are two men who give me confidence in my-

47

self, who make me want to work, and to do nothing unworthy—Copeland and Steffens."

Steffens, concerned about his responsibility to Reed, tried to curb the young man's zeal in some areas.

"Convictions were what I was afraid of," he later wrote. "I tried to steer him away from convictions, that he might play; that he might play with life; and see it all, love it all, live it all, tell it all; that he might be it all; but all, not any one thing. And why not? A poet is more revolutionary than a radical."

Steffens's memory of the exhilaration of their friendship paralleled Reed's. "Great days they were, or rather nights," he wrote, "when the boy would bang home late and wake me up to tell me what he had been and seen that day: the most wonderful thing in the world. Yes. Each night he had been and seen the most wonderful thing in the world."

While Steffens's style could be somewhat pretentious, his observations were not exaggerated. To Reed, the New York of 1911 was an enchanted city. He spent hours wandering its streets, absorbing everything, marveling at everything—"The soaring imperial towers of down-town, the East River docks smelling of spices and the clipper ships of the past, the swarming East Side—alien towns within towns—where the smoky flare of miles of clamorous pushcarts made a splendor of shabby streets."

He learned to know Chinatown, Little Italy, and the Syrian quarter; Sharkey's and McSorley's saloons, the Bowery lodging houses, the German Village, the Haymarket, and all the dives of the Tenderloin. He spent a whole summer night atop a pier of the Williamsburg Bridge and slept, another night, in a basket of squid in the Fulton Fish Market, where he found "the red and green and gold sea things glistening in the blue light of the sputtering arcs."

"The girls that walk the streets were friends of mine," he wrote, "and the drunken sailors off ships new-come from the world's end, and the Spanish longshoremen down on West Street." He found obscure restaurants where he could eat the native food from all corners of the world. He knew where to get dope, where to go to hire a man to kill an enemy, how to get into gambling rooms and illicit dance halls. He came to know Washington Square, with its artists and writers, its bohemians and radicals. He attended balls at Tammany Hall.

Within a block of his Washington Square apartment, he found all the adventures in the world; within a mile's walk, he found "every foreign country." The apartment itself was a collection of ramshackle rooms that Reed shared with three friends from Harvard. After living there a while he persuaded Steffens, who had recently been widowed, to move into rooms below his.

Reed wrote about the things he saw, with what he described as "a fierce joy of creation." He was sure, now, that he could write. Observing and writing, his social conscience was quickening. He read a great deal of radical literature, but the ideas meant little to him until he had confirmed them by personal observation. He attended Socialist and anarchist meetings, met single-taxers and labor leaders, and continued to roam the city, looking for evidence to support their dogma. He found it. "I couldn't help but observe," he wrote, "the ugliness of poverty and all its train of evil, the cruel inequality between rich people who had too many motor-cars and poor people who didn't have enough to eat. It didn't come to me from books that the workers produced all the wealth of the world, which went to those who did not earn it."

Steffens, brought into even closer contact with Reed now that they lived in the same house, began to worry a little about Reed's tendency to fall in love with every new person he met, with every new concept he discovered—with his job, with his friends, with labor, with girls, with strikes, with the IWW, with socialism, with the anarchists, with the bums in the Bowery, with the theater, with God and Man and Being.

"I pulled him out of each such love-affair anxiously at first," Steffens later wrote, "but so easily and so often that I soon felt he was safe. I thought I could trust the next most wonderful thing to save him from the last most wonderful thing."

One love affair Steffens did not have to pull him out of was his engagement to Marguerite Filon. Reed himself changed his mind about that after a few months in New York and broke it off. But the love affair with labor went deeper than Steffens, at the time, realized. Even while Steffens was smiling benignly, Reed was watching and participating in the Paterson silkworkers' strike in New Jersey. The IWW, led by Big Bill Haywood, had sponsored a mass walkout at the Paterson silk mills in the late winter of 1913. Reed, hurrying to Paterson to investigate, was arrested and jailed when he refused to move off the street, where he was talking to a group of strikers.

It was the first time that Reed found himself so deeply involved in a story that he almost forgot he was there to report it. It was also his initiation into prison life—an experience he found horrifying, but not intolerable. The martyr in Reed, which explained a good deal of his subsequent behavior, was already visible. His imagination was so stirred, his sympathy so much engaged by the injustice and suffering he observed, that he found himself compelled to participate in it. Like all genuine martyrs, Reed was unaware of self sacrifice. He courted danger and hardship out of idealistic conviction. He accepted the inevitable cost to himself as a matter of course, and without complaint.

In a magazine article published a few months later, he referred to the Passaic County jail as "Sheriff Radcliff's hotel." Observing that the sheriff was a fairly decent man, as sheriffs went, and that the jail was probably better run than most, he went on to describe what conditions were like in a "good" jail: verminous food, rat-infested cells, minimal sanitary facilities, and an apparently arbitrary system of justice that meted out heavy sentences for minor crimes like begging in the street.

"That strike," Reed later wrote in a personal memoir, "brought home to me hard the knowledge that the manufacturers get all they can out of labor, pay as little as they must, and permit the existence of great masses of the miserable unemployed in order to keep wages down; that the forces of the state are on the side of property against the propertyless." Committing himself unequivocally, Reed also observed that "the IWW dominated the social and industrial horizon like a portent of the oppressed."

Between the energy he devoted to the labor movement, his efforts to make a living by writing, and the half-dozen fringe activities that occupied him, Reed had been leading a hectic life since returning from his European walking tour in 1911. He supported himself on his small salary from the *American Magazine,* supplemented by sales of short stories and non-fiction articles to *Collier's,* the *Saturday Evening Post, Smart Set,* the *Forum,* and the *Century.* The stories were just slick enough to meet the magazines' standards, but were not noteworthy as literature. Reed's forte, as he soon realized, was journalism. Early in 1913 he began contributing pieces to the newly reorganized, barely solvent, but—to Reed—totally felicitous magazine, the *Masses.* It was a Socialist monthly. Housed in a red brick building on Greenwich Avenue, the magazine had been launched at the beginning of 1911 as a forum for anti-capitalist literature by an idealistic but impractical Dutchman named Piet Vlag. After about a year and a half the *Masses* floundered and its tiny staff of contributors, which included the artist, John Sloan, the cartoonist, Art Young, and the poet, Louis Untermeyer, held an emergency session to rescue it.

It was Young's idea to ask Max Eastman, a twenty-nine-year-old Columbia professor who had recently been dismissed for his radical views, to take over the editorship of the *Masses*. Eastman, whose first love was poetry, accepted somewhat reluctantly. There was to be no salary, at least not until the magazine got back on its feet, and the argument of future success and glory was not convincing.

Nevertheless, Eastman accepted. The son of two Congregational ministers from upstate New York, Eastman had been raised in an atmosphere of liberal-mindedness; having a mother who was the first woman to be ordained a Congregational minister in New York State, Eastman found himself perfectly at home and in sympathy with the suffragists and other social reform movements of the day.

He regarded his acceptance of the editorship of the *Masses* as a gamble. As it turned out, it gave him his first influential platform. During the next few years he achieved a reputation as one of the leading American intellectuals and radicals. He was also, like so many of the radicals of that period, a romantic. Boyishly handsome, he was married at this time to an aspiring actress named Ida Rauh, one of several wives and a clutch of mistresses who floated through his life.

By December 1912, Eastman had been able to persuade a wealthy woman, who knew nothing of Socialism, to back the *Masses,* and it was launched on its controversial career.

An editorial in the December issue stated the magazine's policy:

"We do not enter the field of any Socialist or other magazine now published, or to be published. We shall have no further part in the factional disputes within the Socialist party; we are opposed to the dogmatic spirit which creates and sustains these disputes. Our appeal will be to the masses, both Socialist and non-Socialist, with entertainment, education, and the livelier kinds of propaganda."

Eastman asked a recent arrival in Greenwich Village, Floyd Dell, to be his associate editor. Dell, who was the same age as Reed, came from a small town in Illinois and had worked on newspapers in Chicago. He had been a Socialist since he was fourteen, and his ambition was to write novels, though he had tried his hand at playwriting. He was tall and slender, with a broad forehead and pointed chin, and wore long sideburns.

The absence of salary increased rather than diminished the fervor and esprit de corps that ruled the small circle of *Masses* editors and contributors. Editorial meetings were lively and uninhibited, and seldom confined to business. Reed was often there, holding forth on his pet theory of the moment and his articles ran side by side with the contributions of Carl Sandburg, Sherwood Anderson, Bertrand Russell, Maxim Gorky, and Vachel Lindsay.

His first contribution was on his currently favorite topic, the Paterson silk strike. In it he demonstrated that he took to unpaid, advocacy journalism with much greater ease then he did to well-paid, contrived fiction. "There's war in Paterson," he proclaimed. "But it is a curious kind of war. All the violence is the work of one side —the Mill Owners. Their servants, the Police, club unresisting men and women and ride down law-abiding

53

crowds on horseback. Their paid mercenaries, the armed Detectives, shoot and kill innocent people. Their newspapers, the Paterson *Press* and the Paterson *Call,* publish incendiary and crime-inciting · appeals to mob violence against the strike leaders. Their tool, Recorder Carroll, deals out heavy sentences to peaceful pickets that the police net gathers up. They control absolutely the Police, the Press, the Courts.

"Opposing them are about 25,000 striking silkworkers, of whom perhaps 10,000 are active, and their weapon is the picket line. Let me tell you what I saw in Paterson and then you will say which side of this struggle is 'Anarchistic' and 'contrary to American ideals.'"

During this period Reed had become an habitué, along with an assortment of writers, artists, labor leaders, and theater personalities, of Mabel Dodge's salon on lower Fifth Avenue. Mrs. Dodge, a few years older than Reed, was divorced from her second husband, Edwin Dodge, a prominent Boston architect. She was not beautiful; she was completely humorless; and she was staggeringly conceited. But she managed by flattery, a superficial knowledge of the arts and politics, and lavish hospitality, to lure such disparate personalities to her gatherings as Steffens and Emma Goldman. Her friends included Walter Lippmann, Robert Edmond Jones, Gertrude Stein, Isadora Duncan, and Big Bill Haywood. Her Evenings were famous. She seemed, as she candidly admitted, to be able to exert a "free-flowing magnetic influence on all sorts of people." Seldom venturing out of the sheltered luxury of her own house, she joined some friends one evening, out of curiosity, in a visit to the Greenwich Village apartment of Big Bill Haywood's mistress. There she found Haywood, the one-eyed leader of the much publicized silk workers' strike, addressing a group that included Reed. Haywood was complaining of the difficulty of dramatizing for New Yorkers the tragedy in New Jersey. His workers needed money and moral support to win their strike, he said, and their New York comrades would surely help, if they could visualize what was really happening.

Mabel Dodge impulsively suggested putting on a pageant of the strike at Madison Square Garden, re-enacting the police brutality, the poverty-stricken conditions of the silkworkers and their families, and repeating the rallying speeches made by Haywood, Elizabeth Gurley Flynn, and Carlo Tresca. The idea was taken up at once by Reed, who introduced himself to her and volunteered to organize the pageant.

It was at this point that Reed, in Paterson to gather material for the pageant, got himself arrested and jailed. Mabel Dodge did not see him again for three weeks.

Released from jail, Reed quit his job on the *American* and went to work full time getting the pageant on. Mabel Dodge sat in her house, which became the headquarters for the pageant plan, and allowed her magnetic influence to flow over Reed. She had already decided she was in love with Reed, and he with her, but she postponed a declaration until after the pageant, confining herself to soulful glances and tremulous smiles.

The pageant was impressive. A thousand men and women—strikers and their families—were brought from Paterson to act out, before an audience of twenty thousand, what Reed described as "the wretchedness of their lives and the glory of their revolt." But the strike was lost.

Reed collapsed from nervous strain and Mabel Dodge carried him off to her villa in Florence to recuperate. She teased him a bit before taking him as her lover; she enjoyed intellectualizing her emotions. In her autobiography she has quoted herself as saying, "Oh, Reed, darling, we are just at the Threshold and nothing is ever so wonderful as the Threshold of things, don't you *know* that?" She was annoyed that he did not understand her delicacy.

When, at last, Mabel permitted herself to cross the Threshold, she was overwhelmed by her own generosity. "I came to Reed," she wrote, "like a Leyden jar, brimful to the edge, charged with a high, electrical force. . . . He had not known any women like this." Their love affair became, for her, a fabled romantic passion. When Reed seemed disinclined to play Antony to her Cleopatra, she was at first incredulous, then furious. "I hated to see him interested in Things," she wrote. "I wasn't, and didn't like to have him even *look* at churches and leave me out of his attention." Her jealousy and possessiveness bewildered and irritated Reed. He accused her of smothering him. "I love you better than life, but I do not want to die in my spirit," he told her.

Mabel regained Reed's full attention when he fell ill of diphtheria that summer. Weakened and depressed by the illness, he allowed her to install him in her house on Fifth Avenue when they returned to the United States that fall. Living openly with Reed, the liaison accepted by their friends, including Steffens, Mabel was content for a few months. Reed was too overcome by inertia to try to pick up his career. But gradually, as he recovered his strength and his spirit, Mabel observed in him a disquieting tendency to read newspapers. "What the morning paper said was happening in Mexico, in Russia or at the Poles," she observed, "seemed to make Reed's heart beat faster than I could, and I didn't like that."

What was happening in Mexico was the thing that held Reed's interest at the moment.

Francisco (Pancho) Villa was leading a guerilla army with astonishing success against the government forces of Mexico, and the revolution on the United States border was the great news event of the day. Steffens decided it was the perfect assignment for Reed, and suggested to the *Metropolitan* magazine that they send him to cover it.

The *Metropolitan* had been bought in 1912 by the multimillionaire Harry Payne Whitney. It had been a popular fiction magazine, numbering among its contributors Rudyard Kipling, Joseph Conrad, and Booth Tarkington. Whitney installed the British Fabian Socialist, H. J. Wigham, as editor, and Kipling, Conrad, and Tarkington gave way to George Bernard Shaw, Walter Lippmann, and Morris Hilquit. An intellectual New Englander named Carl Hovey had become the *Metropolitan's* editor when Steffens sent Reed to the magazine. Hovey, who had studied with Charles Copeland at Harvard, was married to a Russian-born woman named Sonia Levien, who was a lawyer and later became a Hollywood screen writer. Both Hoveys took quickly to Reed, and the assignment was settled.

Reed, gleeful, said goodbye to Mabel. She did not respond gracefully. She tried tantrums and hysterics to prevent his leaving, and when that failed, followed him to El Paso, Texas. But soon after Reed crossed the border into Mexico, she gave up her pursuit and returned to New York to sulk.

"Jack went, [to Mexico] as a poet, to Villa," Steffens later wrote, "while I went, as U. S. Marshal [C. J.] Reed would have gone, to Carranza's side."

Pancho Villa, in the early winter of 1913, had become a dubious hero. American journalists were flocking to Mexico to follow his progress. Richard Harding Davis, representing the *Tribune*, was among them, and Reed,

57

advised to get accreditation from a daily newspaper in addition to the *Metropolitan,* had wheedled the assignment from the *World.*

When Reed reached the border, Villa had just captured Chihuahua and was getting ready to move on Torreon.

"When I first crossed the border," Reed later wrote, "deadliest fear gripped me. I was afraid of death, of mutilation, of a strange land and strange people whose speech and thought I did not know. But a terrible curiosity urged me on; I felt I *had to know* how I would act under fire, how I would get along with these primitive folks at war."

Reed made straight for Chihuahua and joined an American miner who guided him into the mountains of Durango, then left him for a bandit-general who was moving to the front. For two weeks Reed rode horseback across the desert with the bandit and his undisciplined troops of Mexican cavalry, seeing battles at close range. Several of the battles ended in defeat for his companions, with many killed. The survivors, Reed among them, fled for their lives across the desert. He made it to Villa's headquarters and was allowed to join the march on Torreon and watch its fall.

During his four months with the Constitutionalist armies in Mexico, Reed discovered that bullets did not terrify him and that he could live with the fear of death. He also found the Mexicans "wonderfully congenial." "Sleeping on the ground with *hombres,*" he wrote, "dancing and carousing in looted haciendas all night after an all-day ride, being with them intimately in play, in battle, was perhaps the most satisfactory period of my life. I made good with these wild fighting men, and with myself. I loved them and I loved the life. I found myself again."

Because he was completely swept up in the conflict, his imagination captured by Villa, Reed also wrote better than he ever had.

Few reporters before or since have lived their stories the way Reed lived the Mexican revolution. In one of his dispatches to the *Metropolitan* he laconically reported a noonday meal, taken with some soldiers on the march: "At noon we roped a steer and cut its throat. And because there was no time to build a fire, we ripped the meat from the carcass and ate it raw."

But living under conditions of savage deprivation was only part of it. The exposure to death—from thirst in the desert heat, betrayal by an unpredictable bandit-soldier, or a shot from the opposing forces—became a way of life for Reed. And his writing conveyed all the flavor and immediacy of the hair-raising adventure he was living.

Reed's characterization of Pancho Villa was sympathetic, but not uncritical. His reporting was fresh, vivid, and sophisticated. Unlike much of the journalism of that era, including Lincoln Steffens's, Reed's writing stands up extremely well against today's best journalistic style. This is Reed's description, in part, of the bandit hero, Villa, accepting a medal for heroism in the field from the artillery corps of his army:

"In the audience hall of the Governor's palace in Chihuahua, a place of ceremonial, great luster chandeliers, heavy crimson portieres, and gaudy American wallpaper, there is a throne for the governor. It is a gilded chair, with lion's claws for arms, placed upon a dais under a canopy of crimson velvet, surmounted by a heavy, gilded, wooden cap, which tapers up to a crown.

"The officers of artillery, in smart blue uniforms faced with black velvet and gold, were solidly banked across one end of the audience hall, with flashing new swords and their gilt-braided hats stiffly held under their arms. From the door of that chamber, around the gallery, down the state staircase, across the grandiose inner court of the palace, and out through the imposing gates to the street, stood a double line of soldiers, with their rifles at present arms. Four regimental bands grouped in one wedged in the crowd. The people of the capital were massed in solid thousands on the Plaza de Armas before the palace.

" '*Ya viene!*' 'Here he comes!' 'Viva Villa!' 'Villa, the Friend of the Poor!'

"The roar began at the back of the crowd and swept like fire in heavy growing crescendo until it seemed to toss thousands of hats above their heads. The band in the courtyard struck up the Mexican national air, and Villa came walking down the street.

"He was dressed in an old plain khaki uniform, with several buttons lacking. He hadn't recently shaved, wore no hat, and his hair had not been brushed. He walked a little pigeon-toed, humped over, with his hands in his trousers pockets. As he entered the aisle between the rigid lines of soldiers he seemed slightly embarrassed, and grinned and nodded to a compadre here and there in the ranks. At the foot of the grand staircase, Governor Chao and Secretary of State Terrazzas joined him in full-dress uniform. The band threw off all restraint, and, as Villa entered the audience chamber, at a signal from someone in the balcony of the palace, the great throng in the Plaza de Armas uncovered, and all the brilliant crowd of officers in the room saluted stiffly.

"It was Napoleonic!

"Villa hesitated for a minute, pulling his mustache and looking very uncomfortable, finally gravitated toward the throne, which he tested by shaking the arms, and then sat down, with the Governor on his right and the Secretary of State on his left. . . .

"Then began the many speeches. The Chief of Artillery told Villa, 'The Army adores you. We will follow you wherever you lead. You can be what you desire in Mexico. . . .'

Other officers spoke, calling Villa "The Friend of the Poor," "The Invincible General," "The Inspirer of Courage and Patriotism," "The Hope of the Indian Republic."

"And through it all Villa slouched on the throne, his mouth hanging open, his little shrewd eyes playing around the room. Once or twice he yawned, but for the most part he seemed to be speculating, with some intense interior amusement, like a small boy in church, what it was all about. He knew, of course, that it was the proper thing, and perhaps felt a slight vanity that all this conventional ceremonial was addressed to him. But it bored him just the same.

"Finally, with an impressive gesture, Colonel Servin stepped forward with the small pasteboard box which held the medal. General Chao nudged Villa, who stood up. The officers applauded violently; the crowd outside cheered; the band in the court burst into a triumphant march.

"Villa put out both hands eagerly, like a child for a new toy. He could hardly wait to open the box and see what was inside. An expectant hush fell upon everyone, even the crowd in the square. Villa looked at the medal, scratching his head, and, in a reverent silence, said clearly: 'This is a hell of a little thing to give a man for all that heroism you are talking about!' And the bubble of Empire was pricked then and there with a great shout of laughter."

Reed, who spent a great deal of time with Villa, studied and analyzed him at length and in depth. One of Reed's most effective qualities as a reporter was his ability to disarm his subject, by empathizing with him. Reed was able to get astonishingly candid answers from the revolutionary leader, who was regarded as an enigmatic and almost mythical figure by Americans on both sides of the border. Reed did not hesitate to ask Villa questions of the most personal nature, and he illustrated his conclusions with pertinent anecdotes.

"Villa has two wives, one a patient, simple woman who was with him during all his years of outlawry, who lives in El Paso, and the other a cat-like, slender young girl, who is the mistress of his house in Chihuahua. He is perfectly open about it, though lately the educated, conventional Mexicans who have been gathering about him in ever-increasing numbers have tried to hush up the fact. Among the peons it is not only not unusual but customary to have more than one mate.

"One hears a great many stories of Villa's violating women. I asked him if that were true. He pulled his mustache and stared at me for a minute with an inscrutable expression. 'I never take the trouble to deny such stories,' he said. 'They say I am a bandit, too. Well, you know my history. But tell me, have you ever met a husband, father or brother of any woman that I have violated?' He paused. 'Or even a witness?'

"It is fascinating to watch him discover new ideas. Remember that he is absolutely ignorant of the troubles and confusions and readjustments of modern civilization. 'Socialism,' he said once, when I wanted to know what he thought of it, 'Socialism—is it a thing? I only see it in books, and I do not read much.' Once I asked him if women would vote in the new Republic. He was sprawled out on his bed with his coat unbuttoned. 'Why, I don't think so,' he said, startled, suddenly sitting up. 'What do you mean—vote? Do you mean elect a government and make laws?' I said I did and that women already were doing it in the United States. 'Well,' he said, scratching his head, 'if they do it up there I don't see that they shouldn't do it down here.' The idea seemed to amuse him enormously. He rolled it over and over in his mind, looking at me and away again. 'It may be as you say,' he said, 'but I have never thought about it. Women seem to me to be things to protect, to love. They have no sternness of mind. They can't consider anything for its right or wrong. They are full of pity and softness. Why,' he said, 'a woman would not give an order to execute a traitor.'

" 'I am not so sure of that, mi General,' I said. 'Women can be crueler and harder than men.'

"He stared at me, pulling his mustache. And then he began to grin. He looked slowly to where his wife was setting the table for lunch. 'Oiga,' he said, 'come here. Listen. Last night I caught three traitors crossing the river to blow up the railroad. What shall I do with them? Shall I shoot them or not?'

"Embarrassed, she seized his hand and kissed it. 'Oh, I don't know anything about that,' she said. 'You know best.'

" 'No,' said Villa. 'I leave it entirely to you. Those men were going to try to cut our communications between Juarez and Chihuahua. They were traitors—Federals. What shall I do? Shall I shoot them or not?'

" 'Oh, well, shoot them,' said Mrs. Villa.

"Villa chuckled delightedly. 'There is something in what you say,' he remarked, and for days afterward went around asking the cook and the chambermaids whom they would like to have for President of Mexico."

Reed's capacity for self-dramatization, his youthful tendency to see himself as a romantic hero and to become a participant in the drama he was covering, contributed

63

greatly to the flavor of his reporting. He was occasionally accused by his colleagues of being colorful at the expense of accuracy. But he defended himself by pointing out that it was the mood and spirit he wanted to convey, and that his "truth" was just as valid as an artist's "truth."

He once illustrated this point to the artist Boardman Robinson, when Robinson complained that Reed had slightly altered a sequence of events. Reed retorted that Robinson had drawn a woman's bundle larger than it was, and given a man a fuller beard than he had worn. Robinson explained that he "was not interested in photographic accuracy; he was trying to give the right impression."

"Exactly," Reed replied. "That is just what I am trying to do."

Reed's impressions of his life with Villa in Mexico were read with fascination by the *Metropolitan*'s subscribers. The popularity of his reports was undoubtedly enhanced by the way he wove himself as hero into various dangerous episodes. Here is Reed describing a brush with death in the station hotel in Jimenez, on his way into the interior of Mexico:

"Just then came an unsteady step on the gallery outside and my door was flung violently open. Framed in it stood the pock-marked officer who had been drinking in the bar. In one hand he carried a big revolver. For a moment he stood blinking at me malevolently, then stepped inside and closed the door with a bang.

" 'I am Lieutenant Antonia Montoya, at your orders,' he said. 'I heard there was a Gringo in this hotel and I have come to kill you.'

" 'Sit down,' said I politely. I saw he was drunkenly in earnest. He took off his hat, bowed politely and drew up a chair. Then he produced another revolver from beneath his coat and laid them both on the table. They were loaded.

" 'Would you like a cigarette?' I offered him the package. He took one, waved it in thanks, and lit it at the lamp. Then he picked up the guns and pointed them both at me. His fingers tightened slowly on the triggers, but relaxed again. I was too far gone to do anything but just wait.

" 'My only difficulty,' he said, lowering his weapons, 'is to determine which revolver I shall use.'

" 'Pardon me,' I quavered, 'but they both appear a little obsolete. That Colt forty-five is certainly an 1895 model, and as for the Smith and Wesson, between ourselves it is only a toy.'

" 'True,' he answered, looking at them a little ruefully. 'If I had only thought I would have brought my new automatic. My apologies, señor.' He sighed and again directed the barrels at my chest, with an expression of calm happiness. 'However, since it is so, we must make the best of it.' I got ready to jump, to duck, to scream. Suddenly his eye fell upon the table, where my two-dollar wristwatch was lying.

" 'What is that?' he asked.

" 'A watch.' Eagerly I demonstrated how to fasten it on. Unconsciously the pistols slowly lowered. With parted lips and absorbed attention he watched it delightedly, as a child watches the operation of some new mechanical toy. 'Ah,' he breathed. 'Que esta bonita! How pretty!'

" 'It is yours,' said I, unstrapping it and offering it to him. He looked at the watch, then at me, slowly brightening and glowing with surprised joy. Into his outstretched hand I placed it. Reverently, carefully, he adjusted the thing to his hairy wrist. Then he rose, beaming down

65

upon me. The revolvers fell unnoticed to the floor. Lieutenant Antonio Montoya threw his arms around me.

" 'Ah, compadre!' he cried emotionally."

In February the *Metropolitan*'s Carl Hovey wired Reed, after receiving one of his pieces: "Nothing finer could have been written. We are absolutely delighted with your stuff." Reed's reputation in America was soaring. In April the *Metropolitan* advertised his latest article as "word pictures of war by an American Kipling," adding, "What Stephen Crane and Richard Harding Davis did for the Spanish-American War in 1898, John Reed, 26 years old, has done for Mexico." *Insurgent Mexico*, a collection of his articles, was published in 1914. It put Reed in the first rank of American literary journalists. He dedicated it to Copey.

Reed had some detractors, among them the formidable Theodore Roosevelt, who had been recently defeated for the Presidency by Woodrow Wilson. Roosevelt was a contributor to the *Metropolitan*, and when he and Reed chanced to meet there, sparks always flew.

"Villa is a murderer and a rapist," Roosevelt told Reed.

"What's wrong with that? I believe in rape," Reed shot back.

Roosevelt grinned. "I'm glad to find a young man who believes in something."

Reed spent part of the spring and summer of 1914 with Mabel Dodge in the remote fishing village of Provincetown, Massachusetts. The little town at the tip of Cape Cod had become a summer retreat for New York artists and was beginning to attract writers as well. Reed left Provincetown on assignments for the *Metropolitan* from time to time. Mabel glumly resigned herself to sharing Reed with the world, but she was not pleased when he accepted the *Metropolitan*'s assignment that August to cover the European war.

Reed, with his usual eagerness for any new assignment, sailed for Paris expecting to find the excitement of the Mexican revolution. He spent six months in Europe traveling through England, France, Switzerland, Italy, Germany, and Belgium, visiting battlefronts whenever he could arrange it. He grew steadily more disillusioned with the war.

"In Europe," he wrote, "I found none of the spontaneity, none of the idealism of the Mexican revolution. It was a war of the work-shops, and the trenches were factories turning out ruin—ruin of the spirit as well as of the body, the real and only death. Everything had halted but the engines of hate and destruction. European life, that flashed so many vital facets, ran in one channel."

He could find little to choose between the two sides. He found both sides cynical and callous and he said so in his dispatches.

In a story headed "With the Allies" that ran in the *Metropolitan* in December 1914, Reed chose to illustrate this cynicism and callousness by focusing on the social life in Geneva. Because there was nothing in this unheroic European conflict to catch his romantic imagination, no cause, no leader to idealize, Reed's writing was lackluster, his irony heavy-handed. He was bitter and angry, and articulate about it, but he could never bring his best talent as a journalist to criticism. He was born to be a champion, not a detractor. He wrote at the top of his ability only when he believed himself to be defending a cause.

"At the height of the great European war," Reed wrote, "the cataclysm of Western civilization, Geneva glitters like Monte Carlo at the height of the season—

67

Geneva, mother of the Red Cross; hostess of Humanitarian Congresses for the civilizing of warfare. It has come at last, what all the world dreaded, with the bombarding of open towns, the massacre of non-combatants, murder and mutilation of the wounded—the sack and burning of Louvain—and in Geneva are gathered the gaiety and frivolity of Europe. Germans, English, French dine together, dance together, and throng the gambling table of the Kursaal at night, or crowd to see the latest naughty Revue from Paris. At night the lights along the Lake are a string of jewels. Red-coated orchestras play the lightest, merriest music, drowned in the laughing chatter of extravagant women and men in evening dress—English, French, German. . . . All mention of the greatest war in the world's history is considered distinctly bad taste."

Of Paris in September 1914, Reed wrote:

"The truth is that with two millions of the youth of France fighting a losing battle against the German hordes pouring down the north, Paris, the heart and soul of France, remained tranquil, ignorant, apathetic. As the enemy approached, far from facing them, Paris emptied itself toward the south and west. Almost two million people left the city. The splendid and luxurious hotels, the palaces of the rich, were offered to the Red Cross under the excuse of patriotism, but really so that the Red Cross flag would save them from German destruction. On the shutters of the closed shops were posted notices saying: 'The proprietor and all the clerks have joined the army. Vive la France!' And yet when, after the battle of the Marne, the population poured back into the city, these same shops reopened, and the proprietor and his clerks shamelessly reappeared; even some of the great hotels and houses were withdrawn from the Red Cross when all danger seemed past."

To Reed, the issues of the war were as clear cut as those of the labor movement struggle: On the one hand, there were the victimized working classes, and on the other, the unscrupulous capitalists. The European war was a conflict between the capitalists of several nations—a war between traders—and the workers of these nations were being made to fight and die, knowing nothing about their leaders' motives and destined to suffer, whether their leaders emerged as victors or as vanquished. As for the United States' pro-ally sympathies and indignation over German aggression, Reed thought it absurd and hypocritical. France and England were just as culpable as Germany, and America had no business on either side of the wrangle. "This is not our war," he declared, in an article for the *Masses*.

Depressed and disillusioned with what he saw happening in Europe, he nevertheless found time to fall in love with a married woman living in Paris, break off his affair with Mabel, via an exchange of transatlantic cables, grow bored with and abandon his new love and—as an ironic climax to his disorganized and confusing tour of the western front—to fire a couple of shots with a German rifle in the direction of the French lines.

The episode occurred after he had spent a grisly night seeing the war at first hand from the German trenches. His German guide handed him the rifle and asked if he'd like to have a shot, and this seemed to Reed, at the moment, an appropriately nightmarish gesture in an incredible, nightmarish war. He was no more pro-German than he was pro-English or French, and in firing the rifle he was expressing nothing more than a feverish contempt for the war itself. But word of the episode got back to the United States, and when Reed returned for a breathing spell at the beginning of 1915, he found himself somewhat embarrassed by it. The French government declared him persona non grata and he was unable to return to that country as the *Metropolitan* wished him to do. But he was still a valuable and highly regarded correspondent, and the *Metropolitan* decided to send him back to the war—to the eastern front.

This time, Reed traveled with the artist Boardman Robinson who was assigned to illustrate Reed's stories.

Reed and Robinson became close friends. Robinson, at thirty-nine, was a well-known political cartoonist, whose work appeared regularly in the *New York Tribune.* (He later became a celebrated muralist.) The son of a Nova Scotian sea captain, he had worked his way through art school in Boston and later studied in Paris. Max Eastman once described him as "a big, burly, bluff sort of a character, with dancing blue eyes under bushy red brows, a red beard, and a boisterous way of 'blowing in' as though out of a storm." Everyone called him Mike, "in memory," according to Eastman, "of Michelangelo, whose fury and rapture his powerful and meaningful drawings did recall."

Again, Reed's dispatches were filled with heavily ironic illustrations of the fact that this was a cynical war of the traders. He described a conversation with an American-educated Turk, traveling by train to Salonika:

"Waving a cigar clutched in stubby fingers covered with jewels, he gave his personal views about the Turks, on whose religious prejudices he had battened for years.

" 'Yes, I am a Turkish subject,' he said, 'and my family for generations. They are fine people, the Turks—hospitable, kindly, and honest. I have nothing with which to reproach them, but, of course, I am for the Allies. When England holds the Dardanelles—ah, then there will be good business! Then there will be much money to be made!'"

Reed, like all first-rate war correspondents before or since, found his deepest sympathies engaged by the innocent and ignorant victims of a power struggle about which they could understand little or nothing—the dumbly obedient soldiers sent into slaughter, the civilians dying of malnutrition, disease, and the effects of pillaging. When he could control his anger against the representatives of capitalism, who were callously maneuvering these unwitting victims, Reed wrote skillfully about the war—not with detachment, but with the clarity and compassion of the engaged and articulate journalist.

This is his impression of Nish, in Yugoslavia:

"The stench of the city was appalling. In the side streets open sewers trickled down among the cobbles. Some sanitary measures had been taken—such as the closing of cafes and restaurants from two o'clock until six every day in order to disinfect them—but still it was an even chance of typhus if you stayed in a hotel or public building. . . .

"Such was Nish, as we first saw it. Two weeks later we returned, after the rains had altogether ceased, and the hot sun had dried the streets. It was a few days after the feast of St. George, which marks the coming of the spring in Serbia. On that day all Serbia rises at dawn and goes out into the woods and fields, gathering flowers and dancing and singing and feasting all day. And even here, in this filthy, overcrowded town, with the tragic sadness of war and pestilence over every house, the streets were a gay sight. The men peasants had changed their dirty heavy woollens and sheepskins for the summer suit of embroidered dazzling linen. All the women wore new

71

dresses and new silk kerchiefs, decorated with knots of ribbon, with leaves and flowers—even the ox-yokes and the oxen's heads were bound with purple lilac branches. . . . And I remember five great strapping women with mattocks over their shoulders, who marched singing down the middle of the road to take their dead men's places in the work of the fields. . . .

"We drove to Chere Kula, a mile out of town, late one sombre afternoon in the pouring rain. The name is Turkish, meaning 'Mound of Skulls'; it is literally a tower of skulls of Serbian warriors, erected near the site of a great battle fought more than a century ago. . . .

"Around this sinister memorial were grouped the brick buildings of the typhus hospital, and the wooden barracks where the overflow was lodged. The wind set our way, carrying the stench of bodies sweating with fever, of sick men eating, of the rotting of flesh. We entered a barrack, along whose walls cots lay touching each other, and in the feeble light of two lanterns we could see the patients writhing in their dirty blankets, five and six crowded into two beds. Some sat up, apathetically eating; others lay like the dead; still others gave short, grunting moans, or shouted suddenly in the grip of delirium. . . .

"We passed through fetid ward after fetid ward, smelling of decomposition and death, until we were wrung with the helplessness of these big men, and our stomachs were turned with the stench."

Reed described a battleground, where the Serbian and Austrian armies had recently faced each other, in even more horrifying detail:

"On one side . . . were the Serbian trenches, on the other side the Austrian. Barely twenty yards separated the two. Here and there both trenches merged into immense pits, forty feet around and fifty feet deep, where the enemy had undermined and dynamited them. The ground between was humped into irregular piles of earth. Looking closer, we saw a ghastly thing: from these little mounds protruded pieces of uniform, skulls with draggled hair, upon which shreds of flesh still hung; white bones with rotting hands at the end, bloody bones sticking from boots. . . .

"We walked on the dead, so thick were they— sometimes our feet sank through into pits of rotting flesh, crunching bones. Little holes opened suddenly, leading deep down and swarming with gray maggots. Most of the bodies were covered only with a film of earth, partly washed away by the rain—many were not buried at all. Piles of Austrians lay as they had fallen in desperate charge, heaped along the ground in attitudes of terrible action. . . . In one place the half-eaten skeletons of an Austrian and a Serbian were entangled, their arms and legs wrapped about each other in a death grip that could not even now be loosened."

Living with horror and deprivation was nothing new to Reed, but this seven-month tour of the eastern war zone became more than routinely difficult for him when he had a sudden recurrence of kidney trouble. But in spite of his disgust with the war and his illness, he perked up when his story took him, at the end of May, to Russia.

Reed and Robinson were beset by a series of cloak and dagger mishaps and frustrations, encounters with the Russian secret police and endless bureaucratic snarls, none of which dampened Reed's enthusiasm for the Russian spirit. The same sort of foul-up that would have aroused his scorn and sarcasm in the west, seemed highly entertaining to Reed in the east—particularly since the interminable questions and answers had to be translated and re-translated, often with comical misunderstanding on both sides. In one of his dispatches he described an endless day of waiting in the Russian town of Rovno, in the Ukraine, for travel passes that would get him and Robinson to the front. (They were constantly being arrested by officials who could not read their American credentials as correspondents, and then whimsically released.)

"We were around Rovno station almost all day long, but it was not until evening that the police decided to arrest us. Among others, we appealed to a pompous colonel, named Bolatov [who spoke French], whom we had encountered several times in the course of our travels. He was covered with high decorations, carried a gold honor sword, and had padding in his chest and dye on his ferocious mustache. We never could discover what he did on his leisurely peregrinations around the country. Miroshnikov [a Russian official who knew Reed and Robinson] told Bolatov that Robinson was a celebrated artist.

" 'We shall see!' said Bolatov cunningly. He approached Robinson.

" 'If you are an artist,' said he, 'please draw my portrait.'

"He struck a martial attitude under the arc-light, chest expanded, hand on sword-hilt, and mustache twisted up, while Robinson drew for his life. The portrait was an outrageous flattery. Colonel Bolatov glanced at it with perfect satisfaction. He waved to the police.

" 'Release these gentlemen,' he ordered loftily. 'They are well known journalists—Would you mind signing this sketch?' "

Reed fell in love with the Russian people. "In Russia," he reported, "everyone talks about his soul. Almost any conversation might have been taken from the pages of a Dostoievsky novel. The Russians get drunk on their talk;

voices ring, eyes flash, they are exalted with a passion of self-revelation. In Petrograd I have seen a crowded cafe at two o'clock in the morning—of course no liquor was to be had—shouting and singing and pounding on the tables, quite intoxicated with ideas. . . .

"Russian ideals are the most exhilarating, Russian thought the freest, Russian art the most exuberant; Russian food and drink are to me the best, and Russians themselves are, perhaps, the most interesting human beings that exist. . . . Every one acts just as he feels like acting, and says just what he wants to. There are no particular times for getting up or going to bed or eating dinner, and there is no conventional way of murdering a man, or of making love."

Reed returned to New York in the fall of 1915. He spent several weeks collecting and editing his recent articles. (They were published as a book, *The War in Eastern Europe*, in the spring of 1916.) Then, reluctantly, he turned his back on the exciting bustle of Greenwich Village and prepared for the dutiful, joyless holiday visit in Portland that was to bring him an unexpected romance.

Chapter Five

IN ANTICIPATION OF Louise's arrival in New York in early January 1916, Reed moved into 43 Washington Square, nearby the apartment he had shared with his Harvard classmates. The new apartment was just as ramshackle as the old, with a room to sleep in, a room each for Louise and him to use as a studio, and a small kitchen. To Reed, material comfort was no more important than it was to Louise. Their furniture was sketchy and their housekeeping arrangements were minimal. In order to be free to work and be with Reed, Louise engaged a cleaning woman, a motherly person who relieved Louise of most of the domestic chores.

Reed's new living arrangement caused little more than a flutter of curiosity among his Greenwich Village friends. Most of them were themselves living in inexpensive apartments or furnished rooms, many of them eschewing marriage out of principle, nearly all of them committed to some form of artistic or political activity, and all united by the air of intellectual freedom, moral laissez-faire and camaraderie that pervaded the Village in the years just before the United States entered the First World War.

Many of the Village's inhabitants of that era were, like Reed, already famous in their various fields. Others, like Eugene O'Neill, were about to emerge. Nearly all of them, from the poet Maxwell Bodenheim to the anarchist

Emma Goldman burned with conviction and a sense of mission, certain that they could change the world. It was a period of naive egotism, newly discovered libidos, cheap places to eat and drink. Sex, cubism, anarchism, yellow journalism, and Freud were the chief topics of passionate discussion. Everyone agreed on one point: "Uptowners," symbolizing middle-class conventions and narrow views on literature, art, politics, and morals, were contemptible; and to pursue money or value materialism was unspeakably bourgeois.

The Village represented a spontaneous and vital bohemia, unique in America's history. Its atmosphere was part New York slum, part western boom town, part Paris Left Bank. The area had retained its cozy neighborhood quality, while the rest of Manhattan grew toward the sky and moved north along Broadway and Fifth Avenue. While most of the Village houses were small and shabby, they had an Old World flavor their occupants found charming. Only the north side of Washington Square, the uptown boundary of the Village, was still fashionable. A few blocks south of Washington Arch, which dominated the square, the area ceased to make any claim to elegance. In the early 1900s a Negro slum appeared a few blocks south of the arch, devaluating nearby real estate and placing rentals within reach of artists escaping from middle-class backgrounds all over the country.

Among the favorite gathering places of the Village bohemians was the Liberal Club, an organization of earnest thinkers and tireless talkers that congregated on the ground floor of a MacDougal Street brownstone, adjoining the Washington Square Book Shop—also an informal social center. The club and the bookstore had served, in the winter of 1915, as the birthplace of the Washington Square Players and had, among other one-act plays, presented one by Reed called *Moondown*, which had been published in the *Masses* two year earlier. (Out of this group ultimately came one of the country's most distinguished and long-lived producing companies, the Theater Guild.)

Like other gifted journalists, Reed believed he had it in him to write distinguished fiction. Like most other gifted journalists, he was wrong. His poetry was ardent, but not original; his short stories were, at best, only clever; and his attempts at playwriting were strained. Since he never completed the novel he often thought of writing, it is impossible to know if he could have, eventually, produced a literary work of real merit. On the evidence, it seems unlikely.

Moondown, in all fairness, was no worse than most of the other playlets that American writers were turning out in the innocent theatrical climate of the early 1900s. (The American stage did not approach maturity until 1920, when Eugene O'Neill demonstrated that the native theater could be as valid a literary medium as the novel.) The play has two characters, Sylvia and Mame, pretty, young working girls trying to make their way in what Mame calls "this tough burg"—New York. It is the slenderest of mood plays, consisting of a dialogue between the two girls while Sylvia waits for a young man to call for her at moondown. The young man, being a poet, has forgotten Sylvia and never appears.

"The moon is almost gone and he hasn't come," Sylvia sobs.

"Haven't I been telling you that he's too busy writing up his Romance to remember a date?" says Mame. The moon sets. Sylvia weeps. Curtain.

Reed himself did not take seriously his efforts at playwriting. When he needed extra money he turned out the slick fiction that he could usually sell. But he spent his best effort doing reporting for magazines, and had as many assignments as he wanted. He was also devoting more and more time to lecturing in behalf of political causes.

Professionally occupied as he was, he found time to introduce Louise to all his friends and to recommend her to editors as a potential contributor. She received Max Eastman's encouragement to contribute to the *Masses;* she joined the Liberal Club and impressed Lawrence Langner, one of its charter members, with her beauty and vivacity; she attended anarchist meetings and failed to impress Emma Goldman with her political acumen, although the impression she made was not all bad. Emma Goldman, the fiery, forthright matriarch of the anarchist movement in New York, was a homely, humorless, and fiercely romantic woman who gave and demanded total loyalty. "One had to like [Louise] even when not taking her social protestations seriously," she later recalled.

On Lincoln Steffens, whose rather lofty view of women permitted a strong affection for Mabel Dodge, Louise seemed to have made no impression at all. And on Mabel, predictably, Louise made an unfavorable one. Hearing that Reed was living with a new girl, Mabel decided that the arrangement was a form of revenge on Reed's part. Mabel had herself taken up with a new lover after Reed's final flight, and chose to believe that this had made Reed jealous. "He had to stiffen inside himself and feel coldly toward me so as not to mind too much," she wrote. But Mabel was so curious to see how Reed was consoling himself that she invented a flimsy excuse to look Louise over.

79

"One late afternoon I knocked at [Reed's] door," she wrote. "It was opened by a very pretty, tall, young woman . . . who held a lighted candle in her hand.

" 'Is Jack Reed here?' I asked.

"He appeared suddenly behind her with rumpled hair and hurt eyes. . . .

" 'This is Louise Bryant,' he told me gravely.

" 'How do you do?' I asked her, but she didn't tell me. 'Reed, I came to ask you for your old typewriter, if you're not using it.'

" 'Louise is using it,' he said.

" 'Oh, all right. I only thought . . .' "

Hurrying on after this rather pathetic revelation, Mabel quickly recovered her equilibrium and recorded her acid summary of Louise's character.

"The girl was clever with a certain Irish quickness, and very eager to get on. I think Reed was a stepping stone, and through him she met a lot of people she never would have known otherwise. It had not seemed to me that she cared very much for him."

Mabel's conjecture was not based totally on personal pique. She added, in support of her belief that Louise was not really in love with Reed, "When he was away on one of the writing commissions he always had for the *Metropolitan Magazine* and others, [Louise] had a brief passage of passion with a friend of Reed's and mine."

The actual "passage of passion" was, in fact, some months in the future. But it was true that Reed was away from Louise a good deal. One of his assignments, for *Collier's*, was to accompany William Jennings Bryan on a trip through the South. Reed found Bryan both pompous and fatuous in private conversation; he was, Reed said, insensitive to music, painting, and literature. But listening to his public speeches, he conceded that Bryan was a genuine humanitarian. Reed joined Bryan in Palatka, Florida, and wrote of his speech in the local opera house.

"The opera house's interior was papered in bright turkey red, upon which was a tasty pattern of black and gold fleurs de lis. There must have been about 300 people in the orchestra: retired Confederate generals; courtly gentlemen with fine manners and no collars; blond, fluffy-haired Southern beauties, coquettish and very, very feminine; a Yankee tourist tanned with bass fishing, prosperous looking, garbed in loud checks. . . . Above was the regulation balcony where Negroes are allowed to sit; and there were five or six of them, all solemn and motionless except one, who was evidently a Republican and occasionally slapped his knee with a tremendous guffaw. . . .

"[The speech] was all simple, easily understandable— you felt that there could be no doubt of the man's sincerity."

During Reed's absences, Louise seemed, to many of Reed's friends, to be restless. In her own way, she was genuinely devoted to Reed, solicitous of his career and of his health, which was again beginning to fail. She was also grateful to Reed for the introductions and guidance that were forwarding her writing career. But she and Reed had, like many other Village couples of that era, a tacit agreement that love must be free, that romantic arrangements imposed no moralistic fetters, and that if spontaneous affection became an obligation, it was worthless.

Louise was easily swayed by her emotions. The same romantic impulse that flung her into Reed's arms made her susceptible to other romantic temptations. Indeed, she found it almost impossible to resist anyone who seemed to need her. She believed in herself as a benevolent femme fatale and wanted to be all things to all men.

81

That winter her eye fell on Eugene O'Neill, a brooding, dark young man, whom Reed had befriended and was trying to encourage. Reed had told Louise that O'Neill had talent. With his innate enthusiasm and generosity, Reed had tried to sweep O'Neill into his own creative circle. To anyone but Reed this would have seemed a highly daunting task.

O'Neill at twenty-eight was morose, taciturn, and often drunk. He had few friends among the Village's artists and writers, preferring the company of stevedores, prostitutes, and hoodlums. His closest friend that winter was a middle-aged philosophical anarchist named Terry Carlin, who had given up working as a young man and adopted the life of a hobo.

O'Neill regarded the Village bohemians as mostly poseurs, but he was drawn to Reed as a man of action who managed to pursue a career that did not compromise his lust for adventure. O'Neill had in common with Reed a background of poor health. Both had become excellent swimmers in compensation for their inability to excel at any other sport. Both of them had led lonely childhoods and felt special and set apart. And they shared an affinity for the downtrodden and exploited. But while Reed, with his more conventional middle-class background and his optimistic view of life, had learned how to live in two worlds, O'Neill had cynically submerged himself in the seedy world of Terry Carlin, a world only just removed from skid row. O'Neill was, in fact, close to becoming a hopeless alcoholic.

He had made one attempt at suicide and spent much of his youth in gloomy introspection and in self-destructive adventure at sea. His formal education, in addition to ten unhappy years at boarding schools, consisted of one year at Princeton University in 1906 and one year in Professor George Pierce Baker's postgraduate playwriting class at Harvard in 1914. He had sailed to South America on a cattle ship, lived a derelict's life in Argentina and near the docks of lower Manhattan, sailed between New York and England as an able-bodied seaman aboard passenger ships, toured the country as a minor member of his actor-father's stock company, and spent six months in a tuberculosis sanitarium. The first glimmering he had of a possible literary bent came during his recovery from tuberculosis in 1913, when he began writing poetry and one-act plays.

He briefly held a job on a New London, Connecticut, newspaper, to which he contributed some negligible stories and some humorous poems. He had submitted one of his short plays, *Bound East for Cardiff*, to Professor Baker, who recognized O'Neill's potential talent, but did not think *Bound East for Cardiff* was really a play. He had published, in addition to the New London poems, a long, serious poem called *Fratricide* in a left-wing newspaper, the *New York Call*, in 1914; and a mocking love-poem called "Speaking, to the Shade of Dante, of Beatrices," in F.P.A.'s popular "The Conning Tower" in the *New York Tribune* in the summer of 1915. His only other published work at that time was a privately printed volume of five one-act plays, which, to the ultra-discerning, hinted at a potential dramatic talent.

Apart from his short-lived career as a reporter, O'Neill had never supported himself by writing. During and after his intervals at sea, he lived on an allowance of one dollar a day from his father; the elder O'Neill, a successful and well-known actor, had staked his son to the academic year with Professor Baker, but he was pessimistic about his son's literary aspirations. At the time Reed met O'Neill in the early winter of 1915, O'Neill was living in semi-poverty, existing on the daily dollar and handouts from friends. He was unwilling to commit himself to any kind of steady wage earning; and, depressed by Professor Baker's laconic evaluation of his work, he had little faith in his ability to make an impact on the stage.

But he had not given up writing completely and he could not help responding to Reed's enthusiastic appraisal of his poetry and short plays, or to Reed's contagiously buoyant personality. He accepted Reed as a friend and allowed himself to feel encouraged by Reed's belief in his talent. When Reed was joined by Louise late that winter, O'Neill was one of the first of his friends to whom Reed introduced her.

O'Neill did not frequent many of the places where Reed and Louise saw their other friends. Even if he had not been handicapped by a lack of money, his gloomy state of mind would have kept him to the shabbier saloons. But there was one such saloon, grandiosely called the Golden Swan, that was beginning to lure some of the more adventurous of the Village bohemians. It was on the corner of Fourth Street and Sixth Avenue and its clientele consisted predominantly of truck drivers, teamsters, and gangsters.

The Golden Swan was known to all its habitués as the Hell Hole, and as such it ultimately achieved some fame through the paintings and etchings of a group of contemporary artists, among whom were John Sloan and Charles Demuth. (As Harry Hope's saloon, it also became the setting for *The Iceman Cometh*.)

The Hell Hole was a typical Irish saloon of the period. It had a sawdust-covered floor, rude wooden tables, and was filled with the smell of sour beer and mingled sounds of alcoholic woe and laughter. That winter it served O'Neill as a place to brood drunkenly and, when not drunk, to scribble poetry at one of the scarred wooden tables. In spite of his ragged condition, and without much effort, O'Neill drew women to him. There was a compelling quality of poetic despair in his gauntly handsome face and in the penetrating gaze of his dark, deepset eyes. Louise was instantly drawn to him, and, accepting Reed's evaluation of his talent, let him know that she, too, was ready to be his friend and herald.

O'Neill accepted her friendship warily at first. He was almost as susceptible to romantic impulses as Louise. He was attracted to her, and could not help seeing that she was responsive, but his scruples about her relationship to Reed were stronger than her own. It was understood by Reed's friends that he and Louise would be married as soon as Trullinger divorced her.

For weeks O'Neill was content to adore her silently. And Louise, busy and active in her new life, refrained from an overt invitation to her gloomy admirer.

When Reed was not out of town on a writing assignment, he and Louise were constantly together. Reed believed that he was approaching a crossroad in his professional life and Louise, of course, was vitally involved in the decisions he had to make about where his commitments lay, and how they would support themselves. In spite of Reed's reputation as a radical, he was still in demand as a free-lance magazine writer, and he and Louise could live comfortably on what he earned. But he was beginning to feel that the time had come for him to make a sustained creative effort, to concentrate his talent. He half decided to write a novel and began making notes and outlines. But his interest in both the novel and in popular journalism was constantly being superceded by his passionate involvement in the burning social issues of the day.

85

That spring he was nearly frantic with rage over America's implacable preparations for war. Military training in colleges was becoming commonplace; Theodore Roosevelt was attempting to raise a private army; jingoism was rampant.

Reed attacked the militarist movement in a ferocious article for the *Masses*, condemning America's exploitation of the working classes and concluding:

"The working man . . . will do well to realize that his enemy is not Germany, nor Japan; his enemy is that two percent of the people of the United States who own sixty percent of the national wealth, that band of unscrupulous 'patriots' who have already robbed him of all he has, and are now planning to make a soldier out of him to defend their loot. We advocate that the workingman prepare himself against that enemy. That is our preparedness."

Reed's weak kidney, which seemed to trouble him most during periods of frustration, flared up again in the early spring of 1916, threatening to curtail all of his activities. His doctor believed that an operation would sooner or later be necessary, and he advised Reed to have a rest at once. He and Louise decided to go to Provincetown, where, the summer before, some of Reed's friends had started a theater. A number of these friends were already established there this spring, and late in May, Reed and Louise joined them. O'Neill, too, while rarely inclined to be part of any group, roused himself from his winter doldrums and followed Reed and Louise to Provincetown. Though it was Louise alone who tempted him there with her ambiguous promise of romance, a reward of far greater significance actually awaited him in Provincetown; that summer was to mark the beginning of his career as a playwright.

Discovered only a few years earlier by a small group

of Greenwich Village artists and writers, the Provincetown to which Reed, Louise, and O'Neill journeyed in
1916 was a quiet fishing settlement, proud of its whaling
background. The town's two narrow streets, Commercial
and Bradford—connected by narrow alleyways—ran parallel to the Provincetown harbor. Wharves were strung out
from most of the houses lining the bay side of Commercial Street. Behind Bradford Street stretched miles of
dunes and scrub grass extending to the Atlantic. Provincetown's population was divided among three groups—
families of the early Portuguese settlers, descendants of
the first Puritan arrivals, and "outsiders," who included
such year-round residents as the town doctor, businessmen, and a few artists.

Provincetown had been claimed as a haven for Manhattan's avant garde by Mary Heaton Vorse. Widowed in
1915 for the second time, Mary Vorse supported herself
and her children by free-lance writing. She first visited
Provincetown during the summer of 1906 to give her children sea air, fell in love with the village, and bought an
old house that she later turned into a year-round resi-
dence. Hutchins Hapgood, the journalist, a college friend
of Mary Vorse's first husband, was the second of the writers to arrive, and after him came other New Yorkers in
search of a summer refuge. Two among them were
George Cram Cook and his wife, Susan Glaspell.

Cook, called "Jig" by his friends, was a forty-three-
year-old Greek scholar and university professor from
Davenport, Iowa. He had left a wife and children to
marry Susan Glaspell, a burgeoning writer. Cook had a
mane of white hair and a habit of twisting a shaggy lock
between his fingers when moved or excited. Susan Glaspell, a delicate, sad-eyed, witty woman, worshiped her
husband and devoted herself equally to him and to her

writing; it was she who provided the backbone of their income.

Cook and Susan Glaspell had participated, along with Reed, in the birth of the Washington Square Players in Greenwich Village and had written a one-act play to help launch a summer theater in Provincetown in 1915. Cook dreamed of creating a theater that would express fresh, new American talent, and after his modest beginning in the summer of 1915, began urging his friends to provide scripts for an expanded program for the summer of 1916. None of his friends were professional playwrights, but several, like Reed, were journalists and short-story writers. Their unfamiliarity with the dramatic form was, in Cook's opinion, precisely what suited them to be pioneers in his new theater and to break up some of the old theater molds; Cook wanted them to disregard the rules and precepts of the commercial Broadway theater, and to stumble and blunder and grope their way toward a native dramatic art. The idea appealed to Reed and to other of Cook's friends such as Mary Vorse and Hutchins Hapgood, and a number of them, including Reed and Louise, agreed to write one-act plays for production that summer.

Reed, like Cook, believed that a native American theater could be prodded into being. He was full of enthusiasm for a performance he had seen in a Mexican village that expressed the traditional folk spirit in terms of the contemporary lifestyle of the villagers.

The Cooks and several of their friends commandeered an old fishhouse at the end of a tumbledown wharf owned by Mary Vorse, and christened it the Wharf Theater. Little more than a shell, the building was twenty-five feet square and fifteen feet high. Through the planks of its floor at high tide the bay could be seen and heard and smelled. Under Cook's direction, an ingenious stage was

88

built. Only ten by twelve feet, it was sectional and mobile and could be slid backward onto the end of the wharf through two wide doors at the rear of the theater, to provide an effect of distance.

When Reed and Louise arrived in Provincetown, they found their friends engrossed by the theater project. The company already numbered thirty, each member having contributed five dollars toward the cost of mounting the summer program. Cook wanted to stage Reed's one-act play, *Freedom*, for the opening bill and Louise, urged by Cook, began writing her own one-act play to be staged later in the summer. Both Reed and Louise were swept up in the excitement of the first production. Along with *Freedom*, a satire about four prisoners with divergent ideas on what it means to be free, the opening bill included *Trifles*, by Neith Boyce, the novelist, and a joint effort by Cook and his wife called *Suppressed Desires*, a spoof of the new vogue for psychoanalysis. At fifty cents a ticket, this first bill sold out for its entire run, and Cook, encouraged by the response, sent out a letter asking for a one dollar subscription for the remaining three bills of the season—hoping that nine more one-act plays would materialize.

Louise hurried to finish her play, *The Game*. Though it was a rather stilted attempt at parable—its characters were "Life," "Death," "Youth," and "The Girl"—it caught the interest of William and Marguerite Zorach, both artists, who thought they could create an innovative stage setting, and it was accepted for the second bill. (Reed played "Death.") Cook selected a comedy by Wilbur Daniel Steele, the short-story writer, as the second play; and then he and his colleagues began casting about for a really strong play to give the bill its focal excitement.

It was at this point in the infancy of the Provincetown

Players that O'Neill, with unconscious dramatic timing, stepped onstage. He had not accepted Reed's invitation to stay with him in Provincetown, but had hung back in the adjoining town of Truro. Partly from pride (he preferred to live in a shipwrecked boat on the Truro beach, which cost him nothing) and partly from fear of being too close to Louise, he had avoided Provincetown for the first few weeks of the summer. But he was aware of the theatrical activity taking place there, and finally made up his mind to announce that he had a play to submit.

Reed, Louise, and the rest of the Provincetown Players gathered in the Cook's living room for a discussion of scripts and the final vote that would determine the makeup of the second bill. The only play that had not had a reading was O'Neill's *Bound East for Cardiff*, and Frederic Burt, the actor, was asked to read it aloud to the group. O'Neill sat moodily in the Cook's dining room during the reading, prepared to slip back to Truro without a word if the reception of his play was negative.

The response to the reading was overwhelmingly enthusiastic. To the credit of all those assembled, O'Neill's genius was instantly recognized. (In later years, many members of the group took justifiable pride in writing of their participation in the discovery of the new playwright.) Reed, unsurprised by the talent of his friend, was all smiles; Louise was delighted at the praise showered on O'Neill and secretly elated that he would now be drawn more closely into her circle.

It was part of Cook's philosophy to encourage amateur participation at all levels of his theater, as a statement of rebellion against the slick professionalism of Broadway. Thus, in addition to the playwriting of non-playwrights, he welcomed the acting and directing of non-actors and non-directors. Enthusiasm for the new kind of theater was the chief requirement.

The cast for *Bound East for Cardiff* (all male) included Cook himself in the leading role of the dying sailor, Yank. Reed played another of the sailors, and O'Neill, reluctantly yielding to the group spirit, was persuaded to play the one-line role of the Mate, and to double as prompter (standing behind a flimsy partition where, breathing nervously and loudly, he distracted the other actors). The production of *Bound East for Cardiff* and the emergence of O'Neill provided the impetus for the birth of the Provincetown Players in New York, which, in turn, became the spearhead of the avant garde theater in America.

For Reed, the theater experiment in Provincetown was an exciting distraction, and he eagerly contributed his spare time to it. But he was more absorbed by politics and too busy earning his living by journalism to let it become the center of his life, as it did O'Neill's, the Cooks's, and a handful of others. As for Louise, still uncommitted to a career, and not yet as passionately involved in politics as Reed, she was ready to hurl herself wholeheartedly into the theater project, particularly since it meant an increased rapport with O'Neill.

O'Neill now became a part of the Provincetown social life. Cook urged him to write another play for production that summer and Reed found him a shack, diagonally across the street from his own house, where he thought O'Neill would find it more comfortable to write than in the shipwrecked boat in Truro. O'Neill moved in with Terry Carlin, who that summer consolidated the strong impact he had on the young playwright by filling him in on some of the more colorful details of his life.

A tall, rawboned Irishman with a gaunt face, large nose, coarse white hair, and a lantern jaw, Terry was later immortalized by O'Neill as Larry Slade in *The Iceman Cometh.* Terry's blue-gray eyes had flecks in the irises from a gunpowder explosion, and he had long yellow teeth and long bony fingers. He was unkempt and unclean by choice, but somehow his repulsive appearance was overcome by the effect of his charm. Jack London and Theodore Dreiser liked and admired him. He was a facile, often brilliant talker, and the force of his personality made him welcome anywhere he chose to bestow it. Since his material needs were practically non-existent, he had no trouble maintaining himself on occasional handouts from his friends.

Reed and Louise maintained a disorganized household in Provincetown. They installed as cook an anarchist named Hippolyte Havel, who was a Greenwich Village fixture during the winter. A short, stocky, black-haired man, once likened by a friend to a ragged chrysanthemum, Hippolyte, like Terry Carlin, became a character in *The Iceman Cometh*. In New York, Hippolyte was the lover of Polly Holliday, who owned a cafe in the Village that was a meeting place for intellectuals. He was also nominally her cook, but he spent more time out of the kitchen than in it, and was usually the center of attention at Polly's with his extravagant and profane denunciations of the bourgeoisie and his temper tantrums. He and Polly did not live peacefully, for Polly was inclined to philander, and though Hippolyte was theoretically committed to a tolerant attitude about sexual freedom, he tended to lose his perspective where Polly was concerned. Polly's grievance against Hippolyte was of a different nature. One night, after Hippolyte had made a particularly noisy scene at the restaurant, she complained to one of her customers that Hippolyte was not acting in good faith, because he hadn't committed suicide. "He promised me over and over again," she said, "but he just won't keep his word."

Theodore Dreiser, while living in the Village and

struggling to gain recognition, once told a friend, "Havel is one of those men who ought to be supported by the community; he is a valuable person for life, but he can't take care of himself."

Reed had decided to take care of him for the summer and found that his well-meant gesture subjected him to a houseful of guests week after week, for Hippolyte's menus were widely appreciated and his after-dinner conversation was provocative. Once, after Reed had expounded on some radical cause, Hippolyte furiously accused him of being a "parlor socialist," to which Reed retorted, "And you're a kitchen anarchist!"

Life was quieter, though no less untidy, across the street in O'Neill's shack. He and Terry ate out of cans and threw the empty cans out their back door. Occasionally they varied their diet with fish presented to them by the Portuguese fishermen. O'Neill was trying to work, for he had promised Jig Cook another play for production that summer. And while he was forced into a certain amount of socializing with the Reed household and other neighbors, he attempted to insulate himself for at least part of the day by nailing a sign on his front door that read "Go to Hell."

While Reed was as gregarious as O'Neill was withdrawn, he found the bustle of his own household distracting when he wanted to work. He would often glance enviously at O'Neill's sign across the street, and was grateful to be able to escape from Provincetown occasionally for magazine assignments, even though it meant parting from Louise.

It was during Reed's absences that O'Neill felt himself most endangered. He was aware of Louise watching him, often, as he took his daily swim in the bay. His shack had a long ramp running down almost to the water's edge. After standing in his wide door frame gazing out to sea, sometimes for hours on end, he would move swiftly into the water and swim straight out without swerving to right or left. His next door neighbor, an aspiring actress named Kyra Markham, used to worry about him. She watched as his head became a tiny dot in the distance and sometimes vanished altogether.

Louise was spellbound by O'Neill's marathon swims. Sometimes after watching him from her window, she would join him on the beach. O'Neill could no longer pretend that he was not deeply and unhappily in love with her. Because with him to fall in love was to idealize, he was convinced that Louise, committed to Reed, would be offended by his love. He not only concealed his feelings, but tried his best to avoid her; he was the only one to whom it was not plain that Louise was pursuing him.

One evening after he and Terry had spent a few hours in Reed's house, Louise announced that she was going to New York the following day, and handed O'Neill a book of poetry she said he would enjoy, asking him to read it while she was gone. When O'Neill opened the book in his shack he found a note slipped between two pages in what he recognized as Louise's writing. It read, "Dark eyes. What do you mean?" For the first time it occurred to him that Louise might be encouraging his feelings. But this threw him into an even worse quandary. His sense of loyalty to Reed was doubly outraged at the thought that Louise could be thinking of betraying him—and with a friend whom he trusted.

When Louise returned, she had the satisfaction of seeing that she had thoroughly unnerved O'Neill. O'Neill was torn between his affection for Reed and his desire for Louise. He alternately tried to avoid them both and to watch them together. After tormenting himself a few days in this manner he was handed a note from Louise by Terry. It read, "I must see you alone. I have to explain something, for my sake and Jack's. You have to understand."

It was a summons O'Neill could not resist.

Louise's "explanation" was a characteristic combination of truth and romantic invention, designed to get her what she wanted without sacrifice of her own image as a heroine. She loved Reed, she told O'Neill, and could never leave him. He was seriously ill and was soon going to have a kidney operation that might be fatal. His illness prevented him from having sexual relations, and they were living together as brother and sister. In spite of his apparent good spirits and his continuing capacity for work, he was, in fact, preparing himself for death and she was helping him resign himself. Her own situation was tragic and she was turning desperately to O'Neill for consolation and love. Reed, she said, would understand and not blame either her or O'Neill.

Reed was, in fact, preparing for an operation. But that June his doctor in New York told him his condition was somewhat better and the operation could wait until fall. Reed did realize, though, that the operation could be fatal, and the thought of death occupied him long enough to write a poem about it, which began:

> Death comes like this, I know—
> Snow-soft and gently cold;
> Impalpable battalions of thin mist,
> Light-quenching and sound-smothering and slow.

His ailment, however, had no bearing on his sexuality. He was concerned about the possibility of infecting Louise, and he asked his doctor if it was medically advisable to suspend sexual activity until after his operation. His doctor assured him that there was no danger of infecting Louise. Louise's need, therefore, seems more likely to have been due to the fact that Reed was frequently away from her on writing assignments. And if Reed was, indeed, as complaisant as she promised O'Neill he would be, it was because she told him quite a different story than she told O'Neill; a month or two later she was taking great pains to make Reed believe that O'Neill was only the most casual of friends to her.

O'Neill, in his naiveté, accepted Louise's account without question. Some years later, in confessing the details of the affair to his wife, Agnes, he said that he pitied as well as admired Louise, and that she became for him "a great woman, something out of the old Irish legends, betrayed by life"—exactly what Louise wanted him to believe.

O'Neill and Louise became lovers, and soon most of their friends were aware of it. From observing Reed's behavior to Louise (loving and proud) and to O'Neill (admiring and affectionate), all their friends believed that Reed was in complete ignorance of the affair—that he was simply too trusting and too much in love to suspect it. Only O'Neill believed that Reed knew about and tacitly condoned the affair, and only Louise knew what it was that she had persuaded Reed to believe.

Mabel Dodge, arriving on the scene in midsummer, was quickly apprized of the situation, and, ever undaunted, let Reed know she stood ready to console him. Candid as always, she later recalled, "I thought Reed would be glad to see me if things were like that between him and Louise—but he wasn't."

The affair continued throughout the summer. When Reed was in Provincetown, all three met and worked happily together. O'Neill continued to receive encouragement for his writing from Reed, and was ready with suggestions and help for Reed's dramatic efforts. The Provincetown Players' third bill included another one-act play by Reed called *The Eternal Quadrangle,* a hastily written farce, mocking the vogue for triangle plays on Broadway. He, Louise, and Cook played the leading parts. When Reed was away, he and Louise exchanged love letters, and she sent him a nude photograph of herself, lying against the dunes.

With Louise to distract him, O'Neill did not write much during the rest of the summer. He confided to Terry Carlin, "When Louise touches me with her fingernail, it's like a prairie fire." He wrote some love poetry inspired by Louise, but was unable to finish in time the play he had promised Jig Cook. (It was a monologue called *Before Breakfast,* produced in New York that winter.) As the time for choosing the Provincetown Players' final bill approached, Cook decided to settle for a one-acter called *Thirst* that O'Neill had written two years earlier and that his father had had privately printed in a volume including four other one-act plays by O'Neill, none of them approaching the originality or vigor of *Bound East for Cardiff.*

Thirst was notable chiefly for its ending in which O'Neill indulged himself in his only literary brush with cannibalism. Its symbolic characters were a Dancer, a Gentleman, and a West Indian Mulatto Sailor, adrift on the life raft of a wrecked steamer. The Dancer and the Gentleman, driven mad by thirst, suspect the silent Sailor of hoarding water. The Dancer offers herself to him, but he resists her, stolidly insisting he has no water. The Dancer finally dies, and the Sailor takes out his knife, muttering, "We will live now. . . . We shall eat. We shall drink." The horrified Gentleman pushes the Dancer's

97

body from the raft, the Sailor stabs the Gentleman and loses his own balance, and the two fall into the shark-infested water.

Louise was cast as the Dancer and O'Neill played the taciturn West Indian Mulatto Sailor who entertained the notion of dining on her. The production gave O'Neill and Louise a chance to play (with deadly earnestness) a love scene remarkable for the banality of its dialogue and the luridness of its action:

DANCER (putting her hand on [the sailor's] shoulder she bends forward with her golden hair almost in his lap and smiles up into his face): I like you Sailor. You are big and strong. We are going to be great friends, are we not? (The Negro is hardly looking at her. He is watching the sharks.) Surely you will not refuse me a little sip of your water?

SAILOR: I have no water.

DANCER: Oh, why will you keep up this subterfuge? Am I not offering you price enough? (Putting her arm around his neck and half-whispering in his ear.) Do you not understand? I will love you, Sailor! Noblemen and millionaires . . . have loved me, have fought for me. I have never loved any of them as I will love you. Look in my eyes, Sailor, look in my eyes! (Compelled in spite of himself by something in her voice, the Negro gazes deep into her eyes. For a second his nostrils dilate—he draws in his breath with a hissing sound—his body grows tense and it seems as if he is about to sweep her into his arms. Then his expression grows apathetic again. He turns to the sharks.)

DANCER: Oh, will you never understand? Are you so stupid that you do not know what I mean? . . . I have promised to love *you*—a Negro sailor—if you will give me

98

one small drink of water. Is that not humiliation enough that you must keep me waiting so? . . . Will you give me that water?

SAILOR (without even turning to look at her): I have no water.

DANCER (shaking with fury): Great God, have I abased myself for this? Have I humbled myself before this black animal only to be spurned like a wench of the streets? It is too much! You lie, you dirty slave! You have water. You have stolen my share of the water. (In a frenzy she clutches the sailor about the throat with both hands.) Give it to me! Give it to me!

SAILOR (takes her hands from his neck and pushes her roughly away. She falls face downward in the middle of the raft.) Let me alone! I have no water.

The audience apparently managed to sit through the performance, for there is no record of a mass exodus, but their enthusiasm for their summer theater must have been sorely tested.

The Players' final bill was not a great success and in an effort to end their season with éclat, they presented a "Review Bill" that included *The Game,* which, with its stylized setting and performance had turned out a minor tour de force, and the summer's most enthusiastically received play, *Bound East for Cardiff.*

Toward the end of summer, Cook and Reed began toying with the idea of carrying on with their theater in Greenwich Village that winter. Susan Glaspell was worried that such a project would be laughed at in New York —"new playwrights, amateur acting, somewhere in an old stable. . . . I did not think we were ready to go to New York; I feared we couldn't make it go," she recalled. But Reed, with his usual ebullience, insisted that it could be

99

done. Cook needed only Reed's encouragement to persuade him, and, with these two as the chief proponents of the plan, a meeting of all those who had participated in the summer's productions was called on September 5. In addition to the Cooks, Reed, Louise, and O'Neill, they included Hapgood and his wife, the Zorachs, Mary Vorse, Max Eastman, and his actress wife, Ida Rauh.

A manifesto was drawn up; the name, Provincetown Players, was voted into official being; Cook was elected president and the new home in New York, wherever it might be, was christened by O'Neill the Playwrights Theater. The theater's chief function was to be the encouragement of new American plays "of artistic, literary and dramatic—as opposed to Broadway—merit."

Cook was entrusted with the The Players' total working capital of $320—$80 was left over from the summer's productions and eight contributions of $30 each had been made by the better-heeled members—and instructed to find a theater. Enjoining everyone to "write another play," he happily departed for New York.

With theatrical activity suspended, Reed, Louise, and O'Neill stayed on to enjoy Provincetown's beautiful September weather. Reed was negotiating with the editors of the *Metropolitan* about the possibility of an assignment in China—a country he had wanted, since childhood, to visit. But he was still uncertain about when he would have to have an operation, and increasingly concerned over being able to support himself and Louise if he did have to spend some time in the hospital. A friend, David Carb (one of the founding members, with Reed, of the Playwrights Theater), had recently entered Johns Hopkins Hospital in Baltimore for a similar operation, and Reed wrote to him for advice. "We will make rendezvous at the undertaker's or the cemetery if you don't get some sense knocked into you," Carb wrote back, chiding Reed for his reluctance to have the operation. "I'm quite as broke as you—broker—you can sell your stuff. And it's worth going into debt for. . . . I'm pawning all I ever hope to make, to see it through. Think it over, Jack—you can raise the money easily—about $10 a day it costs—and when you are well, plug like hell to pay up. This is headquarters—and not a bit gruesome. In fact it's quite easy to work here. Bring your typewriter and get well. . . . Won't you do it? It's mere common sense—you aren't well. You can't work much—actually your earning capacity is lessened—If it's the money part that deters you—it's really economy."

Carb's advice made sense to Reed. He took advantage of the relative quiet to which Provincetown had reverted by the departure of many of its summer visitors to turn out a couple of pot boilers for *Collier's* and the *Metropolitan*.

O'Neill finished writing *Before Breakfast* and began another play called *Ile*. And Louise continued to divide her time between the two men, pleased to be regarded as essential by each, and committing herself wholly to neither.

Chapter Six

REED, LOUISE, AND O'NEILL returned to New York at the end of September. One of the first things all three were eager to see was the "theater" Cook had found. It was the parlor floor of an ancient brownstone at 139 MacDougal Street, a block south of Washington Square. It adjoined the Liberal Club and the Washington Square Book Shop, and was rented for $100 a month. Rudimentary renovations were already underway and Cook thought the theater could open at the beginning of November. At a meeting of all the members in Reed's apartment on October 7, it was decided that *Bound East for Cardiff* and *The Game*, together with a play by Floyd Dell, were to make up the first bill.

Since each author was expected to supervise personally the staging of his own play, both O'Neill and Louise were immediately pressed into work. Reed, though he had an assignment from the *Tribune* to report a strike in the Standard Oil plant in Bayonne, New Jersey, found time to rehearse for the role of Death in *The Game*. All through October the three continued their relationship, Louise secretly triumphant in her hold on the two men, O'Neill under Louise's spell, Reed unaware of deception and staunchly promoting O'Neill's career. Early in October he sent a short story by O'Neill, "Tomorrow," to Carl Hovey at the *Metropolitan*, urging Hovey to recognize O'Neill's promise by publishing it. Hovey agreed that O'Neill had talent, but did not like the story. (It was published in the *Seven Arts* magazine the following year.)

O'Neill drew upon the peculiar relationship that existed between Reed, Louise, and himself when he wrote *Strange Interlude* ten years later. The heroine, Nina, is married to a man who cannot have children (symbolically equated by O'Neill with Reed, who, according to Louise, had been rendered temporarily impotent by illness). She secretly takes a lover (who is a friend of her husband) in order to become pregnant (or, in O'Neill's symbolism, to become sexually fulfilled). O'Neill was probably representing Louise's emotions accurately when he depicted Nina's "gloating" pleasure in her hold over her two men.

The opening on November 3 of the Playwrights Theater to a subscription audience of 140 created far more excitement and optimism among the Players themselves than it did among the viewers; while *Bound East for Cardiff* appeared to be the hit of the triple bill, the amateurism of all three productions did not augur a serious challenge to Broadway. Nevertheless, the fuse had been lighted that would eventually result in standing the commercial theater on its ear; within the next two years the Provincetown Players were being credited by leading drama critics with having given birth to a vigorous and innovative era in the American theater. While O'Neill was to link his life and career to the Players, Reed and Louise were destined to be present only at the conception.

Even before the launching of the Playwrights Theater, Reed and Louise had decided they no longer wanted to spend all their time in Greenwich Village. They bought a little house in Croton-on-Hudson, about an hour's train ride from Manhattan, where a number of other writers and artists had settled, among them Boardman Robinson and his wife and Max Eastman. It was an old house at the foot of Mt. Airy, outside the village. Painted white, it had four rooms and a tiny attic, and there was a shack on the grounds that could be used as a studio. They moved in a few pieces of furniture—enough to allow them to spend weekends there—and postponed their final moving, for Reed had been ordered into the hospital by his doctor at the beginning of November. An operation was not yet definite, but a series of tests had been prescribed. Reed reluctantly dropped the project of going to China for the *Metropolitan,* and sent the magazine instead what was to be his last contribution to its pages, a feature story about the strike he had covered for the *Tribune.*

A few days before Reed entered the hospital on November 12, he and Louise decided to get married. Paul Trullinger had waited six months to bring a divorce action against Louise and the divorce had just been granted. According to one friend, Marie Feldenheimer, Louise and Trullinger had agreed to a trial separation. She believed it was Trullinger's intuition, rather than Louise's stated intention, that Louise would not return. Mrs. Feldenheimer said he saw her off on the train to New York— probably unaware that she was going to join Reed—and gave her a bouquet of violets.

When Trullinger finally did divorce Louise—for "cruel and inhuman treatment, personal indignities and desertion"—he seemed more concerned about regaining possession of a piece of real estate he had bought in her name than he did about losing a wife. Nevertheless, he continued to talk fondly of her to Carl and Helen Walters for many years, and, according to them, he never quite recovered from losing her.

Reed and Louise went secretly to Poughkeepsie from

Croton, having agreed to tell only one or two of their closest friends of the marriage. They were married in the city hall, with two strangers as witnesses, and returned to Croton to spend their last few hours together there before separating. On November 12 Louise accompanied Reed to Baltimore and saw him installed in Johns Hopkins Hospital. They had agreed, since their finances were low after the purchase of the Croton house, that Louise should not incur the expense of a hotel room in Baltimore, and that she should await the results of the tests in New York.

According to William and Marguerite Zorach, who were Reed's neighbors in Washington Square, the day Louise returned to the apartment, O'Neill moved in with her. She told Marguerite that she was trying to help O'Neill put his plays into shape; they were fragmentary, she said, but she had deep faith in them and believed that with her encouragement he would produce something truly fine. She also confided to Marguerite that her life with Reed was often trying. "You have no idea what it's like living with Jack," she said. "His war images come back to him at night when he tries to sleep; he goes through hell."

Robert Rogers was another friend to whom Louise implied that she was O'Neill's guide and inspiration. A Harvard friend of Reed, Rogers was an M.I.T. professor of English. Rogers, who had been on a visit to New York while Louise was taking Reed to the hospital, wrote to tell her that he was disappointed to have missed her.

"I saw everybody else," he wrote, "except Gene, whom I should have liked awfully to see. . . . I hope that he is still keeping straight in spite of the temptations of the big city and that you have made a permanent cure of him."

Dorothy Day, a willowy twenty-year-old who worked for the *Masses* as assistant to Max Eastman, was, for a time, a close friend of O'Neill. The vague, mystic urge toward Catholicism that was later to impel her into missionary work and the founding of the *Catholic Worker* was as yet submerged. Although an eager participant in the drinking, talking, and singing of the bohemian community in the village, she would find herself drawn to St. Joseph's Church on Sixth Avenue after a night spent joyously in the Hell Hole. There in the icy dawn, knowing nothing about Catholicism (for she had been raised a Protestant), she would kneel during early morning mass.

"We were all so young," she said. "We all knew that Gene was in love with Louise, and believed that he was nursing a hopeless passion. We regarded him as a romantic figure—a genius unhappily in love." Like most of the group, she believed that Louise, if forced into a choice, would give up the obscure playwright for the successful journalist.

How Louise herself intended to resolve the situation is a puzzle. All through November, while living with O'Neill and encouraging his devotion, she was writing ardent letters to Reed, reaffirming her devotion to him and making slighting references to O'Neill.

Louise wrote to Reed on November 13: "Dearest Sweetheart, please don't be lonesome. I'll come any time you say and stay in a room somewhere. I don't need to stay in a hotel. . . . I'm so anxious to know what they will decide up there about you." An acquaintance had just given her a lecture, she said, about the dangers of a kidney operation and cautioned her to tell him not to let the doctors operate.

Reed answered her, "Dearest of living Honies," saying he had been reading her letter "over and over and over, deary honey," and describing the tests he had been undergoing on "intestines, blood-pressure, heart, lungs, liver, muscles, nerves, etc."adding that tomorrow his kidneys would be "thoroughly overhauled."

"Everybody is very nice and very business-like," he went on, "but a hospital is a hellish place, and this is no exception. If I didn't have books to read and some work to do, I don't know what would become of me. And I certainly do miss my honey so it hurts.

"For two or three days yet I won't know how long I must stay. But if it is any great time I am going to send for my honey, for without her it is getting to be almost impossible." He signed the letter, "your loving hub."

"Oh, darling, it seems so strange and lonesome," Louise answered. "Crowds of people are in this room every minute but it doesn't help any at all. I want my honey!" She was going out to Croton, she said, so she could have the little house "so nice and cheery for you when you come." She really loved having the house, she added.

"I'll come up to see you any minute you say," Louise continued, "because I love you with my whole heart." She said she was working on a story and would send it to him soon. Reed, despite the pain he was undergoing, patiently criticized the story when it arrived and made suggestions for improvement. "The more I read the story, the finer I think it essentially is," he wrote, ending, "Lots of pain. Perhaps more later. Cannot think straight."

Louise, between her writing and her efforts to decorate the Croton house, was not functioning as efficiently as Reed wanted her to in other areas. Although solicitous of her well-being, and trying to face his illness stoically, a gentle note of reproof appeared in his letters to her from time to time. "I am very much embarrassed at not having my check book here," Reed wrote to Louise in mid-November. "You remember I asked you to please get a new one and send it right down? Please do it quickly—you need only to telephone the bank and have them mail it to me. It is costing me money every day because I haven't got a check to send to the Morris Plan Co., etc. and I can't pay the gas bill—and I can't pay my hospital fees, which were due day before yesterday. And how about my laundry? I need shirts, handkerchiefs and nightshirts."

Apologizing for the "hasty note," Reed assured her that he was having no more pain, was feeling fine, and sent "all love, my honey."

Louise, who had been suffering from a throat infection and keeping Reed informed of it, now wrote to tell him that "the abscess has broken and my throat is much better." In another letter she spoke of O'Neill and another friend having dinner with her in the apartment, adding, "I'm so *tired* of their old faces and their old chatter. . . . I do wish you were home."

On November 15 Reed wrote to Louise, "It can't be many more days before I know what's going to happen. I am *so* glad that your little [throat] business is clearing up. When I know what's going to happen to me I'll let you know when to come. I certainly ache to see you." He wrote that he had half finished a short story he hoped the *Metropolitan* would take, and added that the hospital was full of old college friends of his, either patients or doctors, and they had all paid him visits. "But I've got a big aching void which just fits my honey," he went on. "Be a sweet, good dear now, and don't get worried or impatient. I'll either be out, or be having you down, in a very few days."

The next day Reed informed Louise that the doctor would arrange his operation the following Monday, if at last he decided it was necessary, and that she should expect a telegram Saturday or Sunday. He hoped everything was going smoothly with the Croton house, he said, and he wished he could be in New York for the opening of the Playwrights Theater's second bill, which was presenting his play, *Freedom*. "But let me tell you a secret," he added, "If I were to come home tomorrow I'd go off somewhere with my honey and let the theater go to hell."

After receiving an apologetic note from Louise about his checkbook and laundry, Reed wrote back not to worry about it. "I can get along all right until Monday," he said. "By the time you get this I will probably be all over my second torture [the new series of tests]. Then I'll let you know as soon as they have decided what to do."

The second series of tests determined that Reed would have to have a kidney removed. His operation was scheduled for November 20, and Louise went to Baltimore at once to be with him. Walter Lippmann accompanied her. "I don't remember the train ride," Lippmann said many years later, "but I do remember walking down the hospital corridor with Louise, talking about Jack."

Louise stayed in Baltimore until the twenty-fourth, when Reed's doctor assured her that he was completely out of danger. She wrote to him as soon as she arrived in New York to announce her safe return.

"I found everyone in the world living in my room," she said, "and kicked them all out—pleasantly, my dear— no harsh words. . . . Provincetown Players give me a pain in the stomach. . . . Oh darling, the hospital was so white and cold and efficient I hated to leave you there. Please be good and take care of yourself."

A day later Louise wrote again: "I hope you are feeling cheerful. I had a lump in my throat as big as the Woolworth Tower when I left the station and it still comes back any moment." She added that "Gene" and another friend were taking her to dinner. "I'll weep in the middle of it if they aren't careful," she said. She went on to tell him of all the friends who had called to express their concern and sympathy for him. "Oh, honey heart—everyone's been pouring out love over you all day long and it's nice to have the little secret [their marriage] about us when they do."

Reed wrote a few days later saying that though he was "still profoundly uncomfortable and have to take a hypo to sleep at night," the worst of his pain was over.

Louise answered him on Thanksgiving Day. She couldn't believe it was a feast day, she said. "A dismal, cold rain is falling and it is so dark that I have to keep the gas burning to be able to see to write. I don't feel too gloomy, though, because I had a letter from you this morning and you are a little better." She went on to inform him of the progress being made in dismantling their apartment and furnishing the house in Croton. Some of the furniture she was selling, she said, and some had already been shipped to Croton. "I'm just camping out now; I haven't even a desk to write on." As though trying to reassure both herself and Reed for the finality of the step they were taking in giving up their Village establishment, she added, "There's a 'phone at Croton so you can really make appointments from there and if we ever get frivolous enough or can afford to come in to the theater, we can stay at a hotel. That will be fun. . . . I'm perfectly mad to get to Croton and get the house fixed up." She ended with an offhand remark about O'Neill: "He has sold *Before Breakfast*" (to Frank Shay, proprietor of the Washington Square Bookshop, who was bringing out some of the Provincetown Players' works as they were produced).

On the twenty-ninth Reed wrote that he was feeling

better, but was still obliged to lie in one position. He asked Louise to apologize to all the friends who were writing him letters, saying he could manage to answer only one a day, and that one was for her. He also sent a message to Jig Cook that he hoped to have a new one-act play in shape for production in mid-December, but did not think he would be able to produce it himself.

On December 1, Louise packed what was left of her and Reed's possessions in the Washington Square apartment and moved in with a friend to await Reed's release from the hospital. He had suggested she wait in Croton, but she wrote him that she preferred to stay in town and go to Baltimore to pick him up. "I love you, old honey heart, and separations are nix from now on," she added.

Reed wrote back that he thought he would have to stay in the hospital another two weeks. He said he could not afford to pay for a hotel for Louise for more than a few days, and that if she came now, she would have to leave again and wait for him in New York; if she came just before his discharge, they could travel to Croton together. He left the choice to her. Reed wrote again on the same day, overcome by a surge of love: "I feel I must tell you how very much I love you. I don't see, my lover, how I can ever get on without you in my life for very long."

The next day he wrote, "The doctor is tickled to death with my progress . . . you are to come next Friday or Saturday! Then we'll go home together Monday or Tuesday, honey darling."

He rejoiced in a fond and concerned letter from Copey. "I have thought of you often, and am thinking of you so very often now that I feel I must hear," Copey wrote. "Please write immediately or ask Louise to write the details of your health. . . . The note need be only very brief, but I must hear about your health."

Another letter was from Robert Benchley, then writing for the *New York Tribune:* "Allow me to condole with you on your recent bereavement. We never realize, I suppose, what a wonderful thing a kidney is until it is gone. How true that is of everything in Life, after all, isn't it?"

Reed's optimism over the ultimate success of the operation had led him to renew his negotiations with the *Metropolitan's* editor, Carl Hovey, about a trip to China; they had even decided that Louise would accompany him. But now it appeared that his period of convalescence would be longer than he had thought; his doctors told him he might not be able to go for two or three months. "You mustn't be too disappointed if we have to wait for a while," he wrote Louise. "It won't be your honey's fault, and we can have fun waiting, can't we?"

With Reed's recovery now assured, and the prospect of their being united soon—this time less tenuously than before, for they were to settle down in the country as husband and wife—Louise was having an emotional upheaval. She suddenly realized how deeply in love she was with Reed, and became uneasy about the distractions she had allowed to come between them. Without being specific, she wrote telling him that she was unhappy with her past behavior, and had not strictly kept faith with him. Reed replied lovingly and reassuringly. "I don't mind anything in the world if you love me and understand all about everything," Louise wrote back. "When we get back to Croton I hope we can have many long talks. We never really did this summer except once and we were too busy when we came back. It's the best way to keep close to each other and I want to be very close." In the same letter, she told Reed she was having stomach pains and was going to see a doctor.

Louise wrote again a day or two later from Boardman

Robinson's house in Croton, where she had had dinner: "We worked all day at our little house and all traces of former inhabitants have been completely erased so that it really begins to look like us." She said she thought she ought to see a doctor at Johns Hopkins when she came to pick up Reed, "because I do feel that thing inside me a little now and I'd like to be sure that I'm getting the right treatment." (What she had earlier characterized as stomach pain, was actually a uterine infection.) She added that she was not worried because she felt much better, and she was sure that both she and Reed would soon be all well again as soon as they settled down in Croton. "It's *so* quiet and peaceful and happy," she said. She had heard from Carl Hovey's wife, Sonia, that the *Metropolitan* was "crazy" to have Reed go to China. She had also heard from a friend that word that she and Reed were married had got out, but as Boardman Robinson said, "It's a terrible *'scandal'* and is bound to get out." In a burst of enthusiasm, she added, "Oh, my. Just wait until we get well—we will both do *things*—even *I* will—that will be *really good*. You being so ill and my nearly being, made our work seem pretty grave to me. All the weeks before the operation I was so afraid you might not get through with it and I kept thinking to myself—the pity, the unpardonable pity that you had always *wasted* yourself with Greenwich Villagers. . . . Oh darling, I mean this. . . . We never, never can take a chance like that again. That's why I think it will be so fine to do *work* out here, uninterrupted, and play in town."

China was going to be a splendid thing for them both, she went on, and neither of them would ever feel in competition with the other, as was the case with some of their married friends who were both writers. Robinson had just told her of one such couple who had recently arrived back in town and that he said it was "terrible to meet them because they are so *jealous* of each other's work." They came home on separate steamers, five days apart, she said. "We won't *ever* do that. That is just one thing that I love about our being together. You want to see me do my best and I want you to—*at any cost*." She told him to hurry and get well, called him her "sweetest, sweetest darling," and sent him "everything that's best in me."

Reed wrote back of his concern for her health, but seemed reassured that there was nothing seriously wrong. He begged her, though, not to conceal anything. He was euphoric about his own improving condition, and said the doctor had just told him he could probably make the China trip sooner than had at first been thought.

Louise's next letter unsettled him. Although she began with the assurance that she was all right, she went on to tell him that she was in bed. "You remember I told you that I began to feel my insides again," she said. "Well, I got really ill out in the country so I came in and Dr. Lorber examined me and ordered me to bed under special care or in a hospital."

Dr. Herman Lorber was a forty-year-old, Polish-born gynecologist and obstetrician, who had fought his way up from a lower East Side, impoverished childhood to a Park Avenue practice. Always interested in the arts and sympathetic to its young practitioners, he was a favorite of the Greenwich Villagers, to whom he was fondly known as Dr. Harry.

Somewhat incoherently, Louise went on to describe her panic at discovering she had a high temperature. She had no place to stay, was unwilling to enter a hospital, and thought of traveling immediately to Baltimore to enter the hospital there. She was "rescued" by the arrival of an old friend named Becky, who carried her off to her own apartment and agreed to nurse her there under Dr. Lorber's supervision. Louise's symptoms and her garbled account to Reed strongly suggest that her infection was the result of a mismanaged, illegal abortion. Several of her friends were convinced that this was the case. She seemed torn between letting Reed know how ill she really was, concealing what might have been the true cause, and reassuring him that she did not have cancer.

She would have to wait for him at her friend's rather than coming to get him in Baltimore, but she said she was so grateful that Dr. Lorber thought an operation could be avoided that that was all that mattered.

"Oh, my dearest," she wrote, "I'm so sorry to bother you at this time. I've put it off as long as I possibly could —almost too long—just on that account. . . . The little house at Croton looked *so* nice when I left. Oh, darling, I just *ache* to be with you."

Reed replied in considerable alarm: "If you hadn't told me everything, or even if I think you aren't telling me, I'll leave here on a stretcher if necessary, and get carried to New York. You mustn't hold anything back from your honey. You ought to have told me when you first got sick. I was afraid you were ill, and worried a good deal about you." He said he would be able to leave the hospital in a few days, that the doctor had said he had made "a phenomenal recovery," but that he would have to rest for a couple of weeks at home.

The next few days produced bursts of panic and frustration on both sides. On December 11, Reed wrote to Louise that he would be leaving for New York on the following day; he hoped she would be well enough to leave for Croton soon. "I am crazy to be alone with you away from cities and simps." On the twelfth, however, he wired her that he had caught a sore throat and would have to stay another few days. Why hadn't Dr. Lorber written to him explaining her illness, he asked anxiously.

Louise answered telling him of her disappointment at not seeing him. She said Dr. Lorber would talk to him when he arrived, that there was really nothing new to tell, and that no operation would be necessary. Her condition was the same, and all she wanted was to be in the country with him.

Reed's sore throat cleared up more quickly than he had expected and on the thirteenth he wired Louise that he would arrive in New York late that afternoon. Louise met him and they left at once for their house in Croton.

After a joyful reunion that carried them through Christmas and the New Year, the Reeds found that the idyllic existence they had planned was not going to work as well as they had hoped.

In its January issue the *Metropolitan* announced Reed's forthcoming trip to China. "To most of us China is just so many square inches of yellow map," read the house ad. "But not so after 1917. John Reed, the *Metropolitan* war correspondent, is going to China. He will hold up the mirror to this mysterious and romantic country, and we shall see its teeming millions and the big new forces at work there. . . . Imagine Reed in this rich 'copy' empire—the man of whom Rudyard Kipling said, 'His articles in the *Metropolitan* made me see Mexico!' "

Reed and Louise busily went about getting passports and vaccinations, letters of introduction, steamboat passage, and all the other necessary paraphernalia of such a journey. But by the end of January, it looked as though America was on the verge of entering the war.

Chapter Seven

ON FEBRUARY 3, President Wilson announced the severing of diplomatic relations with Germany and that same week Carl Hovey informed Reed that the *Metropolitan* did not believe, in view of the changed world situation, that it could justifiably invest in Reed's assignment to China. Hovey asked Reed dubiously if there was any other more relevant assignment he could propose. But Reed knew, as well as Hovey, that because of his bitterly outspoken opposition to America's entry into the war, his services were unacceptable.

Reed had now lost not only the lucrative employment he had been counting on—for the *Metropolitan* was now closed to him—but the pleasure and romance of the dreamed-of China trip with Louise. He had offers from other magazines, but all of them, wary of his reputation as a radical, stipulated that he keep his personal views to himself and adopt a conformist view in his reporting. He refused to consider this, and made up his mind that he would write nothing in the future that did not express his hatred of capitalism and that did not encourage social revolution. He took an active part in pacifist demonstrations, although realizing that they were not going to prevent America's entry into the war, and he continued to express his views in the *Masses*.

"I know what war means," he wrote in the *Masses* of April 1917. "I have been with the armies of all the belligerents except one, and I have seen men die, and go mad, and lie in hospitals suffering hell; but there is a worse thing than that. War means an ugly mob-madness, crucifying the truth-tellers, choking the artists, side-tracking reforms, revolutions and the working of social forces. Already in America those citizens who oppose the entrance of their country into the European melee are called 'traitors,' and those who protest against the curtailing of our meager rights of free speech are spoken of as 'dangerous lunatics.'

"For many years this country is going to be a worse place for free men to live in; less tolerant, less hospitable. Maybe it is too late, but I want to put down what I think about it all.

"Whose war is this? Not mine. I know that hundreds of thousands of American workingmen employed by our great financial 'patriots' are not paid a living wage. I have seen poor men sent to jail for long terms without trial, and even without any charge. Peaceful strikers, and their wives and children, have been shot to death, by private detectives and militiamen. The rich have steadily become richer, and the cost of living higher, and the workers proportionally poorer. These toilers don't want war—not even civil war. But the speculators, the employers, the plutocracy—they want it, just as they did in Germany and England; and with lies and sophistries they will whip up our blood until we are savage and then we'll fight and die for them."

On April 2, the day President Wilson was to address a joint session of Congress, Reed went to Washington to participate in a pacifist rally attended by thousands. He was to be one of the speakers, but before his turn came, an announcement was made that Wilson had declared war on Germany. Shouting down the turmoil caused by the announcement, Reed declared: "This is not my war and I will not support it."

Reed was called to testify at the House judiciary committee hearings on the conscription bill, which he had characterized as undemocratic. Part of his testimony included the statement that he was not "a peace-at-any-price man, or a thorough pacifist," but that he would not serve in this war. "You can shoot me if you want," he added, probably deriving a double satisfaction from the knowledge (not shared by the committee) that there was little chance of his being drafted in any case, because of his physical disability. "I have no personal objection to fighting," he told the committee. "I just think that the war is unjust on both sides, that Europe is mad, and that we should keep out of it."

By the time he had finished testifying in Washington, Reed was a pariah. The publications that were willing to employ him paid very little; many of his friends, among them a number of former Harvard classmates, avoided or cut him. His family in Portland painfully embarrassed by his views, tried to reason him into a more rational course of behavior. His brother Harry volunteered to fight, and wrote to Reed that it was useless for him "to buck what can't be changed." His mother wrote to him even more emotionally:

"It gives me a shock to have your father's son say that he cares nothing for his country and his flag. I do not want you to fight, heaven knows, for us, but I do not want you to fight against us, by word and pen, and I can't help saying that if you do, now that war is declared, I shall feel deeply ashamed. I think you will find that most of your friends and sympathizers are of foreign birth; very few are real Americans comparatively."

After looking around rather hopelessly for some publication that was willing to hire him and would pay him a decent wage, he found work on the *New York Mail*, a daily paper whose editorial point of view was somewhat critical of Great Britain's role in the war, and willing to resist some aspects of America's war hysteria. (It later evolved that the paper was financed by the German government, but Reed had no idea of this.)

Reed's difficulties during the winter and spring of 1917 were dismaying to Louise. While she agreed in principle with his views, she was not yet ready to throw herself into anti-war activity, for she was still hopeful of establishing herself as a writer and did not want to cut herself off, as Reed had done, from the possibility of working for an establishment publication. She had hoped that the China assignment would give her a chance to file free-lance stories and make her reputation as a journalist, and with that hope shattered, was exploring other possibilities. She was also trying, still, to market her poetry, but without much success.

Somehow, the little house in Croton had lost its charm; with Reed away, attending anti-conscription rallies in New York and Washington, and busy also with assignments from the *Mail*, Louise grew restless. In early spring she told Reed she would like to go to Provincetown by herself for a while to write. Reed, always generous and encouraging about her career, could not spare the time to accompany her to Provincetown, and agreed to let her go alone.

O'Neill was in Provincetown, having left New York after the Provincetown Players' final bill of the season in March. He, too, was trying to escape into an atmosphere more congenial for writing. The five or six months he had spent in New York had been unproductive for him; he had not managed to complete even one short play.

Once in Provincetown, O'Neill found he could concentrate again on writing. In a short period, before the end of April, he turned out four plays—*Ile, The Moon of the Caribbees, The Long Voyage Home,* and *In the Zone* —all of which have stood the test of time. O'Neill worked in a small hotel called the Atlantic House, where he rented a room, and occasionally he wrote on the beach, a blanket wrapped around him, in the belief that the sea air was healthful. The proprietor of the Atlantic House, who was also its chef, amused himself by shouting a customer's order to the kitchen, then hurrying to his stove to cook it himself.

That spring Provincetown, like the rest of the country, was swept up in war hysteria. Threats of German U-boat invasions were a daily topic of conversation on the exposed Cape. O'Neill was not popular among the patriotic villagers for he was identified with Reed and known to be an approving, if not an activist member, of the pacifist movement.

When Louise arrived in Provincetown, she rented a room not far from O'Neill's hotel and kept in touch with Reed by letter and telegram. She took some of her meals at the Atlantic House and soon she and O'Neill picked up their interrupted romance. Their relationship continued, as before, on the basis of love and mutual encouragement of work. Louise was more successful in promoting O'Neill's career than in establishing her own. She was able to persuade Waldo Frank, who edited the literary magazine *Seven Arts,* to buy, for fifty dollars, the story "Tomorrow" which the *Metropolitan* had rejected.

"Our magazine was very serious, almost religious—we considered ourselves the organ of cultural nationalism," Waldo Frank once said. "We were disciples of Walt Whitman and were creating the voice Whitman wanted."

As for Louise, Frank did not take her seriously as a writer. "She was just around," he said. "She was a 'flaming youth' girl, an Irish beauty, thin, with pale skin, very romantic. She was intellectually alive and responsive, although not profound."

While pleased to have O'Neill's story, Frank was less enthusiastic about a poem Louise submitted, called "Spring in Provincetown." "It is a very true and lovely bit of work," was his comment, "but . . ." He did not accept it for publication.

In May, Reed, returning from an assignment, sent Louise a wistful telegram from Croton: "Peach tree blooming and wrens have taken over their house"; he missed her, but was careful not to put any pressure on her to return from Provincetown.

At the end of May O'Neill felt obliged to go to New London, where his family had a house, in order to be near his draft board. He was as determined as Reed not to fight, but chose the easier way out by claiming exemption on the basis of being an arrested tuberculosis case. Louise, discouraged about her writing, unwilling to go back to New York, and bored by the idea of staying in Provincetown without O'Neill, accompanied him to New London.

O'Neill took Louise to dinner at the house of some old friends, Jessica and Emily Rippin. "It was obvious that he thought she was pretty terrific," Jessica Rippin recalled. Emily added that O'Neill made no secret of being in love with her; neither of the sisters was aware that she was John Reed's wife.

After dinner O'Neill asked Jessica and Emily what they thought of Louise. The women were non-committal, but agreed privately that she was "sloppy."

By the end of May 1917, Louise, growing more and more restless and discontented, rejoined Reed in Croton, where she was given the excuse to take an action that she had been vaguely considering. Reed confessed that he had been having an affair while Louise was in Provincetown. Louise chose to apply a different set of standards to Reed's straying than to her own. She and Reed had a bitter quarrel that ended in her decision to go abroad as a war correspondent. Reed was guilty and submissive. Since he knew nothing of Louise's affair, he meekly bore her anger as the righteous indignation of a faithful, injured wife.

He helped her get accreditation as a foreign correspondent to report the war for the Bell Syndicate, furnished her with introductory letters to friends in Europe and paid for her passage. To his cousin in England, Maunsell Bradhurst, he wrote: "I'm sending you with this letter my wife, who is a newspaper correspondent in our Allied Countries. I want her to know you. . . . And of course you must know her—one of America's lovely poets."

Reed's loving description of Louise contrasted sharply with that of the State Department official who reluctantly issued her a passport on June 1. Louise, when she applied for the passport, must indeed have been in a very distraught state. Her passport picture showed an unkempt young woman, hollow-cheeked, with dark rings under her eyes, mouth agape, wearing a wrinkled, open-neck shirt. (She gave her age as twenty-seven, though she would be thirty at the end of the year.)

The notation clipped to her application read: "I suppose I will have to issue a passport to this wild woman. She is full of socialistic and ultra-modern ideas, which accounts for her wild hair and open mouth [on the photograph]. She is the wife of John Reed, a well-known correspondent."

Louise and Reed parted on June 9. Reed stayed in Croton, while Louise went to a friend's in New York to await the departure of her ship, the Espagne. Late that morning she sent Reed a hastily scribbled note: "Please believe me Jack—I'm going to try like the devil to pull myself together over there and come back able to act like a reasonable human being. I know I'm probably all wrong about everything. I know the only reason I act so crazy is because it hurts so much, that I get quite insane, that's all." She told him that if anything should happen to her (which she was sure it wouldn't) he should inform her mother in Nevada. This was merely as a matter of record, she said, for she did not feel herself to be in any way connected with her family. She would work hard when she got to France, she said, and told him to "please do whatever you want to about *everything*."

From the letter, it is hard to determine whether Louise's uppermost emotion was jealousy over Reed's affair, bewilderment at the violence of her reaction, or frustration at finding herself thwarted in some fanciful conception of the ideal triangle. It had not occurred to her, evidently, that the triangle might become a quadrangle. Even in her incoherence, however, one thing was clear: She was intensely attached to Reed and frightened at the thought of losing him. And even before she sailed for France she half regretted her decision. For Reed's distress over her reaction was very apparent, and she feared that she might be punishing him too severely.

"If this thing [Louise's hysterical anger and rush to get away] ever happens again, *don't don't* get despondent," Louise went on in her note to Reed. "Maybe I'll understand better when I get back. I love you so much. It's a terrible thing to love as much as I do. I will try to be decent and sane about it when I get back."

O'Neill, almost as upset as Reed, tried to believe that Louise was, indeed, running away from Reed, rather than from him; but he was hurt by her departure, and reverted to a mood of drunken gloom that lasted until he joined the Cooks in Provincetown, where, encouraged by their approval of his new work, he got back to writing.

Chapter Eight

REED RECEIVED LOUISE'S apologetic note in Croton, read it glumly, wandered about the house and grounds brooding, and decided that he could not bear staying in the country. He took a late train into New York, arriving after Louise's ship had sailed. Knowing she would not reach France for ten days or more, Reed nevertheless felt compelled to answer her letter immediately. He addressed her in care of American Express in Paris. "In lots of ways we are very different, and we must try to realize that, while loving each other," he wrote. "But of course on this last awful business, you were humanly right and I was wrong. I have always loved you, my darling, ever since I first met you—and I guess I always will. This is more than I've ever felt for anyone, honestly. I know that the one thing I cannot bear any more is consciously to hurt you, honey."

He went on to tell her that their house in Croton was "a terrible place" without her, and that he had locked it up and moved into New York.

"I got into town at two this morning, and walked around the streets until almost dawn, thinking of my darling. . . . It is really quite frightfully lonely without you," he wrote. But he added that the very loneliness would probably drive him to work, and he might get something accomplished.

Two days later, on June 13, Reed wrote to Louise

again, from the city room of the *New York Mail*, between assignments. It was terribly hot in town, he said, and he was feeling very restless and lonesome. "I truly wish my little honey were here with me, and we were going out to Croton on the 5:03!" While receiving all his mail and telephone messages at the Harvard Club, and dropping in there every day, Reed was actually living on Fourteenth Street.

"I've put screens on the windows, bought a couple of grass rugs, put a Yale lock on the door and am beginning to feel settled. No one knows where I live." He had seen hardly any of their friends, he said, and was living an isolated life except for dropping into the Brevoort Hotel occasionally after an assignment; the other night at the Brevoort he had run into Emma Goldman and her fellow anarchist and lover, Alexander Berkman. Theodore Dreiser, Djuna Barnes, the novelist and poet, and Benjamin De Casseres, the poet, had also been there. And he had heard from the Irish writer, Padraic Colum, who had asked about Louise.

He was enclosing a note from S. K. Ratcliffe, the English representative of *The New Republic,* who promised to put her in touch with anyone she wished to see in England—"Wells, Galsworthy, etc."

"It seems already as if you'd been gone for months, my little dearest," Reed wrote. "I can't realize it yet. I do hope you'll not stay away from me too long." Everybody he met was so interested in Louise's trip, Reed said, and so envious of her. He hoped that by the time this letter reached her, she had gone through her first few days of discomfort and loneliness at being in a strange place. "It won't last, my dear honey—not for you, so sweet and so lovely. . . . I'm really lonesome for my lover's sweet companionship—and that's beside all the other things.

127

You are really an awfully good friend of mine, honey, and I'd like to live with you for a long time."

The next day Reed wrote again, complaining about the heat and the long working hours he had been keeping. He said that all the friends he ran into felt he had made a "fatal mistake" in going to work for the *Mail*, but that this didn't bother him. He then went on to describe at some length his chance meeting with a girl he had once known, who looked so ill and beaten that he had, out of compassion, taken her to a saloon for a drink. There she had told him that she had just been left by her lover, that she had "the same operation they wanted to do to you," and that she was going to kill herself. Reed said he had persuaded her to go home to her mother's house.

"I just tell you all this stupid history, my honey," he went on, "so you may know all that I've been doing, and that you may believe that nevermore is there going to be any chance of any girl coming between me and my honey, and that I'm perfectly tranquil about how I shall be, waiting for you, old lover."

A day later Reed wrote again, briefly, bewailing his loneliness. "Oh my dear lover, I wish we could have gone together! I don't suppose I'll ever be convinced that you had to go so far away!"

Having still had no letter from Louise by the seventeenth, Reed was beginning to worry about her safety. He should have been spending the day in work, he said; he had two articles to write for the *Mail* and four for the *Masses*, but he was putting all work aside to write some more to her. He had gone to Croton on an impulse late the evening before, he said, and had just now come back to the city.

"When I got out there, however, I didn't feel like

going near the house," he said, "so I ate and slept at the Robinsons' and went up to our house this morning. God but it's lovely! The peonies are all out now, and the irises." He added that he hoped the *Mail* would soon give him an assignment to go abroad and that "the authorities" would permit him to leave the country (a hope that, in view of his political stand, was not realistic).

On the nineteenth Reed wrote to Louise from Baltimore, where the *Mail* had sent him to interview "a damned actress about her damned marriage to a damned prizefighter." After that he was supposed to go to Washington, "arriving there at 4 A.M., and arise again at 8:30 A.M. to interview a lot of damned Congressmen." But he was going to let the story go, he said, for the job was getting to be "a little too much of a good thing." He had had only five hours sleep in two nights and "absolutely no time to write my honey darling for two days."

He had an idea for a story for Louise, he said. A New York City policeman, a detective sergeant, was going to Paris financed by Vincent Astor to drive the New York Police Department ambulance. She should ask him how it felt to be under fire, what he thought of Paris, if he was lonesome for his girl; and she should interview some French cops to see what they thought of the American cop.

"Oh, dearest honey, I'm awful lonesome for you! Really! If I weren't working hard all the time, I think I'd go bugs."

Later that day, in Washington, Reed finally had a cable from Louise announcing her safe arrival.

Louise's passage had been difficult and dangerous, with the constant threat of torpedoes. The ship, picking its way slowly through the submarine zone, had been crowded with apprehensive passengers; the lifeboat drills had been numerous and badly organized, and Louise had been so tormented by her emotions about Reed that the journey had been a nightmare.

Responding to Louise's cable, Reed wrote: "I had worked myself up to such a pitch of worry that I couldn't sleep—although I oughtn't to have [worried], as the French line said they had word the boat was out of all possible danger."

A few days later Louise wrote from Paris, where she had arrived after resting two days in Bordeaux. She had several ideas for magazine stories she said, and had been meeting many people who were giving her information and putting her in touch with news sources. "All my life I've wanted to come to Paris," she said, "and here I am!" But it was disappointing to see it under wartime conditions, and even more disappointing to be seeing it without Reed. She was staying at a hotel on the Place Vendôme, whose rates were fairly reasonable, she said—two dollars and sixty cents a day, including breakfast and dinner.

"Nothing much is left of all that old worry now, dearest," Louise continued. "I don't care about it—I just want more than anything else in the world to see you again." She said she would not be frightened to sail home when the time came, even though everyone was talking about the increasing dangers of such a trip. "Do you know there are loads of Americans in Paris, all of whom are crazy to go back, and they are afraid to do it. They have gotten themselves into an awful mess—I mean mentally—over it, hanging around for months and months." It seemed to her, she said, that the trip back would be less agonizing, as the submarine danger would be over soon after the beginning of the trip. What was awful, she said, was waiting for it at the end of the journey.

On June 21 Louise wrote Reed that she thought her chances of being allowed to go to the front lines were good. After describing the difficulties that had to be overcome and the red tape to be gone through, she went on to more personal matters. "I'm awfully sorry that I haven't been more decent to you, honey, but you know I haven't had much experience in love. I'm not excusing myself. I've been just an ass about it all. I know it.

"Yesterday afternoon I was lying down for a few minutes and I had such a frightful nightmare," she wrote. "You seemed to be in such trouble. Oh, dearest, dearest, *please* tell me if anything is wrong. It matters more than anything else in the world to me. Lots of times I worry over something very terrible you said about getting out of my way if anything happened to you. Darling, for God's sake—you're all I've got . . . and I love you *no matter* what you do. Believe that, honey, always. I love you over and above all this jealousy a million times. The trip has done at least that for me. I'll be a better mate for you when I come back." She did not think Reed should try to come over as a correspondent, she said; there was no point in both of them risking the danger of crossing the ocean. She would be coming back soon, and he must not worry about her. "You say no boat left New York last week. So I probably won't hear from you for two weeks. I'll be quite crazy if I don't. God! How I'd love to *hear* from you—I can hardly imagine *seeing* you—touching you. I do love you so."

Louise had been in Paris less than two weeks when she began having serious doubts about having come. She had been subjected to endless red tape insofar as getting

131

the needed clearance to get to the front was concerned, and she did not seem to be able to file stories about anything else. She was toying with the idea of crossing the Channel to England, but everyone—including Reed—had advised her against the danger of that. It seemed that her journalistic career would never get off the ground. Her high hopes that this trip to France would establish her reputation as a war correspondent were already fading.

On a beautiful Saturday afternoon toward the end of June, she found herself overcome with loneliness and depression. "This is the first time I've really broken down since I left, but it has gradually seemed worse and worse," she wrote to Reed. "The Espagne went back today. I wish I had been on it! . . . We are separated and I cannot bear it. I wonder why such terrible torture doesn't actually kill me." She said she had sat in the garden of the Tuilleries, growing more and more gloomy as she watched "old men, widows, mutilated soldiers" go by. She had struck up a conversation with an elderly Frenchwoman, who said to her, "Ah, mademoiselle, *you* do not look strange in Paris, you are so little and so sad." This had quite undone her, and she had gone back to her hotel and "wept her heart out."

"I feel so *alien*," she said. "Not one person since I left my Honey thinks a thing that I do. Not *one!* Sometimes the conversation drives me almost mad. I try not to argue. Often I have to leave the room. I get more and more isolated, crawl down more inside myself and I miss you so *terribly!* . . . I'm homesick for the first time in my life. It's a queer sensation; beside it, seasickness is quite pleasant. I'm *not* homesick for New York, though, or for any *place*—home is where you are, my dearest. . . . I love you and need you terribly."

Two days later Louise was in better spirits. She had

met a Parisian couple who knew Reed's work and admired him greatly, and had spent the evening talking about him. Her greatest deprivation, she said, was in not having letters from him; she knew that mail-bearing ships were being sunk, but kept hoping something would get through.

Reed, for his part, seemed resigned to the irregularities of the mail from abroad, and continued writing faithfully and regularly to Louise, whether he heard from her or not. On June 27 he told her that his work was going very badly. "I don't like it, and I've made some frightful mistakes—which luckily nobody has noticed but myself. For instance, I wrote a list of Congressmen [for one story] and one of them was dead six months ago!" A day later, he wrote her again, starting out in better spirits:

"I don't suppose there is a place in the world so exciting as this city [Washington] now. Missions continually arriving, uniforms, decorations, swords, all sorts of pageants in Congress when the different ambassadors arrive and are received in the Senate. I had a little talk with the President [Wilson] this morning. He was very cordial."

Reed went on to say that he had had several job offers, one from Arthur Brisbane, the new owner of the *Washington Times*. But he did not think there was much satisfaction for him in newspaper work anymore. "I don't feel like doing much of anything," he added. "Sometimes I feel energetic and interested; other times it doesn't seem worth while. I suppose it's largely the heat."

Lincoln Steffens had just returned from Russia, Reed said, and "asked how it was between us, and I said I'd been a fool and a cad, and he just told me most people were at some time, in some way.

"Sweetheart," he continued, "I do hope you're going to get all over your awful feelings by the time you come back. . . . Think about you and me a good deal, will you?"

Later the same day he wrote again, wistfully supposing, "it will be days before I get any mail from you." He said he didn't like "the desperate grind" of his job, the incessant interviewing of Representatives and Senators and "desperate digging up of facts, figures and statistics."

He had gone swimming with some friends in the Potomac that afternoon but it did not seem to make any difference what he did. "I seem to feel just as restless and aimless and dissatisfied," he said. Again he mentioned that there was a chance of his being asked to go to Europe "with the troops." He would let her know in plenty of time if he was coming over, he said.

On July 1, Reed managed to get himself assigned back to New York. Worn out from the heat and bustle of Washington, "so frazzled in my nerves that I didn't know what to do or where to go," he had headed straight for Croton. "After working in the garden for a few hours I felt much better," he said, "and in the little studio I spent an exquisite night. It is beautiful out there, quiet and cool. We should sleep there instead of in the house in summer." He went on to describe their garden lyrically. "The place looks positively tropical, its vegetation is so luxuriant." A love of flowers was one of the gentler passions Reed and Louise shared. They loved poking about in their garden together, and when separated, each took pleasure in describing to the other the flowers that were blooming along the way.

"I do wish I could stay out in the country a while," Reed said, "instead of this terrible rushing about the city! I wish—Oh I wish—I don't know what—"

Louise received two of Reed's letters on July 2. "I almost wept at the sight of them," she wrote Reed. "Oh, dearest, I *could* talk to you now. I *could* air every part of my heart and brain. I understand you and I understand myself better than you think. We would be happy—more deeply happy than we have ever been—this just had to happen—not this particular little miserable mess but *something* to make us find each other. I love you with all my heart—I can never love anyone else. I want everything about you to be beautiful and fine. You are essentially so wonderful and so big. Artists you do not know at all love you over here. They think you are the greatest man in America."

She went on to caution him to be very careful in what he wrote, not because he might get into trouble, but because he might be wrong. Saying that she could not be any more explicit in a letter, she just wanted him to know that "everything over here has changed—the whole aspect has—*within the last three months*" (presumably she was trying to imply that many former pacifists were shifting to an anti-German view, which justified a pro-ally militarism, quite counter to the view Reed was promoting in America). "You know I am not a conservative," she went on, "you know that I feel exactly as you do. . . . O, if I could explain further! If I could only tell you. But anyway, believe that I know what I'm talking about, believe I've not suddenly lost my vision. The truth is that I've come in alone—everyone, military, anti [military], soldiers, civilians—all have taken me strangely into their hearts. If I could only *tell* you, my dearest dear, what the situation is like right now with France, with Russia and with the little brave land of my own ancestors. Don't write anything that is untrue—better a thousand times silence. On this account the more radical radicals here no longer understand what you will write if I cannot tell you."

135

She ended by asking him to let her know his plans as soon as possible, since it would take weeks for her to arrange passage home, and if he was not coming abroad, she would like to begin planning at once for her return. Louise had been in Paris two and a half weeks, and had filed only one story—a piece accepted by the *American Magazine,* but not published. (She had also sent photographs she had taken herself, which were rejected.) Reed, after reading the submitted article, wrote to tell her "how very fine" he thought her power of observation. "You don't yet write as you will, but you can certainly see awfully straight, my honey," he said. "Your story was so much fuller than [Heywood] Broun's [on the same subject] for example, although, trained reporter that he is, he included some things which you forgot or overlooked."

Louise seemed to feel, though, that the only story worth covering was the battlefront, and she could not obtain the necessary clearance to get near the front lines. Her lack of experience, as much as the fact that she was a woman, impeded her. She spent most of her time talking with other Americans and brooding about her relationship with Reed.

On July 4, Reed, complaining that he had received no letters from Louise, anxiously inquired if she had been receiving the money he had been cabling her for her living expenses. He said he was feeling "a little calmer and better" and had begun work on an article for the *Seven Arts.* "I do hope I can get to feeling like writing again. I seem to be entirely out of it." He mentioned that he had just testified at Emma Goldman's trial. (She and Alexander Berkman had been arrested for holding an anti-conscription meeting in the Bronx. Reed testified as a character witness for Emma Goldman and stated that he had never heard Berkman advise men not to register for the draft.)

Reed told Louise that he had dinner the night before with Lincoln Steffens, who was "full of Russia," adding, "I seem at last to bore him a little, for which I am very sad."

"Well, honey," he said, "it gets more and more depressing here. I feel that I must get to writing, so I can be doing something and forget it all."

Louise also wrote on July 4, full of love and longing for Reed:

"You are the only person in the world I tell everything to and we have been and are such wonderful friends. I'm glad you said what you did about being a good friend, besides a lover. I think that's why we were able to see this through. . . . I'm sorry I wrote you all those blue, hysterical letters. I'm quite ashamed. I want to come home as much as ever but quite tranquilly, sweetheart, quite whole and healthy—not broken. You said I'd forget things if I was normal. I guess I am, because I've forgotten. Sometimes I wonder how I would feel if it all happened again. I can't think—I can't believe it will. I don't have nightmares and things like that any more. Sometimes I feel I can't bear it away from my honey—but it's a different feeling—not the awful mad need I used to have when I first left."

She went on to caution him again about participating in radical activity in New York, knowing his proclivity to rush into battle without heed for personal consequences, such as arrest and jail. "You are too precious to waste your energy in that way," she said. "All of your best strength you'll need a little later for big, big things and it would be too terrible if you were out of the running by some rash deed when you are needed most—and you will be needed." She went on to tell him again of the great admiration in which he was held by some of her new friends in Paris. One man, she said, asked if her husband was the John Reed who had written the story "Endymion," and when Louise said yes, he jumped up and began shaking her hand. "Great God," he cried, "it was marvelous, marvelous! I read it aloud to my wife and tears ran down our faces. It's the best story I've ever read."

"Endymion, Or On the Border," had appeared in the *Masses* in December 1916. It was a character sketch of a drunken old doctor, self-exiled in the border town of Presidio, Texas. Its poignancy lay in the fact that the doctor had been a highly cultivated, well-travelled and successful man, who, since his wife's death by drowning thirty years earlier, had buried himself in this semi-primitive town. The odd thing about the story is that Reed, in casting his tale as fiction, seemed to lose all his spontaneity. He was describing the same sort of setting and characters as appeared in his journalistic accounts, but here the writing was forced and strangely lifeless.

A sculptor named Storrs, Louise said, called Reed "the greatest writer in America," and wanted to do his bust. She was bringing home with her some of Storrs's etchings for the *Masses*, she went on, adding that he would love them—they were strong, like Boardman Robinson's.

Her friends wanted to see a picture of Reed, she said, and she showed them one of him taken in a bathing suit in Provincetown; Storrs declared that his head had "much the same moulding as Beethoven's."

"Oh, sweet old honey," Louise went on, "You are all over Paris, all over the world, and you *must* go on with your work. . . . I'm quite well now and I don't need anyone to cook at Croton when I come back. Couldn't we be awfully economical and quiet so you could do more work —so you could begin your novel?" She said she would like to leave for home in about two weeks; she was still hoping to get to the front, and wanted to wait a little longer for permission.

On July 5 they both wrote to each other again. Reed had just received several of Louise's letters in one packet and said he was reading "your very heart from the time you left me."

"It makes me feel sick to my stomach, with relief, and love and shame and all kinds of terrible emotions. As for me, my darling, I have been frozen for a long time, and am still a little frozen." To illustrate his "frozen" state, he went on to describe an incident with a young woman he had met in Washington. "I burst out and talked of you and what you meant to me for about an hour—why, I don't know. That's all, my darling. I was decent and nice to a girl and pitied her—she wanted to make love. I didn't and couldn't. I've been true all right. But I think perhaps there's something terribly wrong about me—that I may be a little crazy, for I had a desire once, just the other day. I can't tell you how awful, how wretched that made me feel—how I have looked into myself and tried to know why those things happen."

Reed went on for several almost incoherent pages, trying to explain and rationalize his conflicting emotions. "I know why it is that people run to vice when they feel loss—I know that—I can imagine it—I should do it.

"You see, my dearest lover, I was once a free person. I didn't depend on anything. I was as humanly independent as it is possible to be. Then along came women, and they set out deliberately, as they always instinctively do, to break that armor down, to make the artist a human being and dependent upon human beings. Well, they did it, and so now without a mate I am half a man, and sterile." He was under repression and dared not let himself go, he said. He felt that he was always on the verge of something "monstrous." He hastily added that this was not as bad as it seemed.

"It's just that no one I love has ever been able to let me express myself fully, freely and trust that expression." Louise was probably right, though, he said, in feeling that "it would wreck things to let nature take its course," and he admitted that his nature was not to be trusted.

But if they were to have a workable life together, he went on, Louise must allow him to resolve the conflict in his nature by himself. He would do nothing to hurt her, but he could not help his "feelings and thoughts," and she must trust him to fight them out successfully.

It would be intolerable to both of us," he continued, "if you felt you had to direct and censor my thoughts, my actions—as you have in the past—as you did even in your letter telling me not to drink."

Ending on a note of confusion and despair, he said, "There is with me—and I suppose with you too—a kind of uncurable bitterness running through my veins, and a taste of ashes in my mouth. *Come home soon!*" A few days later he added, "I have discovered with a shock, how far I have fallen from the ardent young poet who wrote about Mexico. . . . But please God I intend to get back to poetry and sweetness, some way."

By July 17, Louise had finally decided to leave for home, and was making plans to sail on a French Line ship because it was the fastest; she begged Reed to try not to worry about the safety of the passage. In her final letter to him before sailing, she tried to reassure him, and possibly herself, that she was rational and clear-headed about her own feelings, prepared to be tolerant about his, and that they could pick up their lives together and go on in tranquility and love.

"Nothing matters so much as my love for you—I don't

know what you have said to [Dr.] Lorber or he has said to you [presumably with regard to the emotional complications of her illness]—I don't love any one else. I am dead sure of that. I just love you. I can talk everything out now with you. . . . Oh, dearest, please, please let's not make any more complication in our life until we do talk things out. . . . All my love dear and please don't worry. I'm quite sane now and reasonable."

While awaiting Louise and anticipating a turning point in his life, Reed, who was going to be thirty years old on October 20, wrote an autobiographical essay, "Almost Thirty" (which was never published).

"I am twenty-nine years old," he began, "and I know that this is the end of a part of my life, the end of youth."

"Sometimes it seems to me the end of the world's youth, too; certainly the Great War has done something to us all. But it is also the beginning of a new phase of life; and the world we live in is so full of swift change and color and meaning that I can hardly keep from imagining the splendid and terrible possibilities of the time to come.

"The last ten years I've gone up and down the earth drinking in experience, fighting and loving, seeing and hearing and tasting things. I've travelled all over Europe, and to the borders of the East, and down in Mexico, having adventures; seeing men killed and broken, victorious and laughing, men with visions and men with a sense of humor. I've watched civilization change and broaden and sweeten in my lifetime; and I've watched it wither and crumble in the red blast of war. And war I have seen, too, in the trenches, with the armies.

"I'm not quite sick of seeing yet, but soon I will be—I know that. My future life will not be what it has been. And so I want to stop a minute, and look back, and get my bearings." He went on, briefly, to describe his grow-

141

ing up, and then continued: "And now, almost thirty, some of that old superabundant vitality is gone, and with it the all-sufficient joy of mere living. A good many of my beliefs have got twisted by the Great War. I am weakened by a serious operation. Some things I think I have settled, but in other ways I am back where I started—a turmoil of imaginings . . .

"I must find myself again. . . . The War has been a terrible shatterer of faith in economic and political idealism. And yet I cannot give up the idea that out of democracy will be born the new world—richer, braver, freer, more beautiful. . . .

"As for me, I don't know what I can do to help—I don't know yet. All I know is that my happiness is built on the misery of other people, that I eat because others go hungry, that I am clothed when other people go almost naked through frozen cities in winter; and that fact poisons me, disturbs my serenity, makes me write propaganda when I would rather play—though not so much as it once did. . . .

"I am waiting, waiting for [the War] to end, for life to resume so I can find my work.

"In thinking it over, I find little in my thirty years that I can hold to. I haven't any God and don't want one; faith is only another word for finding oneself. In my life as in most lives, I guess, love plays a tremendous part. I've had love affairs, passionate happiness, wretched maladjustments; hurt deeply and been deeply hurt. But at last I have found my friend and lover, thrilling and satisfying, closer to me than anyone has ever been. And now I don't care what comes."

Chapter Nine

LOUISE FOUND REED in a state of high excitement when she rejoined him in New York late in July of 1917. His gloom about the future, his doubts about the turn his career should take, had been wiped away. He was focused with a singleminded and burning intensity on Russia. All of his personal hopes and dreams for social reform through the rising of the working classes was embodied for him in what was taking place in Russia. With Russia lay all the promise for a new world order, untainted by the domination of what he regarded as the corrupt capitalist system. And the professional challenge of covering what he was convinced would be a world-shattering chapter of history had restored him to a vigor and high-pitched optimism about writing he had never felt even at the height of his journalistic career.

He had been watching, with the rest of the world, as the revolution gathered momentum at the beginning of July. Reed, like many other American socialists, had at first viewed the events in Russia that followed the abdication of the Czar on March 15 as a "bourgeois revolution." Alexander Kerensky's provisional government did not fire him with any hope for a real liberation of the oppressed working classes. But by mid-May, with the emergence of Lenin leading a suddenly revitalized Bolshevik party of opposition, Reed anticipated a genuine revolution of the workers. The possibilities inherent in this rising thrilled him. It could, he wrote in the *Masses* that May, evolve into "the establishment of a new human society upon the earth."

In this state of purposeful enthusiasm his emotional difficulties with Louise were blown away. Louise was delighted to find her husband in such good spirits and eagerly joined in his plans. "When the news of the Russian revolution flared out across the front pages of all the newspapers in the world," she later wrote, "I made up my mind to go to Russia."

Symbolic of the Reeds' reconciliation in both love and work, was their collaboration on an article for the *Masses*, which appeared under their joint byline in the October 1917 issue. "The uninteresting war begins to be interesting to liberals," it began. "Out of the dull twilight that has hung over the world these three years like a winter mist in Flanders, tremendous flames begin to leap, like bursting shells. Events grand and horrible are brewing in Europe, such as only the imagination of a revolutionary poet could have conceived. The great bust-up is coming.

"Russia has shaken off the evil spell that bound her, and arises slowly, a gentle giant, hope of the world. Not a day passes without revolt in Germany. . . . British labor and British soldiers are chafing under the platitudes of Lloyd George. In Italy people talk openly of refusing to suffer another winter without coal, for the doubtful rewards of imperialism. And France is at the end of her men, resources and patience."

Louise had no difficulty in getting herself hired by the Bell Syndicate, which was pleased to send a correspondent for "the woman's point of view of the revolution." But Reed had two problems to overcome. He had to be legally exempted from the draft in order to get a passport, but getting his exemption on the basis of physical disability was against his principles; he preferred the stand of refusing to serve in the war out of moral conviction. However, he decided finally to sacrifice that particular bit of idealism for the larger mission ahead. He applied for and was granted a "Certificate of Discharge Because Physically Deficient"; nephrectomy, it was ruled by the Surgeon General, disqualified him from serving in the army.

The more serious problem was finding a publication that would send him. None of the major newspapers or magazines in New York or other big cities to which he applied would trust him to represent them, because of his well-advertised socialist tendencies. Max Eastman was eager to send him for the *Masses,* but the magazine had no money for such a trip. Eastman finally asked a close friend of his, Eugen Boissevan, if he could raise the money for Reed's expenses. Boissevan, (who later married Edna St. Vincent Millay) found a wealthy society woman who was willing to provide $2,000; Eastman was just as convinced as Reed that the revolution would furnish him with the material for his greatest journalistic achievement. As it turned out, no story of Reed's from Russia ever appeared in the *Masses,* since the magazine was suppressed by the government a few months later. In its November-December issue, not knowing it would be the last, the *Masses* announced in large type on the back cover: "John Reed is in Petrograd. . . . His story of the first proletarian Revolution will be an event in the world's literature." Although the *Masses* did not print the story, the prediction was accurate. When Reed returned from Russia he wrote the classic, on-the-spot account of the revolution, *Ten Days That Shook the World.*

With the *Masses* as his support and having also agreed to file stories for the *Call* and *Seven Arts,* Reed left New York with Louise on a small Danish ship on August 17.

"From my elevation on the first-class deck the first night out I could hear people in the steerage singing revolutionary songs," Louise later wrote in one of her articles expressing the woman's point of view. "In the days that followed I spent most of my time down there. They were the only persons on the ship who weren't bored to death. There were about 200, mostly Jews from beyond the pale. Hunted, robbed, mistreated in every possible manner before they were exiled, they had retained the most touching love for the land of their birth."

Bored or not, most of the first class passengers—Russian exiles being repatriated, Scandinavians returning home, a couple of diplomats, and some American college boys on their way to jobs with an American bank in Petrograd—enjoyed a good life on the ship. The Danish food was plentiful and delicious and the ship's band played all day. There were a few inconveniences. The ship was delayed for a week in the British port of Halifax, while English inspectors gave it a thorough going over. A Socialist congress was scheduled to meet soon in Stockholm and the British were nervous about it. Reed had with him some letters from American Socialists for delivery to conference members, and he enjoyed playing the spy game by hiding the letters under the rug in his cabin and diverting the searchers with whiskey and friendly conversation.

According to Louise's account, it was the steerage passengers in whom the British inspectors were most interested. "Every day British officers came on board and examined and re-examined. Pitiful incidents occurred. There was an old woman who clung frantically to some letters from a dead son. She secreted them in all sorts of strange places and brought down suspicion upon herself.

"The whole of them—more than 100 in number—were in a state of nervous excitement. Russia was so near and yet so far."

The ship arrived in Christiania, Norway (now Oslo), early in September. Here the passengers, who were to proceed by train to Stockholm, were again detained.

"In Christiania," Reed wrote in a newsletter to the *Masses*, "the gardens of the king's palace are given over almost entirely to the raising of potatoes, and Christiania's glory as the cheapest place to live in Europe has departed." A bottle of whiskey cost seventy-five dollars, he reported, and while the wealthy could still buy white bread, it was in short supply. "As for the peasants, fishermen and workers, they never had much to eat but raw fish and black bread anyway, and now they have less of that than ever. As in all the little neutral nations, a few speculators and ship-owners have grown fabulously wealthy, and the workers haven't enough to eat or to wear—with the terrible northern winter coming down."

Nevertheless, Reed found Christiania "a brisk little city," reminiscent of Sophia, Bulgaria, in its newness— "the overhead telephone wires, the king's palace contiguous to the Grand Hotel and the Grand Cafe—where everybody goes and the general unpretentiousness of things. And the people, too, are of the Bulgarian temperament; friendly, honest, virtuous and a little slow in the head. . . . There are hundreds of new apartment houses everywhere, of hideous design and color."

The sun shone brassily in a pale sky, Reed wrote, and there was a hint of frost in the air. "The linden trees are faintly yellowing. In the parks, in the little gardens before every house and apartment building, in countless window-boxes, are wonderful masses of flowers—asters, geraniums, golden-glow, dahlias, heliotrope, gladiolas, nasturtiums—of immense size and dazzling color. Over the house-tops and at the end of streets can be seen the deep-green forested mountains, all around the city, and westward the blue fiord winding seaward like a mountain lake."

Finally permitted to continue their journey, Reed and Louise boarded a train for Stockholm. What had been in pre-war days a six-hour trip on an express train with sleeping and dining cars was now a seventeen-hour journey in an overcrowded coach train, with a change at midnight to an even more crowded Swedish train. Reed and Louise had to stand in the aisle from midnight to ten the following morning. They were held for an hour at Charlottenberg, on the Swedish frontier, where they were searched.

"I shall never forget that awful hour," Reed wrote. "Passports overhauled, long documents to be filled out as to whether your father had brown hair and your mother's political affiliations—hand baggage gone through, heavy baggage dumped out on the platform and pawed over, bread cards to be procured from the police."

On the trip from Christiania there had been two second-class and two third-class cars. From Charlottenberg there were two second-class cars and only one third-class car for one hundred passengers.

"In that car aisle, upon impassable mountains of baggage, we dozed and smoked and fought with orderly conductors all night. And in the morning we looked out upon chill fields lying blanketed with white mist, through which spiked up the wisps of barley hung upon poles above the emerald grass. A hearty old wench got on, with an enormous basket full of bread, sugar and thermos bottles of hot coffee. With her scissors she snipped off bits of our bread-cards, and gave us each a few small slices of brown barley bread and a brittle biscuit made of potato flour—and coffee brewed from roasted grain of some kind."

Many of the returning Russian exiles who had been with the Reeds on the ship were on board the train, hoping they would be allowed to stay over for the Stockholm conference, but knowing that the Swedish government preferred to ship them through directly to Russia.

"At dawn," Reed wrote, "someone got hold of a newspaper, and we read that the conference was indefinitely postponed. In the cold twilight they gathered around these dwarfed, voluble, pale men and women, their cheeks sunken from driven labor in East Side sweat shops, dejected and bewildered. . . . All of them had helped to bring about the Russian revolution, that most splendid manifestation of the possibilities of the human spirit; they had lost all their worldly goods in its service, had risked their lives and suffered imprisonment and exile. And at last the new Russia had come to them in America and asked them to come home.

"Then their troubles began. American secret service agents harried them to the boat; at Halifax the British searched them, refused to allow some of them to proceed; when they landed at Christiania they were met with furious hostility by the Russian consul, an appointee of the old regime; the American representative would not help those who were naturalized Americans; the Swedish government shunted them along through and out of Sweden —and at the Russian frontier interminable changes of the balance of power made difficulties. And it is said that when they got to Petrograd many were forced into the army and sent to the front. . . . Massacred in Galicia and Bukovina by both armies, jailed in America and deported, truly the Russian Jews were never more a homeless and wandering race than they are now."

In Stockholm the Reeds' hotel room was searched every time they left it. Reed was known as a Socialist and he did, indeed, go about dutifully contacting the Socialist leaders to whom he had letters, taking the constant surveillance he was under as a matter of course.

"Stockholm is the last great spy-city," he wrote, "the last go-between of the belligerents. Its population is between three and four hundred thousand, and fifty thousand are foreigners, and three-quarters of these are spies of various sorts." For example, there was the genial young Englishman who professed to work for the *Manchester Guardian*—and who perhaps did—but who was also on a secret mission for the French government; and the German princess, ostensibly in Stockholm for her health, who traded in diamonds with various furtive-looking individuals of different nationalities; and the Russian who infiltrated the groups of exiles as they passed through, noting down their political sympathies.

"The strangest conferences and congresses are proceeding," Reed continued, "some openly, others with a good deal of privacy. . . . There is the conference of the Poles, and the conference of the Ukranians, and the Finnish meeting and the meeting of the Czechs; then there is the third conference of the Zimmerwaldists, and a Jewish conference, not to speak of the organizing committee of the Stockholm International Conference, which has tremendous hopes. And almost every month there are private meetings between diplomats and the belligerents—which generally take place in some little country town nearby."

In spite of all the spying and politicking, the Reeds found Stockholm very gay. September marked the opening of the cultural season, and operas and plays were performing to capacity audiences and American movies were being shown in many film houses.

"Cloudless day follows cloudless day, and in the parks and public gardens the flowers are glorious, banked richly in the thick lawns around playing fountains. Everywhere are open-air restaurants and sidewalk cafes; in the evening the bands play under the lindens, in the glare of yellow arcs, and all the world, brightly uniformed or civilian, of twenty different nationalities, sips its coffee or schnapps or beer on the terraces, or strolls around under the trees. . . .

"The hotels are jammed to the corridors, with prices at about the New York level and there is not room in the restaurants to sit down. And the strange people—Turks, Russians, Caucasian princesses, English diplomats, convalescing German nobles, South American Socialists. . . . That thin, wiry dark man with the rat-tail mustache thinks he will be the first president of the new republic of Poland; and the large, black-bearded gentleman with his hat rakishly on the side of his head, who looks so much like Ferdinand of Bulgaria, is sure that he will be king of the Ukraine very soon. The pale, gaunt man in shabby clothes with the sparse beard of a Tartar and slanting, slow eyes, is an exiled Bolshevik. . . . Lenin is said to be hiding here, somewhere." (In fact he was hiding in Finland.)

One day in Stockholm as Reed wandered by himself down the narrow alleys of the old city behind the royal palace, a group of husky blond workmen shouldered past him. All wore their shirts open at the throat, revealing bright tattoos on their chests. As they passed, one looked back and said something to his companions, gesturing toward Reed. He came back, tapped Reed on the shoulder, stuck out his tongue, pointed at his throat and made thirsty, drinking noises. Reed obligingly handed him a crown and the others, grinning hugely, surrounded him, talking animatedly in Swedish, of which Reed did not understand a word. Reed, grinning back, gestured his lack of comprehension and said "Americaner." One of the workmen noticed that Reed was wearing a red tie and, pointing to it, asked, "Socialista?" Reed nodded affirmation and instantly the workmen burst into delighted cries of, "Ik Social Democrat! Ik!"

Plunging their hands into trouser pockets, they brought out greasy, red Social Democrat membership books and thrust them under Reed's nose. He understood that they wanted him to join them in a drink. They turned into a dark, evil smelling alley and one of the Swedes dove into a doorway, emerging with a bottle of yellow schnapps. With much eye-rolling and toasting the schnapps was quickly consumed, and Reed was hustled through the door, down a dark hallway and up four flights of stairs to a small room containing several tables and a wooden bar. The place smelled foul and a stout blonde woman stood leering at them from behind the bar, a bottle clenched in her hand, ready to strike. The workmen shouted conciliatory phrases, pointing at Reed, and Reed understood that the treat was to be on him once more. Again, Reed produced a crown, and beer was brought to them at a table. They drank and then the workmen looked carefully about them and began singing softly. Reed did not recognize the tune, but he caught the words, "bomba" and "dynamita" and knew it was a song of revolution. They drank more beer and sang more songs, sounding to Reed progressively more bloodthirsty and violent, pounding their chests for emphasis, gesturing at Reed to indicate that they accepted him as a fellow revolutionist.

At length, Reed beckoned to the barmaid for his bill. Grinning, she held out her hand for more after Reed had given her a crown. Reed's companions noisily protested, and when the barmaid persisted, one of them shoved her, sending her flying halfway across the room. From where she landed, she began cursing them loudly and at length, while the workmen and Reed shook hands all around. Suddenly one of the workmen dashed into a rear room, returning with an old, white-bearded man carrying an accordion. Standing him in a corner with a shouted instruction to play, the workman grabbed the barmaid and danced her around the room. The other men followed in pairs, one of them seizing Reed, and the afternoon ended in rowdy good humor and fellowship.

Later that day Reed called on Camillo Huysmans, Secretary of the Internationalist Socialist Bureau, and on Socialist representatives of Russia, Holland, and other European Socialist groups. From them he heard for the first time the details of the rise and fall and rise of the Soviet in Russia. He found it "Infinitely more inspiring than the history of the Romanoffs," and was convinced, now, that the Russian revolution "was not and could not be a failure." Russia's greatest days, he was sure, were to come, and soon he would be there to see with his own eyes.

Reed and Louise boarded a train in Stockholm on September 8 for the long journey through northern Sweden. At Haparanda, on Sweden's northeast coast, it was raining when they arrived at dawn. Wearily they ate a meager breakfast of sour black bread and weak coffee, chatting with those of their fellow passengers who spoke

English or French, asking for and imparting what bits of news had arrived from Russia; word had leaked into Sweden that the Russian army's commander in chief, General Kornilov, had marched on Petrograd, but nobody knew with what result. Before they could board the ferry that would take them across to Tornio in Finland, the passengers were searched by Swedish authorities. In Tornio they were again searched. Louise was herded into a small, ill-lighted, unheated room, guarded by six soldiers with fixed bayonets, and told by a stocky young Russian woman to undress. Louise complied and when all her clothes were off, the woman ordered her to put them on again, without having examined her or searched the clothes. What was the point, Louise asked the woman. "It's just a rule," she said, smiling at Louise's bewilderment.

When she rejoined Reed she found him talking to the British consul and an American official. They were telling Reed what a dangerous place Petrograd was at the moment. When they understood that Louise was going to accompany him they were shocked; Petrograd was no place for a woman, they said. "But she wants to go," Reed told them.

Rain beat down on the little ferry boat that carried the Reeds and the rest of the trainload to Tornio, on the Finnish border, and the rain continued all morning as they boarded the train that would carry them across the flatlands of Finland. They traveled through the night, heading south again for the city of Vyborg on the Russian border, where, at last, they entrained for the short trip to Petrograd.

The Reeds took a room at the Hotel Angleterre, which was expensive, and immediately began hunting for a small apartment. Lodgings were very scarce and food prices high, but Reed found that in spite of all the war-time hardships the population suffered under, an aura of joyous excitement pervaded the city.

"The old town has changed!" he wrote to Boardman Robinson, who had accompanied him to Russia a year and a half earlier. "We are in the middle of things, and believe me it's thrilling. There is so much dramatic to write about that I don't know where to begin—but I'll have a tale to unfold if ever—For color and terror and grandeur this makes Mexico look pale." He and Louise, he said, hoped to travel all over Russia.

Everyone except Louise and himself, he told Robinson—diplomats, newspapermen, and all the foreign visitors—felt that the revolution was "the worst possible taste." But he was exuberant about the revolution, was getting a hearty welcome from all the Russians he met, and had already found "thousands of comrades." He asked Robinson to tell Max Eastman that he felt he must stay in Russia at least four months and that he did not think his money would last more than two.

The Reeds moved into a small apartment at number 23 Troitskaya Ulitza, that was well heated and furnished with a samovar, and began the job of collecting information. Reed had picked up a few Russian phrases on his earlier visit to the country, but neither he nor Louise spoke the language. Nevertheless, they rarely encountered much difficulty in communicating with the Russians, for the educated Russians spoke French and English and interpreters were available for communicating with the workers and peasants. The Reeds could always find a fellow journalist (American or European) who spoke some Russian, or a friendly Russian who spoke French or English, to accompany them.

Together and separately the Reeds attended meetings,

strolled the streets, interviewed Bolsheviks, Cadet members, soldiers, and members of the Red Guard, and exchanged information and opinion with other journalists. With all his close daily attention to the rapidly changing political situation, Reed offered to do some shopping for a friend of Sally Boardman's who was an interior decorator. Beautiful crystal, amber, Siberian emeralds, embroideries, textiles, and furniture were to be had very cheaply, he said, and it was "a marvelous chance for somebody with a few hundred dollars to invest."

Reed perceived that the revolution by mid-September had settled down to the class-struggle "pure and simple." After the failure of Kornilov's attempt to impose himself as a military dictator earlier that month, all the Socialist groups had drawn together in what Reed called "a passionate impulse of self-defense." While there were splinter groups ranging from right to left among all the different factions struggling for power, Reed believed that the main fight was between the Bolshevik party and the Cadets, whose members and sympathizers, while representing many shades of thinking, basically favored a capitalist republic, and would have settled for a constitutional monarchy. In Reed's opinion, the intellectuals and romantic revolutionaries were shocked by the reality of revolution —Lenin's singleminded and consistent advocacy of terrorism was unpalatable when put into practice—and had either joined the Cadets or quit the battle. With the repulsion of General Kornilov, Kerensky had once again emerged, however tentatively, as the leader of the government; Russia was irreversibly established as a republic, Reed believed, and the present struggle was taking the shape of an economic revolution.

"Through the tempest of events tumbling over one another which is beating upon Russia," Reed wrote, "the

Bolsheviki star steadily rises." On September 12 the Bolshevik members of the Petrograd Soviet outnumbered
their opposition by 279 to 115 and were able to pass a
resolution demanding that Russia be formally declared a
republic, that the government consist entirely of Socialists, that all land be handed over to the peasants, that in-
dustry be controlled by the workers, and that a peace
treaty with Germany be signed immediately at any cost.

Although Lenin was still in hiding, Trotsky was released from jail and on October 8 replaced the Menshevik
chairman of the presidium. The Bolsheviks now demanded that a meeting of the Second All-Russian Congress of Soviets be called in Petrograd on November 2,
confident that with a majority in the congress they would
be able to force their program on the government and
possibly to take over the government itself. Lenin, meanwhile, from his hiding place in Finland, was writing
angry letters to the Petrograd Bolsheviks decrying their
political maneuvering and urging them to plan a takeover
by force, insisting that to delay such a measure would be
death. On October 22 he secretly entered Petrograd to
take charge of the uprising.

Unaware of, or ignoring, the brewing storm, the Petrograd public went about its daily life as usual. "The poets
made verses—but not about the Revolution," Reed later
wrote in *Ten Days That Shook the World*. "The realistic
painters painted scenes from medieval Russian history—
anything but the Revolution. Young ladies from the provinces came up to the capital to learn French and cultivate
their voices, and the gay young beautiful officers wore
their gold-trimmed crimson bashliki and their elaborate
Caucasian swords around the hotel lobbies. The ladies of
the minor bureaucratic set took tea with each other in the
afternoon, carrying each her little gold or silver or jew-

elled sugar-box, and half a loaf of bread in her muff, and wished that the Czar were back, or that the Germans would come, or anything that would solve the servant problem. . . . The daughter of a friend of mine came home one afternoon in hysterics because the woman street-car conductor had called her 'Comrade!' "

But for much of the populace life was difficult, Reed noted. September and October were the worst months of the Russian year, especially the Petrograd year. "Under dull gray skies, in the shortening days, rain fell drenching, incessant," he wrote. "The mud underfoot was deep, slippery and clinging, tracked everywhere by heavy boots, and worse than usual because of the complete break-down of the Municipal administration. Bitter damp winds rushed in from the Gulf of Finland, and the chill fog rolled through the streets. At night, for motives of economy as well as fear of Zeppelins, the street lights were few and far between; . . . It was dark from three in the afternoon to ten in the morning. Robberies and house-breakings increased. In apartment houses the men took turns at all-night guard duty, armed with loaded rifles."

Food was becoming scarcer every week, and one had to stand in queues for hours in the rain to get milk, bread, sugar, and tobacco. Coming home from attending an all-night meeting, Reed saw one such queue beginning to form at dawn, composed mostly of women with babies in their arms. But the crowds tolerated these hardships with miraculous good nature, Reed found.

Reed did not know until later of the secret meeting that took place on the night of October 23 among the members of the Bolshevik Central Committee. Lenin, his beard shaved and wearing a wig, had slipped secretly into Petrograd to preside at the meeting and urge an immediate Bolshevik rebellion and take-over of the government. Trotsky and Stalin were among those of the inner group of the party who attended. The conference lasted for ten hours, with Lenin finally persuading a majority of the group to his plan of action. The meeting disbanded at three in the morning, and Lenin again went into hiding.

Reed did attend the stormy all-night meeting of the Petrograd Soviet on October 30. (Earlier in the day he interviewed Kerensky, in French. "The Russian people," Kerensky told Reed, "are suffering from economic fatigue —and from disillusionment with the Allies. The world thinks that the Russian Revolution is at an end. Do not be mistaken. The Russian Revolution is just beginning." It was Kerensky's last public statement in Russia; within two weeks he had been forced into hiding, finally escaping the country disguised as a sailor.) At the all-night meeting of the Petrograd Soviet the moderate faction of the Socialist party, intellectuals and army officers, were present in force. Against them, Reed wrote, "rose up workmen, peasants and common soldiers, passionate and simple."

Petrograd was in turmoil. Street robberies increased to such an extent that it was dangerous to walk in most sections of the city; one afternoon Reed saw a crowd of several hundred people beat and trample to death a soldier caught stealing.

"At Smolny . . . the committee rooms buzzed and hummed all day and all night, hundreds of soldiers and workmen slept on the floor, wherever they could find room. Upstairs in the great hall a thousand people crowded to the uproarious sessions of the Petrograd Soviet." In contrast with the political fervor, gambling clubs were jammed every night until dawn, and richly dressed prostitutes strolled about the center of the city.

159

Sunday, November 4, was announced as the Day of the Petrograd Soviet; its avowed purpose was to raise money for the organization, but actually it was planned as a show of Bolshevik strength. Suddenly the Cossacks announced that on the same day they would hold a Procession of the Cross. "The atmosphere was electric," Reed wrote. "A spark might kindle a civil war." The Petrograd Soviet issued a manifesto, headed "Brothers—Cossacks!" In it the Cossacks were exhorted not to demonstrate against the workers and soldiers, and told that their procession was being incited by their "common enemies," the privileged classes of generals, bankers, landlords, former servants of the Czar. The procession was called off.

During the last days of October and the early days of November, Reed spent a great deal of time at Smolny Institute, Bolshevik headquarters. Security had tightened, and it was becoming more difficult to get in. Passes were issued to those who could satisfactorily explain their business, but the pass system was changed every few hours, for spies were constantly sneaking through.

One day as Reed approached the outer gate of the building, which was guarded by double rows of sentries, he saw Trotsky and his wife just ahead of him. They were halted by a soldier and Trotsky searched his pockets for a pass, but could not find it. A journalist friend of Reed's, who understood Russian, translated the ensuing dialogue. "Never mind," Trotsky told the sentry, "You know me. My name is Trotsky."

"You haven't got a pass," answered the sentry. "You cannot go in. Names don't mean anything to me."

"But I am the President of the Petrograd Soviet."

"Well," said the soldier, "if you're as important as all that you must at least have one little paper."

"Let me see the Commandant," said Trotsky. The soldier

As a 21-year-old senior at the University of Oregon in 1908, Louise Bryant did not appear to be destined for a life of high drama.

The Reeds bought a country cottage in Croton-on-Hudson shortly before their marriage on November 9, 1916. It was to be their refuge from the bustle of Greenwich Village.

Bursting with energy at 29, John Reed in 1916 was a leading journalist and political activist. That year he also became a fledgling playwright and founding member of the Provincetown Players. It was Reed's colorful coverage two years earlier of the Mexican "bandit" leader, Pancho Villa, *below*, that brought him overnight fame as a journalist.

Louise was sent to Russia by an American news syndicate to cover the Revolution "from the woman's viewpoint." On her return in 1918 she compiled her newspaper reports into a book, *Six Red Months in Russia*.

Reed's account of the Revolution, *Ten Days that Shook the World*, became a classic. Reed found the Russian lifestyle "the best." He dedicated his first book, *Insurgent Mexico*, to his Harvard English teacher, Charles Townsend Copeland, *below left*.

Lincoln Steffens, *right*, was the celebrated muckraking journalist who strongly influenced Reed's career.

Left, Smolny Institute in Petrograd, commandeered by the Bolsheviks as their Revolutionary headquarters. "At Smolny," Reed wrote, "the committee rooms buzzed and hummed all day and all night. In the great hall a thousand people crowded to the uproarious sessions of the Petrograd Soviet."

Below left, the storming of the Winter Palace in Petrograd. It was here, "in a back room on the top floor," that Louise visited and interviewed "Babushka." The aging Revolutionary had been offered "her choice of the beautiful apartments" in the Winter Palace, Louise wrote, but "Babushka" had insisted on a small, bare room.   UPI PHOTO

Below, street fighting in Petrograd in July 1917. The Reeds had been watching, with the rest of the world, as the revolution gathered momentum. "When the news of the Russian revolution flared out across the front pages of all the newspapers of the world," Louise wrote, "I made up my mind to go to Russia." The Reeds began their month-long journey from New York to Petrograd that August.

Above, Russian soldiers and workers demonstrating in Petrograd. Scenes like this, duplicated in Moscow and other cities throughout Russia, became a familiar sight to the Reeds. *Below*, Bolshevik military patrol on the Nevsky Prospekt, Petrograd.

A street barricade in Moscow in the late fall of 1917. The Reeds witnessed scenes such as this when they visited Moscow together for the first time.

Bolshevik leaders reviewing a parade in January 1919 honoring those who died in the Revolution. Behind them is a wall of the Kremlin.

EXCLUSIVE NEWS AGENCY, LTD.

The faces are grim, but it is nonetheless a "celebration" honoring Bolshevik leaders in Moscow, 1920, about the time the Reeds were reunited in that city.

Below, grinning triumphantly, Red Cavalry troops pass before the Kremlin. American newspapers described the Russian Army in 1920 as well equipped and "a formidable menace."

Lenin, his beard just beginning to grow back after he had
shaved it off to disguise himself, in a moment of oratorical
eloquence. A poor linguist, he spoke to the Reeds, who did not know
Russian, through interpreters. HERMAN AXELBANK

Below, Katherine Breshkovsky, known as "Babushka" and "the
grandmother of the Russian Revolution," with Alexander Kerensky,
whom she had hoped to see as Russia's leader. Louise interviewed
"Babushka," and Reed interviewed Kerensky. ASSOCIATED PRESS PHOTO

Trotsky, fluent in English and French, granted Reed a lengthy interview while working on strategy for the Bolshevik takeover. "Few questions from me were necessary," Reed later wrote.

Below right, Angelica Balabanoff, whose disillusionment with the Bolshevik experiment paralleled Reed's, posed at the International Congress in 1919.

Grigory Zinoviev, a master of the double cross, was a constant thorn in Reed's side and came to symbolize for Reed the ugly and corrupt aspect of Bolshevism.

Eugene O'Neill fell in love with Louise and basked in her encouragement of his early efforts as a playwright. Their love affair ended bitterly. MURAY

Above right, Reed loved Mabel Dodge, but squirmed under her possessiveness. That affair, too, ended with rancor. BETTMANN ARCHIVE

Reed, *left,* and Boardman Robinson in Washington Square Park after the publication of *The War in Eastern Europe,* written by Reed and illustrated by Robinson. It was while gathering material for this book that Reed first visited and fell in love with Russia.
CULVER PICTURES, INC.

Max Eastman was Reed's close friend, his editor on the *Masses*, and his staunch supporter to the end.

Above right, Morris Hillquit, the prominent Socialist, was the defense lawyer in the first *Masses* trial. Reed, unable to leave Russia in time, was tried *in absentia.*

Below left, Emma Goldman on her way to Ellis Island for deportation. Her cheery look vanished when she reached Russia. The celebrated anarchist shared her sense of shock and despair over applied Bolshevism with the Reeds in Moscow.

Right, William Bullitt, wealthy, socially prominent, a friend of Presidents, and a diplomat, married Louise three years after Reed's death. The marriage did not work. They were divorced in 1930.

Louise stands by Reed's coffin in the Labor Temple. "The Russians let me take my grief in my own way," she wrote. "I wished to walk according to the Russian custom, quite by myself after the hearse." HARVARD UNIVERSITY

The plaque near the Kremlin wall marking Reed's grave and that of two others regarded by the Soviet Union as Revolutionary heroes. Reed's name is second. "All foreigners will visit his grave for all time here," Louise wrote to Reed's mother. It was, she said, "the most honored spot in Russia." SOVFOTO

АРМАНД Е.Ф. ИНЕССА 1875-1920
ДЖОН РИД 1887-1920
РУСАКОВ И.В. 1877-1921

muttered something about not wanting to disturb the Commandant for everyone who came along, and finally called over the soldier in command of the guard.

Again, Trotsky explained who he was.

"Trotsky?" the soldier repeated. "I've heard the name somewhere. I guess it's all right. You can go in, comrade."

Reed followed him into the corridor and met there a member of the Bolshevik Central Committee, who explained to him what the new Government would be like: "A loose organization, sensitive to the popular will as expressed through the Soviets, allowing local forces full play. At present the Provisional Government obstructs the action of the local democratic will, just as the Czar's Government did."

On October 30 Reed went, by appointment, to meet Trotsky in a small attic room in Smolny. He found Trotsky seated in the middle of the room on a wooden chair at a bare table. "Few questions from me were necessary," Reed wrote. "He talked rapidly and steadily for more than an hour." Trotsky was an accomplished linguist, and while Reed did not record what language was used during the marathon interview, it is a fair assumption that it was English, since that was one of the languages in which the Russian leader was fluent.

The Provisional Government was absolutely powerless, Trotsky told Reed. The Army was with the Bolsheviks and the "conciliators and pacifists," Socialist revolutionaries and Mensheviki, had lost all authority because the struggle between the workers and the employers, between the soldiers and the officers, had become more bitter, more irreconcilable than ever. Only by the concerted action of the popular mass, only by the victory of proletarian dictatorship, could the Revolution be achieved and the people saved.

Counter-revolutionary schemes of all sorts were now being hatched in the corridors of the Council of the Russian Republic, Trotsky went on. The Cadet party represented the counter-revolution militant. On the other side, the Soviets represented the cause of the people. Between the two camps there were no groups of serious importance. The bourgeois counter-revolution was organizing all its forces and waiting for the moment to attack the Bolsheviks. Their answer would be decisive.

On November 3 the Bolshevik leaders held a meeting behind closed doors and Reed waited outside in the corridor for word of what was taking place. At length, one of the members emerged and told Reed what was planned. Lenin had decreed that the rising would take place November 7. In a remote, upstairs room, Reed was told, a careful plan was at that moment being drawn by a party strategist for the seizure of the capital.

The Bolsheviks were making no secret of their intended uprising (only of the details), and the Government had ample time and opportunity to plan for defense. A number of army regiments, believed by the Government to be loyal, were ordered to Petrograd. Artillery was drawn into the Winter Palace.

On Wednesday, November 7, Reed rose very late. The noon cannon boomed from Peter-Paul Fortress as he walked down the Nevsky. In front of the State Bank he stopped to talk with some soldiers who were standing with fixed bayonets at the closed gates.

"Which side do you belong to, the Government?" he asked.

"No more Government," one of the soldiers answered, grinning, "Glory to God!"

Reed bought a copy of the Bolshevik newspaper, *Dyen,* to find out what had happened during the night.

The Bolsheviks, he read, had captured the Telephone Exchange and the Telegraph Agency; the Government troops had been unable to reach Petrograd; the Cossacks were undecided which side to join; some of the Government Ministers had been arrested.

On the corner of the Morskaya Reed ran into a Menshevik official and asked him if an insurrection had actually taken place.

"The devil knows!" he said. "Well, perhaps the Bolsheviki can seize the power, but they won't be able to hold it more than three days. They haven't the men to run a government. Perhaps it's a good thing to let them try—that will finish them."

On November 8 Petrograd was filled with rumors about Kerensky, who, Reed heard, was at Pskov, marshalling a huge army to march on the capital. One of the Government newspapers published that day ran Kerensky's proclamation: "The disorders caused by the insane attempt of the Bolsheviki place the country on the verge of a precipice, and demand the effort of our entire will, our courage and the devotion of every one of us, to win through the terrible trial which the fatherland is undergoing."

On the same day placards issued by the All-Russian Congress of the Soviets appeared on the walls of public buildings, declaring that the ministers of the Provisional Government had been arrested by the Military Revolutionary Committee, that Kerensky had fled Petrograd, and that any assistance given to the Kerensky regime would be punished as "a crime against the state."

The Bolshevik revolution had, in effect, been accomplished. The "Ten Days" that Reed was later to assign to its achievement—November 6–17—were now being played out. Yet on November 8 few people in Petrograd,

let alone the rest of Russia, really believed that the Bolsheviks could remain in power for more than three days.
"Perhaps [only] Lenin, Trotsky, the Petrograd workers
and the simpler soldiers" were sure that the Bolsheviks
had won, according to Reed.

On the afternoon of November 8, Lenin, finished with
hiding, appeared at a meeting of the Petrograd Soviet at
Smolny. Reed and Louise were there and Reed recorded
his impression of Lenin for posterity:

"A short, stocky figure, with a big head set down in
his shoulders, bald and bulging. Little eyes, a snubbish
nose, wide, generous mouth, and heavy chin; clean-
shaven now, but already beginning to bristle with the
well-known beard of his past and future. Dressed in
shabby clothes, his trousers much too long for him. Unim-
pressive, to be the idol of a mob, loved and revered as
perhaps few leaders in history have been. A strange popular leader—a leader purely by virtue of intellect; colour-
less, humourless, uncompromising and detached, without
picturesque idiosyncracies—but with the power of explaining profound ideas in simple terms, of analysing a
concrete situation. And combined with shrewdness, the
greatest intellectual audacity."

At dawn Reed and Louise returned to their apartment
house and were stopped, as usual, by an armed patrol of
citizens. Their landlady heard them and stumbled out in
a pink silk wrapper.

"The House Committee has again asked that you take
your turn on guard-duty with the rest of the men," she
told Reed.

"What's the reason for this guard-duty?" Reed asked.

"To protect the house and the women and children."

"Who from?"

"Robbers and murderers."

"But suppose," said Reed, "there came a Commissar from the Military Revolutionary Committee to search for arms?"

"Oh, that's what they'll *say* they are. . . . And besides, what's the difference?"

Reed solemnly told her that the American Consul had forbidden all American citizens to carry arms, and that he could not do guard duty.

Reed continued attending meetings, interviewing leaders and the man in the street, and making careful and vivid notes on all he saw. On November 21, having heard ominous reports of violent street fighting and destruction in Moscow, he and Louise decided to go there and see for themselves what was happening. "Petrograd, after all, in spite of being for a century the seat of Government, is still an artificial city," he wrote. "Moscow is the real Russia, Russia as it was and will be; in Moscow we would get the true feeling of the Russian people about the Revolution. Life was more intense there."

The Reeds, together with several other American and European journalists, were given passes from Smolny, without which no one was permitted to leave Petrograd. When the train backed into the station, a mob of soldiers carrying huge sacks of food forced their way through the doors, smashed windows, and swarmed into the aisles of the train. Soon the train was so crowded that people began climbing up onto the roof. Reed and Louise managed to squeeze into a compartment designed for four people, but within seconds twenty soldiers had shoved themselves into the cubicle. Reed tried to argue them into leaving and the conductor tried to come to their aid, but the soldiers laughed in their faces, asking why they should bother about the comfort of the bourgeoisie. The Reeds showed their passes from Smolny, and the soldiers changed their attitude.

"Come, comrades," one soldier said, "These are American tovarishtchi. They have come thirty thousand versts to see our Revolution, and they are naturally tired." With friendly apologies the soldiers backed out of the compartment. A little later, the Reeds heard them breaking into a compartment occupied by two well-dressed Russians who, they had learned, had bribed the conductor to let them have the compartment to themselves.

At seven in the evening the train pulled out of the station.

"In the corridors, so jammed that it was impossible to pass, violent political debates raged all night long," Reed wrote. "Occasionally the conductor came through, as a matter of habit, looking for tickets. He found very few except ours, and after a half-hour of futile wrangling, lifted his arms despairingly and withdrew. The atmosphere was stifling, full of smoke and foul odors; if it hadn't been for the broken windows we would doubtless have smothered during the night."

At the Moscow station there were no cabs, but a few blocks down the street they found a drowsing sleigh driver, who offered to take them and one of their fellow journalists who spoke Russian into the center of town for a hundred rubles. Reed was indignanat; before the Revolution it had cost *two* rubles, he said. But it was very dangerous now to drive a sleigh in the streets of Moscow, the driver answered. Finally they agreed on fifty rubles, and during the ride the driver told them about the recent six days' fighting in Moscow: "Driving along, or waiting for a fare on the corner, all of a sudden pooff! a cannon ball ex-

ploding here, pooff! a cannon ball there, ratt-ratt! a ma-
chine gun. I gallop, the devils shooting all around. I get
to a nice quiet street and stop, doze a little, pooff! another cannon ball, ratt-ratt! Devils! Devils!"

In the center of town the snowy streets were quiet
and a bitter wind blew. The Reeds entered the lobby of
the first hotel they saw, and were told that there were
comfortable rooms available, but all the windows were
shot out; if they wouldn't mind a little fresh air . . .?
Finally they found rooms at the Hotel National, with
windows intact.

Late that night the Reeds were taken to Red Square
in front of the Kremlin and shown the two huge pits
being dug by hundreds of soldiers and workers that were
to serve, on the following day, as the mass graves of the
five-hundred proletarians who had been killed during the
fighting—the Brotherhood Grave, they were told by their
guide, for those who died for the Revolution. This was
the holiest place in all Russia, he said, and here would be
buried Russia's most holy.

After watching the impressive funeral procession that
lasted all of the following day, Reed noted: "I suddenly
realized that the devout Russian people no longer needed
priests to pray them into heaven. On earth they were
building a kingdom more bright than any heaven had to
offer, and for which it was glory to die."

Back in Petrograd, the Reeds continued their sympathetic observations of the progress of the Bolshevik Government. The American ambassador, David R. Francis,
was having them watched; other American officials and
private citizens in Petrograd on business, with whom the
Reeds came in contact, did not hesitate to express their
disapproval of the Reeds' partisan views. But there were

some Americans, including the Socialist, Albert Rhys Williams, and the journalist, Bessie Beatty, who often went to the Reeds' apartment for sympathetic talk.

Williams, a thirty-four-year-old clergyman and writer from Ohio, had come to Russia as an advocate of the Revolution and been welcomed by the Bolsheviks as a propagandist; he was given an appointment to the Commissariat for Foreign Affairs. Bessie Beatty, a Californian in her early thirties, was on assignment in Russia for the *San Francisco Bulletin*. Unlike Reed and Louise, she did not become a convert to Communism, but her journalistic enthusiasm and willingness to take risks for her job made her welcome to the Reeds.

The little apartment was frequently cold now with fuel in short supply, and food had become even scarcer; sometimes Reed built a fire on the tiled bathroom floor to heat cans of soup to serve his guests. Sympathetic Americans continued to invite the Reeds to social functions, in spite of the hostility this sometimes aroused on the parts of other guests. Colonel Raymond Robins, Commander of the American Red Cross in Russia, included the Reeds in his invitation to Christmas dinner, to which he also invited members of the American diplomatic staff.

Robins's qualifications for the Red Cross command were somewhat unorthodox. Forty-four years old, he was a New Yorker who moved to San Francisco to practice law and gave up a promising career there to look for gold in Alaska. He found it, and also found a mission as a crusader. Returning to New York, he became active in progressive politics and social reform, joining Theordore Roosevelt in the Progressive Party movement in 1912. He left politics in 1917 to head the Red Cross mission to Russia.

Louise and Reed often discussed between themselves

the difficulties they knew they would encounter when they returned to America. But they were firmly committed to their espousal of the Bolshevik cause and prepared to face whatever social and legal difficulties might await them. Since their arrival in Russia they were more united in love and work than ever before. Louise's Christmas present to Reed was a poem expressing her joy at being with him in this great adventure. It read, in part:

> It is fine to be here in the North
> With you on Christmas
> In a land where they really believe
> In peace on earth
> And miracles
> . . . . .
> What I want most to tell you
> Is that I love you
> And I want more than anything
> To have you stay strong and clear-visioned
> In all this world madness . . .
> You are the finest person I know
> On both sides of the world
> And it is a nice privilege to be your comrade.

Chapter Ten

In New York that November 1917, Max Eastman closed the *Masses* office "on the very date, almost of the Bolshevik revolution in Russia," he later recalled. "It was as though we had achieved the revolution and could now take a rest!" While Eastman did not mind having a vacation from his editorial obligations, he was not happy about facing the impending trial on espionage charges that had been brought against him and other members of the *Masses* staff. He got word to Reed of the trial in the usual tortuous way—a hand-carried message by someone with business in Moscow. Reed answered, by the same route, that he would leave Russia in time to attend. When the trial was postponed, Reed decided to stay in Russia until after the Constituent Assembly had met on January 18, 1918. He and Louise would leave for America on January 20. But on the twentieth, having become more and more personally involved in Russian politics, he postponed his departure once more, in order to attend the third All-Russian Congress of the Soviets on the twenty-third.

Louise was eager to get back to America and begin writing her account of the revolution, and decided to leave on the twentieth alone, assured that Reed would follow within two weeks. This decision later prompted some of Reed's friends to abuse Louise for ill-natured competitiveness; they claimed that she wanted to beat

Reed to a first-hand account of the Revolution, and that she bullied him into taking a back seat. But the evidence of Reed's correspondence with Louise does not support this claim. Reed was much too secure in his own journalistic reputation to fear being overshadowed by his wife. Indeed, he was eager for her to establish a reputation, and always encouraged and praised her work. It is more likely that Louise felt herself to be in competition with Bessie Beatty, who was also hurrying home to write an account of the revolution. (Both women published books about their Russian experiences later that year and both created a brief stir. But it was Reed's *Ten Days that Shook the World*, published a year later, that became the classic.)

Louise made as many notes as Reed, and collected copies of newspapers and official documents, as Reed had done. The opportunity to work alongside him did much to advance her journalistic training. Her enthusiasm for her subject was equal to Reed's and her willingness to take risks and endure hardship was, perhaps, even more remarkable than his, considering the added difficulties under which she had to operate because of her sex. Her style, however, was not as sharp as Reed's. At times she wrote more breathlessly than forcefully. She was not, like Reed, a born writer. But she was a brave and resourceful woman, swept up in an adventure much bigger than even she, with her romantic imagination, could have conceived. And on her own terms, she did it justice.

Louise took seriously her commission from the Bell Syndicate to gather "the woman's point of view," and many of her observations were quite poignant.

One of the first people she looked up was "Babushka," known, as she pointed out, as "the Grandmother of the Russian Revolution."

"Katherine Breshkovsky!" she exclaimed in one of her articles. "What richness of romance that name recalls. What tales of a young enthusiast who dared to express herself under the menacing tyranny of a Russian Czar. An aristocrat who gave up everything for her people; a Jeanne d'Arc who led the masses to freedom by education instead of bayonets; hunted, imprisoned, tortured, almost half a century exiled in the darkness of Siberia, brought back under the flaming banners of revolution, honored as no other woman of modern times has been honored, misunderstanding and misunderstood, deposed again, broken . . . and when the quarrels of the hour are set aside her page in history will be one of honour and she will be known to all posterity."

Louise visited this paragon in the Winter Palace, where she was established in a small, bare room. Babushka was delighted to tell Louise her life's story, discuss her relationship with Kerensky, whom she loved as a son, and hoped would be Russia's first president, and to share her meals of tea and black bread.

"I saw Babushka a good many times . . . and found out why she lived in this back room on the top floor of the Winter Palace," Louise wrote. "First, it was because she chose to live there. They had offered her the choice of the beautiful apartments and she had refused anything but this simple room. She insisted on having her bed and all her belongings crammed into the tiny place, and ate all her meals there. I don't know whether it was her long years in prison that made her assume this peculiar attitude, or if it was just because she was a simple woman and very close to the people. . . .

"Babushka is an old lady and is very forgetful. Often she did not remember in the afternoon what she had said in the morning. I once spent a most amusing day in the

Winter Palace, accomplishing none of the things I had set out to accomplish. I had had an appointment with Babushka at ten o'clock. At ten she was asleep. At eleven-thirty I went in and we began to talk. Five minutes later three French officers came to pay their respects. Babushka said they would stay but a moment. They stayed two hours. . . . I waited in the adjoining room with a young Caucasian officer, three girls, two old women and several miscellaneous officials. We discussed everything from psychoanalysis to the reason why American writers don't produce better literature. . . . The Caucasian officer gave me letters to his people in the South, and with true Russian hospitality—not knowing anything about me—invited me down there to stay for an indefinite period.

"At three o'clock Babushka appeared and was amazed to see me. We went back to her room and had tea and black bread.

Another woman revolutionary who impressed Louise even more—perhaps because, being young, attractive, and daring, she had something in common with Louise—was Marie Spirodonova. Louise wrote of her with both greater restraint and sharper insight.

"Marie Spirodonova looks as if she came from New England. Her puritanical plain black clothes with the chaste little white collars, and a certain air of refinement and severity about her seem to belong to that region more than to mad, turbulent Russia—yet she is a true daughter of Russia and of the revolution. She is very young—just past thirty—and appears exceedingly frail, but she has the wiry, unbreakable strength of many so-called 'delicate' people, and great powers of recuperation.

"Her early history as a revolutionist is exceptional even in the minds of the Russians, and they have grown used to great martyrs. She was nineteen when she killed Lupjenovsky, Governor of Tambov. Lupjenovsky had as dark a record as any official ever possessed. He went from village to village taking an insane, diabolical delight in torturing people. When peasants were unable to pay their taxes or offended him in any way at all, he made them stand in line many hours in the cold and ordered them publicly flogged. He arrested anyone who dared hold a different political view from his own; he invited the Cossacks to commit all sorts of outrages against the peasants, especially against the women.

"Spirodonova was a student in Tambov; she was not poor and she suffered no personal discomfort, but she could not bear the misery about her. She decided to kill Lupjenovsky.

"One afternoon she met him at the railway station. The first shot she fired over his head to clear the crowd, the next she aimed straight at his heart, and Spirodonova has a steady hand as well as a clear head. Lupjenovsky was surrounded by Cossacks at the time. They arrested Spirodonova.

"First the Cossacks beat her and threw her quite naked into a cold cell. Later they came back and commanded her to tell the names of her comrades and accomplices. Spirodonova refused to speak, so bunches of her long, beautiful hair were pulled out and she was burned all over with cigarettes. For two nights she was passed around among the Cossacks and the gendarmes. But there is an end to all things; Spirodonova fell violently ill. When they sentenced her to death she knew nothing at all about it, and when they changed the sentence to life imprisonment she did not know. She was deported to Siberia in a half-conscious condition. None of her friends ever expected to see her again.

"When the February revolution broke out eleven

years later she came back from Siberia and offered her life again for freedom. . . .

"I once asked her how she managed to keep her mind clear during all the eleven years that she was in Siberia.

" 'I learned languages,' she said. 'You see, it is a purely mechanical business and therefore a wonderful soother of nerves. It is like a game and one gets deeply interested. I learned to read and speak English and French in prison.'

"No other woman in Russia has quite the worship from the masses of the people that Spirodonova has. Soldiers and sailors address her as 'dear Comrade.' . . . She was elected president of the first two All-Russian Peasant Congresses held in Petrograd and she swayed those congresses largely to her will. Later she was chairman of the executive committee of the Peasants' Soviets and she is an extremely influential leader in the Left Socialist Revolutionist party. . . .

"Spirodonova is barely five feet tall. She may weigh 100 pounds. She has big grey eyes circled with blue rings, and soft brown hair which she wears in a coronet braid. She works on an average of about sixteen hours a day and everybody in Russia pours into her office to ask advice."

Louise and Spirodonova discussed the reasons why there were so few women in public office in Russia. Spirodonova thought it was because women were more idealistic than men, and found it difficult to square political expediency with their consciences. "I wish I could believe it," Louise wrote parenthetically, "but I can never see any spiritual difference between men and women inside or outside of politics. They act and react very much alike; they certainly did in the Russian revolution. It is one of the best arguments I know in favour of equal suffrage."

Spirodonova gave Louise a photograph of herself when they parted. "She hates publicity and it is the only photograph she ever gave to anyone," Louise wrote. "This one she tore off her passport but she refused to say good-bye. 'You must come right back,' she said, 'when you have written your story. And never mind saying anything good about me, but do say something about the revolution. Try to make them understand in great America how hard we over here are striving to maintain our ideals.'"

Louise's investigation of Russia's women soldiers also furnished her with good copy.

"No other feature of the great war ever caught the public fancy like the Death Battalion, composed of Russian women. I heard so much about them before I left America that it was one of the first things I investigated when I got to Russia. In six months I saw them go through a curious development which divided them into two bitter hostile camps. Their leader, Leona Botchka-rova, was severely beaten and had to be taken to a hospital. Hurt, uncomprehending, she declared: 'I do not want to be associated with women! I do not trust them!' If she had been a thinker as well as a fighter she would have known that sex had little to do with the matter. Class struggle permeated everything and it hurled the women's regiments into the maelstrom with everything else."

Louise began her research into the women's army at a recruiting station near Smolny Institute.

"Inside were half a dozen girls sitting on stools in the hallway. They were arrayed in the strangest attire; one had on dancing slippers and a frivolous waist; another high-heeled French shoes, and still another wore brown buttoned shoes and green stockings—the only universal note was short hair and men's trousers.

"They looked like the chorus of a comic opera in various stages of make-up. They all began to talk to me at

176

once, as is the Russian custom. 'Who are you?' 'Are you English or American?' 'Are you going to join the regiment?'

"A very intelligent and lovely girl by the name of Vera, who was in charge that day, came out and invited me into her office. I often went back after that and had lunch with her. She was well read and spoke five languages. The only thing I didn't like about her was that she loved to salute so much that she kept doing it all the time, and as she was the superior officer, she couldn't very well salute anyone else but me. This I found very droll after coming from France, where war correspondents are not treated like commanders-in-chief.

"Vera explained about the variety of shoes. She said that they had ordered boots, but had never heard any further word. There was a very good reason, which I found out afterwards; there was no leather. Everyone was 'just waiting,' as everyone does in Russia."

Louise wrote affectingly about the plight of the Russian children.

"Conditions have been unbearable for the children. Transportation, never very efficient, was almost completely upset as soon as mobilization began and it was never reorganised. Children in the cities have been without proper nourishment for four years because milk and other necessities have not been brought in from the rural districts. At first, the country children were not greatly affected, but as the war went on and disorganisation spread, King Hunger claimed them all. I wondered how any of them survived. I once asked a doctor who has had experience in caring for children in six warring countries and he said that the only explanation he could offer was that Russian children have more resistance than other children. 'I was forced to give them food in my hospital,' he said, 'that American babies would have died on in a few days.'

"If it is true that Russian children are so strong it only makes the statistics regarding their mortality more tragic. On the retreats in Galicia, out of Riga and other places, they died at the rate of 800 out of every 1000. In the charitable institutions, over-crowded, disease ridden, unsanitary, lacking almost every medical necessity, only 15 per cent survived. . . .

"I came to realise with horror that everybody in Russia is grown up. Those young in years, who we still called children, had old and sad faces, large, hungry eyes burned forth from pale countenances, wretched, worn-out shoes, sagging, ragged little garments accentuated their so apparent misery.

"On the retreats confusion and terror swept along with the refugees. Last autumn when they were fleeing down the muddy roads before the advancing Germans, parents had no time to stop to bury their dead children. Mothers fell exhausted and died with live babies in their arms. . . .

"The children showed remarkable courage, standing all sorts of hardships without whimpering. This was especially true of the children who were sent ahead of the parents in order that, even if the parents perished, the children at least might be saved. In the strangeness and turmoil of the new life, individuals asserted themselves. One little boy or girl, often by no means the oldest, might lead a band of twenty or thirty. He would make himself a self-appointed chief. . . .

"Life was not all serious in those sad little armies. The children found time to play jokes on the doctors, to tease the nurses and to mimic the revolutionary leaders. They formed committees and issued proclamations of defiance, pretending to refuse orders from superiors. This aping of the new life was true in the schools of Petrograd. Little boys laboriously wrote out long documents and pasted them on the walls, 'just like Lenin and Trotsky.' One of the teachers told me an amusing tale about a committee of youngsters who came to her with the portentous information that thereafter the students in the school would receive no orders 'unless countersigned by the committee,' the oldest member of the committee being twelve years old."

In a lighter vein, Louise described one of the off-beat aspects of Petrograd, the Alexander Market, which never failed to astonish foreign visitors.

"It is known as 'Thieves Market,' because obviously most of the things that are for sale there are stolen goods. . . . More antique treasures can be bought there than anywhere else except in old markets in Constantinople. . . .

"The range of loot is amazing. There are old Bokharas, ikons of wood, brass and iron, amber, carved silver chains, old enamel, tapestries, Bristol glass, Chinese porcelains, furs and great trays of precious and semi-precious stones. It is situated in a remote corner of Petrograd, and no guidebook ever mentions it. It seems to be entirely overlooked by tourists. I once took the American consul and Somerset Maugham, the playwright, to see it. The consul was shocked at the idea of such an open market for thieves, but like most foreigners, he decided to have no scruples, since it was not his country and it was none of his business what peculiar customs alien peoples had. He found a pipe owned by Peter the Great, and Maugham picked up two marvelous bead purses."

One of the most effective bits of descriptive writing Louise turned out was her eyewitness account of the mass burial, in Moscow, of "the last martyrs of the revolution." She watched, during most of the night, in twenty degrees below zero weather, as the huge grave was dug near the Kremlin wall.

"It was terrifyingly still and lonesome. There was no sound but the clatter of spades and the sputter of torches. . . . I asked the soldiers [digging the trench] why they had chosen this spot for the Red Burial. They said it was because they wished to bestow the greatest possible honor on their dead comrades . . . it is the holiest spot in all Russia. . . .

"About five o'clock we climbed stiffly over the edge and straggled wearily home. The task was completed; the gaping hole was ready to receive five hundred bodies. . . .

"The procession began at eight. The Executive Committee of the Soviet was to head the procession, and they kindly invited me to march with them. . . .

"From early morning I stood on a mound of newly turned earth watching an immense sea of people pouring through the white, arched gateway of the old Tartar City —flooding all the Red Square. It was bitter cold. Our feet froze to the ground and our hands ached under our gloves. But the spectacle before us was so magnificent that we forgot everything else. . . . Women all around began to sob and one quite near me tried to hurl herself after a coffin as it was being lowered. . . . With all her frenzied strength she fought against the friends who tried to restrain her. Crying out the name of the man in the coffin, she screamed, bit, scratched like a wounded wild thing until she was finally carried away moaning and half unconscious. Tears rolled down the faces of the big soldiers."

Louise devoted a long piece of writing to Lenin and

Trotsky, both of whom she met and interviewed. Both were, in the early days of the Bolshevik take-over, remarkably accessible to foreign correspondents. It was in her writing about these two formidable figures (whose impact on history she clearly recognized) that her weakness as a reporter was most evident. She wrote brief descriptions of both men, based on her personal impression of them, and described, at length, their various programs and projects with transparent advocacy. But she never managed, as Reed did, to connect them, as human beings, with their ideas and performance. She had not learned Reed's trick of putting the reader on the scene, with the subject in action.

Only in one brief passage did Louise put the two Russian leaders onstage:

"Lenin and Trotsky are always menaced by assassination. I once was present when three shots were fired at Lenin. He was as cool as if he had been made of stone."

Packing to leave Russia, Louise worried about her papers and notes. Since both she and Reed were under surveillance, she feared that her papers would be examined and possibly confiscated by American or British officials at some point on her return voyage. She applied to the Assistant Foreign Minister, Zalkin, for help, and Zalkin offered to make her a courier for the Soviet Government. He gave her a document stating, "The bearer of this certificate, Louise Bryant, is going to Stockholm as a courier of the People's Commissars of Foreign Affairs and is taking along sealed bags and packages. It is requested that all those in authority show her assistance on her journey and particularly with her baggage." The document was issued in both Russian and French.

She also obtained a letter from Colonel Raymond Robins to the Naval Attaché of the American Legation in

Christiania, requesting his assistance in getting her passage on a ship to the United States.

The night before she left Petrograd Louise took her bags to the Foreign Office. "Three old servants, who had seen many years of service under the Czar, and who still wore the same old uniforms, stood stiffly at attention ready to perform the ceremony," she later wrote. "One held a flaming taper, one the long wax sticks and one the official seal, which never left his person while he was on duty and reposed in the great safe at night.

"They were very solemn and never changed the expression on their faces as they pasted over my heretofore inconspicuous baggage large white cards that proclaimed in black letters that I was about to depart on an official expedition. They treated me with all the deference due an emissary of his Imperial Majesty. Only the soldiers and sailors shuffling through the building looked in at the door and grinned broadly."

Louise encountered various degrees of scornful or indignant behavior on the parts of anti-Bolshevik Russians and Scandinavians, but her trip to Stockholm was otherwise uneventful, and her baggage remained intact. She arrived in New York on February 18, 1918, aboard the Norwegian ship, Bergensfiord. While the passengers were held on board for a search by customs officials, reporters interviewed some of them. Louise was startled to find that she had become something of a celebrity during her absence, due to recent newspaper accounts of Reed's activities in Russia. The first question put to her was, what did she think about her husband's dismissal, just announced, as Russian Consul to the United States. Louise, who knew nothing about Reed's appointment, let alone his dismissal, said, truthfully, that she was surprised. She refused to discuss her stay in Russia, saying she would be writing about it.

Soon after debarking Louise learned from friends some of the details of Reed's appointment, but it was not until Reed's return that she heard the entire story.

On January 29, while Louise was en route from Russia, *The New York Times*, among other newspapers, carried a story announcing Reed's appointment as Consul. The appointment resulted from Reed's request to Trotsky that he be made a courier, like Louise; Trotsky had—perhaps with ironic intent—decided to go one better. Reed was delighted, even though some of his friends warned him that the Bolsheviks were merely exploiting him, and that the appointment would very likely lead to his arrest for treason when he arrived home. Reed was willing to face this, believing that the publicity would call attention to the Bolshevik cause and arouse sympathy for the new government. The American officials in Petrograd were indignant over the appointment. What means they used to have it revoked have never been made clear, but some sort of persuasive argument was evidently put before Trotsky, who apologetically cancelled it.

On February 19, the day after Louise arrived in New York, *The New York Times* carried a story announcing that Ambassador Francis had notified the State Department that the Russians had withdrawn Reed's appointment as Consul. Reed was in Stockholm, the story continued, and was traveling in his private capacity, without any Bolshevik credentials.

Evidently Louise assumed that, despite the flurry about his status, Reed was safely on his way home. It was not until early March that she began to worry about his non-arrival and the absence of any communication from him.

Chapter Eleven

ALMOST IMMEDIATELY after reaching New York, Louise did a somewhat mystifying thing. She wrote to O'Neill in Provincetown, urging him to come to New York to see her. Apparently she had decided to re-establish the triangle, in spite of her protestations of loyalty to Reed.

To some of Louise's women friends, who advocated and practiced free love, her attachment to two men was perfectly understandable. But these women, for the most part, conducted their affairs quite openly. If they had more than one lover, they took no pains to conceal the fact from either one. Louise's maneuvering and deception puzzled them.

Louise's motives were complex. She seemed to have a compulsive need to court danger. Risk stimulated her. When she was not enduring such realistic dangers as traveling through a war or revolution, she created a situation in which she could evoke stress. Keeping an intense romance going with two men simultaneously, concealing the truth from both, was a way of creating such a situation. In spite of her earlier and perfectly sincere conviction that Reed was the man she wanted, it seemed that monogamy was not, for her, a fulfilling state.

But she could not confront this difficulty. She had married Reed, and apparently needed the security of that marriage. Therefore, she could not be honest with Reed and chance losing him. And she had to entice O'Neill by inventing a false picture of her relationship with Reed—or lose him. For her, it seemed to be less a question of being torn by two loves, than of playing an exciting game for its own sake.

Louise had heard that O'Neill was living in Provincetown with a woman named Agnes Boulton, and that they were planning to be married. Mutual friends in Greenwich Village assured Louise that O'Neill's affair with Agnes was a direct result of his bitter disappointment at Louise's going off to Russia with Reed. Agnes, she was told, bore a strong physical resemblance to her, and O'Neill had persuaded himself he was in love with her. For weeks after Louise's departure for Russia O'Neill had brooded in New York, making no secret of the fact that he was carrying a torch; he would make melodramatic references about his broken heart to almost anyone who would listen. Then, late in October, he met Agnes Boulton. She was a pretty, dark-haired writer of pulp magazine fiction in her late twenties. He began seeing her regularly and it was not long before she fell in love with him. In January O'Neill began talking about going to Provincetown to settle down to serious writing, but he kept putting off his departure. On January 22 one of O'Neill's closest friends, a man named Louis Holliday (Polly's brother), killed himself by taking an overdose of heroin. Terribly shocked, O'Neill packed up Agnes and himself and fled from the Village.

By the end of January he and Agnes were living somewhat primitively but not unhappily in a couple of furnished rooms in Provincetown, and O'Neill was seriously at work writing *Beyond the Horizon*—the tragedy about two men in love with the same girl that had its inspiration in the Reed-O'Neill-Louise triangle. (O'Neill's reputation was still minor. The Playwrights Theater was producing his one-act plays, but it was not until two years later, when *Beyond the Horizon* was produced on Broadway, that he was hailed as a dramatist of major talent.)

And then, abruptly, the summons came from Louise.

An acquaintance of O'Neill who lived in Provincetown, a middle-aged woman named Alice Woods, recalled the impact that Louise's arrival had on O'Neill's ménage. Privately, she thought Agnes and O'Neill mismatched, although she liked them both. Agnes, she felt, was out of place in the bohemian lifestyle O'Neill had established. "Agnes seemed to be a typical young American girl," Miss Woods said. "She wasn't subtle enough to play the game that Gene seemed to be playing."

O'Neill and Agnes went to tea at Miss Woods's house one day in late February. Agnes was in tears. She told Miss Woods that O'Neill wanted to marry her but that she would not agree.

"Why not?" asked Miss Woods. Sobbing, Agnes said that O'Neill was still in love with "that girl." O'Neill looked haggard, said nothing, and stared out the window at Miss Woods's orchard, covered with melting snow.

According to Agnes Boulton's memoir, *Part of a Long Story*, O'Neill gave her Louise's letter to read.

"Louise wrote that she must see him—and at once. She had left Jack Reed in Russia and crossed three thousand miles of frozen steppes to come back to him—her lover. Page after page of passionate declaration of their love—of hers, which would never change; of his, which she knew also would never change. She had forgiven him. What if he had picked up some girl in the Village and become involved? There was no use writing letters—she had to see him! It was all a misunderstanding and her fault for leaving him, for going to Russia with Jack."

186

Agnes said she was trembling when she finished the letter. She was frightened, for she saw "some sort of uncertainty" in O'Neill's face.

"What are you going to do?" she asked O'Neill.

"I'll have to see her—to explain. I can't let her suffer like this. I can't do this to her . . . now!" O'Neill said.

"*See her*—"Agnes gasped.

"I should go to New York, I suppose. After all, she made a trip of three thousand miles."

"Three thousand miles of frozen steppes—yes! She knew that phrase would get you!"

Bitterly, Agnes recalled, "Already this woman was invested, in my mind, with all the wiles of the serpent. I had read in her letter such assurance, such surety of her hold over this man. I had already begun to suspect that he liked to suffer. He was beginning to suffer already before my eyes, looking away from me, looking deep into himself. I could see him remembering all the dark passionate travail of their love."

Agnes tried to reason with O'Neill: "She loves John Reed. She is his wife. She chose to go with him—not to stay with you!"

"You don't understand. She's not—there has never been any physical relationship between them."

"Oh, you fool—you *fool!*"

Why hadn't she told him that, Agnes mused, when he had first confessed his love affair with Louise? Why had she listened quietly and understandingly, though privately she had immediately put her down as a very artful woman?

"Perhaps it was because I had wanted to protect him, not to destroy his belief in anything—even a rival woman," Agnes said. "But at that time she was a figure in the past, a nonentity so far as Gene and I were concerned. Now she was a threat, living and possessive—ready to claim her own. Her pride had been hurt. She would stop at nothing."

While Agnes was remembering, the postman arrived with another letter from Louise. O'Neill looked at it in dismay and said, "I don't want to read it, *she's crazy!*"

But he did read it, and told Agnes that he must go to New York to see Louise, to tell her that the affair was finished; she would never understand, unless he explained it to her face to face. Agnes began weeping.

"You're not afraid I'll go back to her—it's impossible you could think such a thing," O'Neill said.

"But you *are* going back if you go down there now. And your work, what about that?"

"I won't drink. Is that what you're afraid of?"

Agnes paused to think. Suddenly she knew that she did not believe O'Neill would give her up for Louise; it was her pride that was hurt, "an unseen contest between this woman and me, in which I didn't even want her to have the satisfaction of winning the first round by summoning him to her side." But still, the idea of his leaving his work, exposing himself to the temptations of the city, taking "that long, boring and uncomfortable trip to explain to this woman that he loved me and no longer loved her" upset her.

That night O'Neill decided to try, after all, to explain in a letter. Agnes watched scornfully as he labored over phrases, rewriting, discarding and editing, "spending twenty minutes or more on paragraphs which, when read, would sound as if they had been torn from his heart and from the depth of his soul." She wondered what "the fair Louise would think, could she see him doing this."

O'Neill insisted that Agnes read the letter when he had finished.

"It began with a review of their love and their torture —a searing memory of the past but bringing a great beauty to it, too, so that here and there I seemed to catch a cadence of Irish words, a memory of the Aran Islands and, of course, the sound of the sea." Agnes was both moved and jealous as the image of Louise was evoked— "this menacing and determined hussy . . . a half-mythical symbol of the great old and mystic Irish legends."

The letter went on to review their relationship of secrecy, betrayal, and torment, and to accusations of Louise's playing with him "as a cat plays with a mouse." Finally, he wrote about his love for Agnes. He ended by saying he wanted to see Louise, but could not leave Provincetown because he was finishing a long play, and asked her to come to Provincetown. Agnes did not like that, but accepted it as preferable to O'Neill's going to New York; she half-believed that Louise would refuse to come.

The next morning O'Neill was back at work, apparently having dismissed the whole thing.

According to Agnes, letters from Louise continued to arrive at intervals. O'Neill and Agnes were married on April 12, and soon after a letter came from Louise saying that she understood about the marriage; it was "both escape and revenge, but she would forgive that, there were more important things in the world than marriage."

Questioning O'Neill now, secure in her marriage, Agnes found that Louise and O'Neill had agreed before she left for Russia that they would resume their relationship when she returned. Louise had promised O'Neill that she would tell Reed she was in love with them both, that she was convinced that O'Neill now needed her more, and that they must reverse roles—she would live with O'Neill, while still remaining Reed's companion and friend. Still according to Agnes, subsequent letters from

Louise "hinted broadly" that Reed had agreed to this arrangement "for love of her" and that the proof was that she had left Reed behind in Russia and was here to put the plan into effect. Again, Louise insisted that O'Neill come to New York to see her. At Agnes's suggestion, O'Neill wrote back offering to meet her halfway, in Fall River, Massachusetts.

"Her reply was quick and imperious—a vibrant assault upon and belittlement of me," Agnes wrote, "and a denunciation of Gene for his weakness and lack of understanding. She made it clear that he had fallen greatly in stature in her eyes; and also that there were other and greater concerns on her mind than going to Fall River. She implied that as she was a clever journalist and writer there was a greater orbit in which she circled—of world happenings and important events—than that to which Gene in his Provincetown flight had relegated himself." Soon after, a letter came saying that Reed was on his way back from Russia. "So she revolved back into her orbit of exciting events, of glamour and journalism and many admirers," wrote Agnes.

While claiming that she "had no animosity" toward Louise and "at times even admired her brilliant escapades and journalistic prowess," Agnes summed up the affair somewhat spitefully. Louise, she wrote, went about telling her friends that she had broken O'Neill's heart, that O'Neill had rushed to New York on her return from Russia, that she had to turn him out of her apartment, that she found him drunk, morning after morning, on her doorstep. That Louise believed she had broken O'Neill's heart is likely, in view of her romantic nature. That she would have wished to malign him is less believable; malice was not a part of her makeup.

But Louise's pride must have been rather severely wounded when nothing resulted from the lengthy, impassioned dialogue with O'Neill, for she had taken time out from a busy schedule to try to rescue him from Agnes. Eugene O'Neill never re-entered Louise's life. At the height of his fame, in 1926, he left Agnes Boulton and their two children for a beautiful, thrice-divorced woman named Carlotta Monterey, to whom he was married in 1929, and with whom he lived until his death in 1953.

During March and early April Louise was busy writing the series of articles for which she had contracted in August 1917, trying to find out where her husband was and what had happened to him, and fulfilling speaking engagements.

The articles began appearing in the *New York American*, the *Philadelphia Public Ledger*, and other newspapers on April 14, 1918. Later that year the collected articles were published as the book *Six Red Months in Russia*. Louise had actually spent four months in Russia —from mid-September to January 20; the other two months were spent in transit. But the articles were vague about dates, stressing rather an anecdotal, chatty view of the momentous period of Russian history she had witnessed, and she probably reasoned that six months sounded more substantial than four.

In addition to her writing and speaking engagements, Louise found herself sought after to endorse various political causes. On February 25, Lincoln Steffens asked her to co-sign a cable he was sending to Reed in Christiania, asking him to return to Russia and try to change Lenin's mind about signing a separate peace treaty with Germany; President Wilson wanted Russia to continue fighting with the allied countries. "If you can and will change

Trotsky's and Lenin's attitude you can render historical international service," the cable read. Louise refused to sign it, knowing Reed would be angered by the request. She was right; Reed cabled back his refusal.

Chapter Twelve

REED HAD PLANNED TO SAIL from Christiania on February 22, 1918, but when he arrived there on the nineteenth, the American consul informed him that the State Department had ordered him detained indefinitely. Having missed the sailing on the twenty-second and finding that there was no ship scheduled to sail for the United States until April 15, he rented a room and started work on *Ten Days that Shook the World*.

In Christiania he met Angelica Balabanoff, a Russian woman in her early sixties, who had recently been appointed First Secretary of the Third International. European educated, Miss Balabanoff had been a close friend of the young Benito Mussolini, whom she had converted to Socialism, and later broken with when he formed his own Fascist Party. Soon to break with the Bolsheviks in disillusionment over their repressive rule, she was still, when she met Reed, a staunch supporter of the revolution.

"I had only to talk [with Reed] a few moments to understand that here was one of the most devoted and genuine revolutionists I had ever met," Balabanoff wrote, in *My Life as a Rebel*. "I was amazed to find in an American such a profound understanding of the Russian Revolution and such love for the Russian masses. As a journalist and a poet, as well as a revolutionist, it was probably natural that he should have been stirred by the dramatic boldness of the Revolution itself. But there was something more than an appreciation of the color and drama of the Revolution, hero-worship of its leaders and sympathy with its aims in Reed's enthusiasm for Russia. He loved the country itself and the great anonymous mass that had made the Revolution possible by its suffering and endurance."

Reed and Balabanoff spent many evenings together talking, and Reed, fascinated by the stories she told him, urged her to write her memoirs (which she later did). On one of their evenings Reed took her to see a Charlie Chaplin movie; the solemn socialist, who had never seen Chaplin, "enjoyed it immensely."

For over a month Reed received no word from Louise, nor did she hear from him. Both were writing regularly, and it was not until much later that they realized their mail had been intercepted, although they never discovered by whom. By mid-March Louise was growing anxious and she appealed to the State Department for word about her husband. On March 15 she received a note from the State Department saying that their "last information, received in a telegram from Christiania, indicated that Mr. Reed is in that city." On the same day, she addressed an audience of 300 in New York. Describing her trip to Russia, she said that accounts of violence there were greatly exaggerated. She said she had "never met a people so kind and generous as the Russians, who refused to hate anybody, and dislike to kill anyone except their officers and oppressors."

On March 27, Louise received a note from the sympathetic chairman of the Committee on Public Information in Washington: "This afternoon the State Department received information that your husband was still in Christiania. No word came as to his plans—only the bare fact of his presence there. I shall take pains to give you any further information as I receive it.

"You must expect visits from the investigating branches of Government, and try not to be worried by them."

Early in April, Louise finally heard from Reed; somehow, this letter, written on March 27, slipped through the censor. He addressed her in care of Carl Hovey's wife at the *Metropolitan*, not knowing that she was living at the Brevoort. Calling her his "dearest little honey in the world," Reed wrote that he was greatly relieved to have just gotten word of her from his friend, Robert Minor, who had arrived in Christiania on his way to Russia. Minor, a thirty-four-year-old Texan, was a newspaper writer and cartoonist. Like Reed, he had been a war correspondent in Europe. He was also a dedicated Socialist and was soon to become a leader of the American Communist Party and, later, the editor of the *Daily Worker*.

Reed had been terribly worried about Louise, he said, and still was worried at the thought of her working so hard and carrying "all those loads" on her shoulders.

"I do so want you to come over here and be with me," Reed wrote. "But how can we support ourselves here, or in Russia?" Some people in Norway were deciding about giving him a job, he said, and if that came about, they would have enough to live on. However, the authorities did not want him to stay in Norway. On the other hand, Max Eastman (who, with his sister, Crystal, had started a new magazine called the *Liberator*) wanted him to return to Russia as their correspondent, in which case he hoped she would join him there. "Anyway, my dearest, don't fail to come *immediately* if you can arrange some way of settling the money question. I do so want to see you!" (Reed's letter did not sound as though he had agreed with Louise that she should "reverse roles" and live with O'Neill; nothing in his behavior now or in the ensuing weeks gave any indication that he had the least suspicion of what Louise was up to.)

Reed told Louise that he was hard at work on his book and that he would try to stay in Norway until the book was "more or less in shape"—about another month. He had asked Eugen Boissevan, who had raised the money for his trip, for additional funds, he said, which he needed in spite of the fact that he had made a little money selling articles on Russia to local newspapers, and working as a stenographer. He ended by asking her to keep in touch with Morris Hilquit, the prominent Socialist Party leader and lawyer in New York, to whom he would communicate his plans if the authorities would give him permission.

Hilquit, who was to be the defense lawyer in the *Masses* trial, had made his legal reputation as a defense lawyer in many of the most celebrated labor union disputes of the 1900s. Then forty-nine, he was one of the most highly regarded members of the Socialist movement in America. A few months earlier he had run for mayor of New York City and received the largest vote (150,000) ever cast for a Socialist candidate in any city of the United States. Latvian born, Hilquit emigrated with his family to the United States in 1886. He received his law degree from New York University at the age of twenty-four and began defending labor union leaders. Like Eastman and Reed, he had been under attack during the last few years for his pacifist views.

In mid-April, Reed was suddenly informed that he could return home. The *Masses* trial was scheduled to begin April 15, and Reed hoped to arrive while it was still underway; he preferred facing the charges in person rather than being tried in absentia.

The trial, by now something of a cause célèbre, opened at 10:30 in the morning of April 15, 1918, in the old Post Office building of Manhattan, opposite City Hall. War fever ran high and public opinion was not on the side of the group of editors and writers who had steadily opposed American participation. However, as Max Eastman recalled, there were two things in their favor: "There was not a drop or recollection of German or Austrian blood in our veins; we were all, absolutely and from way back, American, and we looked it." And the presiding judge was Augustus N. Hand, a man who, according to Eastman, "could have upheld in a hurricane the dignity of the law. He was less genial and less patriarchal than his cousin, Learned Hand, but he had a like unshakeable integrity."

Outside the courtroom windows was a Liberty Bond booth, in front of which a brass band periodically struck up patriotic songs. Just as the proceedings in the courtroom got underway, the band began playing "The Star Spangled Banner," and the *Masses* business manager, Merrill Rogers, leaped up and stood at attention. In the face of this display of patriotism on the part of an accused traitor, the judge seemed to have no choice but also to rise to his feet and within seconds the entire courtroom was standing at attention. When the band repeated its performance twenty minutes later, the same thing happened. A few hours later, it happened again. When the music began a fourth time, Judge Hand found the courage to resist, and told the courtroom that the ceremony would have to be dispensed with.

The spectators in the courtroom, many of them hostile, believed that Eastman had arranged the whole thing as a satirical comment on the trial. "I've never heard the last of this cleverly impudent trick I played on a judge who was trying me for treason," Eastman wrote.

"To me it was, in simple truth, an appalling disaster. My flag was still the red flag, and I was not in the habit of standing up for 'The Star Spangled Banner.' . . . We had been indicted for 'conspiring to cause mutiny and refusal of duty in the military and naval forces,' and 'obstruct the recruiting and enlistment service' of the United States. To call the *Masses,* and above all its editorial meetings and general mode of parturition, a conspiracy, was about the most cockeyed fantasy the war psychosis produced. I had no wish . . . to spend twenty years in jail for a crime I did not commit; but to avoid this without betraying my convictions was, in the existing hysteria, an extremely delicate operation. I was planning to devote my most discriminating efforts to it, and this witty stunt of Merrill's scotched my plans completely. If I rose, I would be subscribing to that 'Religion of Patriotism' which I had analyzed and rejected in a recent essay in the *Masses;* if I refused to rise, with the whole court standing, I might as well withdraw my plea of 'not guilty' and hand myself over to the sergeant-at-arms. I did get up, of course—reluctantly, and, no doubt with a very solemn expression, for my thoughts as I stood there were concerned with the relative merits of different ways of murdering Merrill Rogers."

Art Young, on the other hand, was, in Eastman's view, the hero of the trial. Young, at fifty-two, was a nationally famous political cartoonist, who had been the Washington correspondent for the *Metropolitan* until 1917, and a contributor to *Life, The Saturday Evening Post,* and *Col-*

lier's, in addition to the *Masses.* A member of the Socialist Party, he was a crusader for women's suffrage, labor unions, and racial equality.

One of the prosecution's pieces of evidence was a cartoon Young had drawn, showing a capitalist, an editor, a politician, and a minister dancing a war dance, while the devil directed the orchestra; it was captioned, "Having Their Fling." The prosecutor asked him what he meant by the picture.

"Meant? What do you mean by meant? You have the picture in front of you."

"What did you intend to do when you drew this picture, Mr. Young?"

"Intend to do? I intended to draw a picture."

"For what purpose?"

"Why, to make people think—to make them laugh—to express my feelings. It isn't fair to ask an artist to go into the metaphysics of his art."

"Had you intended to obstruct recruiting and enlistment by such pictures?"

"There isn't anything in there about recruiting and enlistment is there? I don't believe in war, that's all, and I said so."

After hearing the bulk of the testimony, Judge Hand dismissed the part of the indictment that accused the *Masses* staff of conspiring to cause mutiny and refusal of duty in the armed forces; the only charge for the jury to weigh was that of a "conspiracy" to obstruct the draft.

In summing up, Hilquit said, in part: "Constitutional rights are not a gift. They are a conquest by this nation, as they were a conquest by the English nation. They can never be taken away, and if taken away, and if given back after the war, they will never again have the same potent vivifying force as expressing the democratic soul of a nation. They will be a gift to be given, to be taken."

The prosecuting attorney, Earl Barnes, was "sincerely convinced" that the *Masses* staff should go to jail, Eastman recalled. Yet he seemed equally sincere in his reluctance to send them there, and in his summation to the jury, made numerous complimentary references to the individual talents of the defendants.

The jury retired on the afternoon of April 26; they could not reach a decision and on April 27, the jury was dismissed. A re-trial was ordered.

Reed arrived in New York on the morning of April 28. *The New York Times*, observing the military secrecy imposed by a jittery government, datelined the arrival "An Atlantic Port." In its headline *The Times* characterized Reed, for some mysterious reason, as a "Trotsky Envoy" (although it had carried the story of his dismissal as a Russian representative on February 19). Louise was at the pier, watching as the passengers debarked, but Reed was not among them. He was kept aboard for more than eight hours, while Federal agents picked over every item in his possession and confiscated most of his papers, including the unfinished manuscript of *Ten Days that Shook the World*.

Finally, at eight o'clock in the evening, he walked onto the pier, to be greeted by his exhausted wife. He was under arrest on the *Masses* conspiracy charge—the new trial was scheduled for later that year—and Morris Hilquit, who had come to meet him, promised Earl Barnes to produce Reed for formal arraignment on the following morning. To *The Tribune* reporter who interviewed him briefly on the pier, Reed "appeared to be in the best of health and showed a great deal of cheerfulness at reaching once more a land of plenty and comparative security." In the style of personal journalism that was prevalent in the press of the day, the reporter continued: "For what is a mere indictment, compared with practical starvation and a good chance of a merry Bolshevik bullet in the back?"

Reed declined to answer any questions, saying he could make no statement until he knew what his status was. He and Louise drove off in a taxi.

Freed on bail the following morning to await trial, along with the rest of the *Masses* staff, Reed was now technically at liberty to go about his business. But without his notes and manuscript, he had to postpone indefinitely the work he wanted most to finish—his account of the revolution. He did, however, resume writing for the *Call*. He also joined the staff of the *Masses'* successor, the *Liberator*. And, even more than Louise, he was much in demand as a public speaker.

On May 31, 1918, he went to Philadelphia to keep a lecture date, and found that the hall where he was to speak had been locked by the police. A crowd of 500 had gathered outside, and Reed led them around a corner and began addressing them from the street. The police attempted to arrest him, and a member of the crowd, a shipyard worker named Kogerman, took it on himself to "rescue" Reed. Both men were finally marched off to the police station and Reed was charged with inciting to riot and making seditious remarks. At his hearing the following morning, Reed protested that he had delivered the same speech on fourteen previous occasions. "I've given it in Boston and other places, and no accusation of treason followed. It is made up of notes taken by me on Bolshevik conditions in Russia."

The assistant district attorney hearing the plea was unimpressed. "Reed defied the police," he said. "Disorder

and riot resulted. He made seditious remarks." He asked
to have bail fixed at $5,000; the trial was postponed until
fall.

Except among the acknowledged radicals, Reed was
not popular. A letter he received on June 12 from Upton
Sinclair illustrates the somewhat gingerly interest with
which some of his friends now regarded him. Saying that
he had read "with great interest" Reed's article in the
Liberator describing the Bolshevik program and dismissing stories of Bolshevik terrorism, Sinclair went on to
point out that Maxim Gorky "directly contradicts everything you have to say."

Sinclair, at forty, was a world-famous advocate of social justice. The year before he had written *King Coal*,
describing the tragic strike of the Colorado Coal and Iron
Company. His most recent book, *The Profits of Religion*,
was an exposé of the avariciousness of clergymen. He was
a lifelong defender of the underdog and had been a member of the Socialist Party since 1902. But he supported
America's war policy (it was not until later, with hind-
sight, that he condemned it). And his chief source of difference with Reed was over the failure of the new Russian government to stand with the allies against
Germany.

Later that month, Reed had a letter from Lincoln
Steffens, who also disapproved of Reed's stand. "You do
wrong to buck this thing. . . . I must wait. You must wait.
I know it's hard, but you can't carry conviction. You can't
plant ideas. Only feelings exist. The public are bewildered. I think it is undemocratic to do much now. Write,
but don't publish."

Walter Lippmann, too, held aloof from Reed. He had
been annoyed with his former college classmate ever
since the episode of Reed's firing the famous bullet from

the German lines.

"Reed was a great talent, the great descriptive journalist of our era," Lippmann later said, "but as a descriptive, romantic writer, not a political thinker. He was Byronic. But he was not a politically oriented man. Once the war began, we drifted apart."

Possibly to counteract his growing sense of isolation in his own country, Reed made formal application in June for membership in the Socialist Party.

Another friend, William C. Bullitt, angered Reed by ignoring his letters requesting help in getting back his confiscated papers. Bullitt, who was later to become Franklin D. Roosevelt's ambassador to Moscow, was a wealthy young Philadelphian whom Reed had met when he was bureau chief for the *Philadelphia Public Ledger* in Washington in 1916. Bullitt, at twenty-six, was now head of the State Department's Bureau of Central European Information, and its specialist on the Russian Revolution. Reed thought it logical that Bullitt should, out of friendship, pull a few strings; Bullitt thought it expedient to ignore him.

On July 20, Reed addressed the future ambassador irately:

"I don't see any reason why you should simply ignore my letters, just because I wrote and asked you if you couldn't *please* find out where my papers had gone, and whom to write to. I've certainly not bothered you a hell of a lot; and you know how damnably important to me it is to get those papers.

"Why should they have disappeared—why should no one know where they have gone?

"Why is the government *sabotaging* me? If they have anything on me, why not say so?"

While Reed tried, fatalistically, to accept the snubs

and open enmity of former friends and acquaintances, he could not help feeling bitter. He became defensively arrogant, sometimes attacking friends who might have remained sympathetic, but who, in his state of near paranoia, Reed was sure had turned against him.

All through July, August, and September of 1918, Reed continued to make speeches, extolling the Bolshevik revolution, criticizing America's war policy and encouraging the class struggle in America. Although not yet ready to say so publicly, Reed had by now convinced himself that a revolution should and would take place in America. He was, as yet, vague about how to organize such a revolution. He envisioned a political upheaval without bloodshed, and saw his own role as that of an orator, but he did not delude himself that he had the practical or technical knowledge to lead the actual revolt.

Continuing to write for the *Call*—Bolshevism as the "foe of all Imperialism," and the heroism of the Russian army were his chief subjects—Reed resigned in July of 1918 from the *Liberator*. He thought it was sidestepping the radical issues, and he did not want his name to appear in the masthead. But he continued to contribute articles to the magazine—"How the Russian Revolution Works," was one; a piece about Eugene Debs, then in jail for criticizing the government's prosecution of persons charged with violation of the 1917 Espionage Act, was another.

In September Reed managed to get himself arrested again—this time in the Bronx, where he was accused of "wilfully, knowingly, and feloniously uttering scurrilous and abusive language" about United States military policy. His bail, as in Philadelphia, was set at $5,000.

When not traveling to speaking engagements, Reed and Louise stayed in their Croton cottage; united in their dedication to a cause that had now become a single-minded way of life for both, they cherished the times they had together in this peaceful rural setting. Louise had finally persuaded herself that she had chosen the man who needed her most. For the time, Louise's earnings were their chief support and she tried to follow up her successful newspaper series on Russia with other assignments. But she soon ran into the same difficulty as Reed. The *Philadelphia Public Ledger*, which had run her Russian articles, turned down her suggestion that she write a series on Ireland. "In view of the fact that your husband has again been arrested," wrote a *Ledger* representative, "I think it would be wiser for you to let the matter rest a while. Your identity as Mrs. Reed has been pretty widely established, and I am afraid the newspapers would not go in for a series from you until Mr. Reed has cleared up all his troubles."

The first of the three charges under which Reed stood indicted was tried at the beginning of October. The defendants in the second *Masses* trial found themselves virtually without counsel; Morris Hilquit was engaged on another case and the lawyer who had assisted him, Dudley Field Malone, had joined the Navy. The lawyer they engaged, Seymour Stedman, an attorney prominent for his defense of Socialists, became ill on his first day in court. Suffering from a high fever, he dragged himself into court from time to time, but was unable to contribute more than a symbolic objection or two. The job of defending the *Masses* staff fell on a willing but inexperienced young lawyer named Charles Recht—and on the accused staff members themselves.

In Eastman's view, the second trial was enhanced "as a dramatic performance" by the presence of Reed.

"I think we had all quietly made up our minds we

were going to jail this time," Eastman wrote, "and the conclusion was not weakened when one of the talesmen, to an inquiry whether he had any prejudice against social- ism, answered: 'I don't know what it is, but I'm opposed to it.'" Eastman and his colleagues were not happy about the new judge, either. He was Martin Manton, "hard, brisk, and mean-looking, unpossessed of dignity, and al- ways in a hurry as though he had larger interests else- where."

The judge seemed impressed, however, with Reed's testimony, and listened attentively as Reed described his experiences as a war correspondent in Mexico and Eu- rope, and how his observations of the exploitation by the capitalist class of the workers had led him to socialism and to sympathy for the Russian revolution.

"I've been on all but two battlefronts," Reed told the judge and jury. "I have seen men frozen, starved, scream- ing, dying in the mud on these fronts—and then I came back to find American society women knitting socks for soldiers, with Caruso singing at the knitting parties. I came back to find that war was fashionable and that so- ciety people and rich people wanted to get into this new- est fashion. And because I knew what war was I opposed the entrance of the United States into the war."

In response to a question from the prosecution as to whether he was interested in the "war of the people against capitalism," Reed answered, "To tell the truth that is the only war I am interested in."

According to Eastman, Reed was "very boyish and high-voiced and inept and uneasy in his clothes, but all the more likeable and believable because of it."

"Some people," Eastman wrote, "you look in their eyes and you say, 'This man is honest and kind,' and you feel that no further question need be asked. Jack had such eyes."

Eastman wrote that an air of general informality pervaded the courtroom, due partly to the absence of a formal defense by an established lawyer and partly to Judge Manton's "brisk and unjudicial manner." (Manton later served a year and a half in jail for having accepted bribes.) Earl Barnes was again the prosecuting attorney, and, again, his evident personal liking for the defendants robbed him of the traditional attitude of severity. (In a letter to Louise written after the trial, Barnes said, "My dear wife says that nature never designed me for a prosecuting attorney anyhow—and she is usually right.")

Eastman took it upon himself to make the summing up. He spent several nights preparing it. "The judge had ruled against our attempt to bring in testimony as to what was happening in Russia, but I assumed the right, as relevant to our intent, to state *our opinion about what was happening in Russia,* and he did not stop me," Eastman wrote. "This permitted an exposition of the entire socialist philosophy."

Stedman, still ill, made a short speech to the jury, that appealed, according to Eastman, to "the one thing we had a ray of hope in, their good-humored common sense."

Barnes made a trite and maudlin speech, ending with the sad story of a friend of his who had died in the trenches of Europe "so that the world might be made free."

"Somewhere in France," said Barnes, "he lies dead, and he died for me. He died for Max Eastman. He died for John Reed. He died for Merrill Rogers. His voice is but one of a thousand voices that demand that these men be punished."

"Art Young," wrote Eastman, "who had been quietly sleeping at the counsel table, awoke at this point. He listened for a moment with growing perplexity, then leaned across the table and said in a loud whisper: 'Didn't he die for me, too?' "

Young himself did not recall that he was "quietly sleeping." In *his* autobiography, he wrote: "I was waiting for [Barnes] to mention me, but he didn't, and I leaned over and asked Reed: 'Who was this hero who didn't die for *me*?' . . . Reed said: 'Cheer up, Art, Jesus died for you.' "

Judge Manton, evidently swayed by the defendants' combined eloquence and sincerity, told the jury that every American had the right to criticize his government and oppose its policies. Eastman and his colleagues were, on the whole, sanguine about the outcome of the trial after hearing his address. The trial had lasted five days. Again, it resulted in a hung jury—eight for acquittal, four against.

Writing in the next issue of the *Liberator,* Reed said: "How inevitably, how clearly in all these cases, the issue narrows down to the Class Struggle! District Attorney Barnes' opening address to the jury implied one chief crime—that of plotting the overthrow of the United States Government by revolution; in other words, the crime of being, in the words of Mr. Barnes, 'Bolsheveeka,' addicted to what he called 'Syndickalism.' An immortal definition of the Socialist conception which he made to the jury remains in my mind:

" 'These people believe that there are three classes— the capitalists, who own all the natural resources of the country; the bourgeoisie, who have got a little land or a little property under the system; and the proletariat, which consists of all those who want to take away the property of the capitalists and the bourgeoisie.'

"We were described as men without a country, who

wanted to break down all boundaries. The jury was asked what it thought of people who called respectable American businessmen "bourgeoisie."

"In no European country could a prosecuting attorney have displayed such ignorance of Socialism, or relied so confidently upon the ignorance of a jury.

"I was not present at the first *Masses* trial. In prospect, it did not seem to me very serious; but when I sat in that gloomy, dark-paneled court-room and the bailiff with the brown wig beat the table and cried harshly, 'Stand up!' and the judge climbed to his seat, and it was announced, in the same harsh, menacing tone, 'The Federal Court for the Southern District of New York is now open. . . .' I felt as if we were in the clutches of a relentless machinery, which would go on and grind and grind. . . .

"I think we all felt tranquil, and ready to go to prison if need be. At any rate, we were not going to dissemble what we believed. This had its effect on the jury, and on the Judge. . . . When Seymour Stedman boldly claimed for us, and for all Socialists, the right of idealistic prophesy, and repudiated the capitalist system with its terrible inequalities, a new but perfectly logical and consistent point of view was presented. The jury was composed of a majority of honest, rather simple men, the background of whose consciousness must have contained memories of the Declaration of Independence, the Rights of Man, Magna Charta. They could not easily, even in war time, repudiate these things; especially when all the defendants were so palpably members of the dominant race.

"Two weeks later I saw in that same court the trial of some Russian boys and girls on similar charges. They did not have a chance; they were foreigners. An official of the District Attorney's office was explaining to me why the

Judge had been so severe upon these Russians, while our Judge in the *Masses* case had been so lenient.

" 'You are Americans,' he said. 'You *looked* like Americans. And then, too, you had a New York Judge. You can't convict an American for sedition before a New York Judge. If you'd had Judge Clayton, for example, it would have been equivalent to being tried in the Middle West, or in any other Federal Court outside of New York. You would have been soaked.'

"It has been said that the disagreement of the jury in this second *Masses* case is a victory for free speech and for international Socialism. In a way this is true. International Socialism was argued in court, thanks to the curiosity and the fair-mindedness of Judge Manton. [Reed, of course, could not know that his "fair-minded" judge would turn out to be a spectacular crook.]

"Free speech was vindicated by the charge of Judge Manton, who ruled that anyone in this country could say that the war was not for democracy, that it was an imperialist war, that the Government of the United States was hypocritical—in fact, that any American had the right to criticize his government or its policies, *so long as he did not intend to discourage recruiting and enlistment or cause mutiny and disobedience in the armed forces of the United States.*

"But the one great factor in our victory was Max Eastman's three-hour summing up. Standing there, with the attitude and attributes of intellectual eminence, young, good-looking, he was the typical champion of ideals—ideals which he made to seem the ideals of every real American. . . . Max boldly took up the Russian question, and made it part of our defense. The jury was held tense by his eloquence; the Judge listened with all his energy. In the courtroom there was utter silence. After it was all over the District Attorney himself congratulated Max."

The signing of the Armistice in November alleviated somewhat the pressure on Reed. The charges against the *Masses* staff were formally dropped; and Reed's impounded papers were finally released. His pro-Bolshevik views did continue to get him into trouble, however.

In the November 1918 issue of the *Liberator*, Reed once again attacked the folly of government persecution of those who saw clearly what Russia was up to. "My point is," he wrote, "that the American people are misinformed about conditions in Europe, and especially in Russia, and that in the case of Russia our Government is acting upon false information. Moreover, people who are in a position to inform the public concerning the Russian situation are either ordered to keep silent, or, if they speak in public, arrested by the Department of Justice, and if they write in the press, barred from the mails by the Post Office Department. . . .

"The kind of Russian news usually fed the public is illustrated by the frequent newspaper reports stating that the Soviet Government has fallen, that Lenin and Trotsky have fled to Germany and that chaos and anarchy are universal in Russia—statements which the very reports of the Allied commanders in Russia have again and again demonstrated to be false. . . .

"The gravity of the situation is intensified by the recent release for publication by the Committee on Public Information of a series of documents purporting to prove that the leaders of the Russian Soviet Government were in the pay of the Imperial German Government, and that their actions were directed from Berlin. The fact is, that the authenticity of many of these documents is very doubtful. And the documents have been in the hands of the United States Government for more than six months.

211

Why were they not given out before this time? Or, more pertinently, why have they now been released? Was it to give color or excuse to an uninvited intervention in the affairs of a friendly people, and, moreover, a people which has appealed to us for help against Germany?

"There is definite evidence now in the United States sufficient, I believe, to prove that the leaders of the Soviets have not been pro-German, but, on the contrary, if anything, pro-Ally. Strangely enough, this evidence is not allowed to reach the public. . . .

"I, myself, and certain other Americans, who have had the opportunity to observe closely the character and actions of the Soviet Government, have been shut up by the simple expedient of taking away all documents and corroborative papers which we brought back with us from Russia, on the pretext of 'examination.' Only those officials and correspondents who are opposed to the Soviets, for one reason or another, are allowed freely to speak or write their erroneous facts and their baseless opinions."

Reed's bank closed his account early in December, claiming that he was overdrawn; according to Louise, the bank seized the excuse because it did not like Reed's politics. And the Board of Managers of the Harvard Club ordered him suspended for six months on a flimsy technical infraction.

But Reed could overlook these petty annoyances, grateful to be able to get back to work on *Ten Days that Shook the World*. The prestigious firm of Boni and Liveright gave him a cash advance, and he secluded himself in a rented room in Greenwich Village, letting no one but Louise know where he was. He discarded the beginning he had made in Norway and started over again. He now had a broader project in mind—a series of three books that would cover the history of Bolshevism. The first book—*Ten Days*—he described as "a slice of intensified history—history as I saw it."

In the book's preface, Reed wrote: "It does not pretend to be anything but a detailed account of the November Revolution, when the Bolsheviki, at the head of the workers and soldiers, seized the state power of Russia and placed it in the hands of the Soviets.

"Naturally most of it deals with 'Red Petrograd,' the capital and heart of the insurrection. But the reader must realize that what took place in Petrograd was almost exactly duplicated, with greater or lesser intensity, at different intervals of time, all over Russia.

"In this book, the first of several which I am writing, I must confine myself to a chronicle of those events which I myself observed and experienced, and those supported by reliable evidence."

Ten Days that Shook the World was finished in January and published in March 1919. It was an instant popular success, going into its fourth printing in July. It has been widely translated and published abroad, and continues to be printed in various editions in this country. An undisputed classic, it is used as a source and quoted from by almost every major book dealing with modern Russian history. (The Boni and Liveright edition published in 1922 included a short introduction by Lenin, written at the end of 1919. "Unreservedly do I recommend it to the workers of the world," Lenin wrote. "Here is a book which I should like to see published in millions of copies and translated into all languages. It gives a truthful and most vivid exposition of the events so significant to the comprehension of what really is the Proletarian Revolution and the Dictatorship of the Proletariat.")

While the book clearly expresses Reed's sympathy

with the revolution, it is nevertheless a minutely accurate and penetrating description of the events, seen at first hand from the inside. It contains Reed's most incisive and vivid writing. But the book, predictably, did not receive unqualified praise from contemporary critics. It was reviewed in the "Literary Section" of *The New York Times* on April 27, 1919, by Charles E. Russell, once a prominent member of the Socialist party and a man who had made a reputation almost as formidable as Lincoln Steffens's, as a muckracking journalist. This would seem a commendably fair choice on the part of *The Times*'s book editor. But Russell, at fifty-nine, had recently been expelled from the Socialist party over the same issue that caused many such splits; he refused to adopt the Socialist's pacifist stand and actively supported American entry into the war. And he was a personal friend and booster of Woodrow Wilson.

Russell reviewed the book together with one written by John Spargo called *Bolshevism: The Enemy of Political and Industrial Democracy*. (Spargo, too, was a recent defector from the Socialist Party over the war issue.) He was restrained in his admiration of the Spargo book (pointing out that Spargo had not been to Russia), but cited the thoroughness of its research and clarity of its conclusions. "It is a book of a thinker for thinkers: Serious, adequate and worthy of the man and the occasion," Russell wrote.

He had grave misgivings about Reed's thesis in *Ten Days that Shook the World*, which he understood to be: "All revolutions are good; some revolutions are better than others; the Bolshevik revolution was of the best." But he obviously enjoyed reading it.

"There is no doubt that [Reed] writes of [the revolution] brilliantly and entertainingly. His familiar powers of graphic description and moving narrative are here at their best," Russell wrote, immediately qualifying his praise by adding, "It cannot be said that he adds anything to the essentials of the narrative already told by his talented wife."

In the next breath, however, Russell declared, "Many of the incidents he relates afford new and convincing sidelights upon the Bolshevist spirit and methods." Uneasily, Russell settled for the somewhat lame complaint that Reed had not really answered the key question, "What is Bolshevism?" and that his readers had a right to know the answer to that question.

By February 1919, Reed had plunged back into speech making. He was trying to arrange an extended lecture tour for Louise and himself; a lecture bureau was interested in booking them both into six cities—Louise to speak first, followed two weeks later by Reed. Their guaranteed fee was to be $300 apiece for each lecture, with the probability of higher payment, depending on how well-attended the lectures were.

On February 2, Louise spoke in Washington, with Albert Rhys Williams, on "The Truth About Russia." A few days later she participated in a rally that was climaxed by the burning in effigy of President Wilson and was arrested and jailed. Reed, in New York, wrote to her anxiously: "The papers are full of your exploits. . . . I *do* hope you are not hunger-striking. I am lonely without my honey, and very worried about her."

Louise was, in fact, hunger-striking; it was a device, she had learned, that was the quickest way to be released from jail. "If you go without food and become weak," she later explained, "the authorities let you out because they do not want you to die in jail." Reed was alarmed.

"Why did you do that?" he wrote. "You said you

wouldn't hunger-strike. It makes me sick to think you are feeling so badly. It is a mere waste of energy and time to do things like that."

As soon as she returned from Washington, Reed wrote, they would go to Croton together to rest. His trial in Philadelphia (on the charge of inciting to riot) was scheduled for February 26, so they would have a few peaceful days. Their little vacation, he said, would be financed by a check for seventy-five dollars that had just come to Louise from *McCall's*—without it, they could not have gone away. A speaking date in Yonkers that Sunday would bring Reed twenty-five dollars and a propaganda pamphlet he was finishing would bring in another hundred dollars.

"By that time my book ought to be bringing in something. . . . I am awfully lonesome, honey, and don't feel very well. I have been trying to work, but I don't get much done."

A few days later Louise wrote that she could not leave Washington. She was trying to arrange a hearing for both herself and Reed before the Senate Committee investigating Bolshevism. Originally implemented to look into pro-German activities, the committee had recently shifted its focus to Bolshevism as a result of the publicity given the February 2 meeting addressed by Louise and Albert Rhys Williams. Louise, Reed, Williams, and others who had a first-hand knowledge of the Bolshevik regime, felt that they ought to be allowed to testify before the committee on the "true" conditions of that regime, in order to counteract the anti-Bolshevik testimony being heard.

The Senator in charge of the hearings was Lee S. Overman, a sixty-four-year-old North Carolinian, who had been a member of the Senate since 1902. A former school teacher and lawyer, Senator Overman was a close advisor to President Wilson and a highly influential figure in Washington. As author of the Overman Act, he had been responsible for giving Wilson extraordinary and unprecedented powers in carrying out his war policy. He had also been instrumental in getting the Espionage Act passed by Congress.

"I saw Overman today and he said he would tell me tomorrow when I could be heard," Louise wrote to Reed. "I want to meet you in Philadelphia and then come back here with you for a day or so if I can arrange a hearing for you about Wednesday of next week." She said that she had notes on all the testimony that had been heard by the committee "with all the blunders and misstatements" and that she and Reed could correct them with "real evidence."

The hearings, she added, were "tragically funny." "One feels the smell of decay and the utter impossibility of the old to comprehend the new. I feel that [Albert Rhys] Williams is a fool not to be here. They cast slurs on him all the time."

Louise had written Senator Overman a note that he had not answered, she told Reed, so she had walked into the hearing and confronted him. Obliging him to take her offered hand, she announced, "I am Louise Bryant, Mrs. John Reed, you know. I have written you I am at the services of your committee. I feel that, since it was the meeting at which I was one of the speakers that brought about this hearing, I ought to be allowed to testify." Overman seemed "temporarily embarrassed," Louise said, but finally agreed to fix a date for her to testify—"and the whole room heard [him say] it."

She told Reed that she thought her recent hunger strike had done her good. "My legs are a little shaky but that is my only remembrance of the horrors of prison."

She would try to persuade Sonia Hovey that the *Metropolitan* "really needed" a story from Louise about her prison experience.

Louise was called to appear on February 20 and spent the whole day on the witness stand. Reed had joined her in Washington and accompanied her to the hearing. Senator Overman ordered the room cleared of all spectators when a noisy storm of applause and hisses greeted Louise's first remarks. Only the witnesses and reporters were allowed to stay—and Reed, when he explained that he was Louise's husband.

"Do you believe in God?" Louise was asked.

"There may be one."

"I asked if you believed in God. A person who does not believe in God has no conception of the sanctity of the oath."

"I will concede that I believe there is a God."

After being asked if she was a Christian, if she believed in "a punishment hereafter and a reward for duty," Louise complained, "It seems to me as if I were being tried for witchcraft."

The questioning proceeded to her first marriage and divorce, Louise protesting that she had been called to testify about Russia. The committee was trying to establish her character, she was told, so that it would know how much credence to give her testimony.

"Did you participate in the burning in effigy of President Wilson, recently?" she was asked. Louise said she had.

"Now is it not a fact that when you secured your passport from the Department of State you made an affidavit that if permitted to go to Russia you would not indulge in political propaganda?"

"I did."

"Did you violate that oath?"

"I did not."

"Did your husband take the same oath in the State Department?"

"Yes, but he is here to answer for himself."

"In Russia, was your husband employed by the Bolsheviki?"

"Yes, but why not ask him those questions?"

"Is it true that when you left Russia and went to Sweden on your way back to America you traveled under the protection of a passport issued by the Bolshevist military committee, and are you not referred to on that passport as a comrade of the Bolsheviki?"

"Yes, all people in Russia then, as well as now, are comrades unless they are enemies."

"How about another passport issued to you by the Bolsheviki in which you are stated to be a Bolshevist courier, and that your progress is to be facilitated because you are the bearer of 'sealed bags and packages.'"

"I had such a certificate."

"Were you a bolshevist courier?"

"No. They simply gave me the certificate so I could get through the lines. Madeleine Doty [another American journalist] also came out as a courier."

"Now, is it not a fact that every person who opposed the Bolsheviki is considered a traitor in Russia?"

"Yes."

"Does chaos rule in Russia?"

"Not at all. Not while I was there."

"Do you consider the Bolshevist Government a dictatorship?"

"Yes, for the transitory period. I think the Russians should be permitted to settle their own affairs and to determine what sort of government they want. It is untrue that the peasants are against the Bolsheviki. They are for the Bolsheviki."

After further questioning about various Americans who had served in Russia as propagandists for the Bolsheviks, and more details of the conditions of Russian life, one of the questioning senators dismissed Louise for the day, calling her "deluded."

"You are young, too, and I am sorry for you," he said.

Louise's questioning continued the following morning. She began by making a statement complaining of her treatment by the committee, which she characterized as "discourteous," said that she had been gratuitously lectured on her morals and declared that the Bolshevik government was doing "great work."

Reed was questioned for two hours in the afternoon. He was succinct, logical, and authoritative, and the questioning senators found him to be a formidable witness. When asked if he had ever publicly advocated a revolution in the United States, he calmly replied, "I have always advocated a revolution in the United States."

"You are in favor of a revolution in the United States?" was the astonished response.

"Revolution does not necessarily mean a revolution by force. By revolution I mean a profound social change. I do not know how it will be attained."

"Do you not in your speeches leave the impression with your audiences that you are talking about a revolution by force?"

"Possibly."

"Do you mean to leave that impression?"

"No. My point is that the will of the people will be done; the will of the great majority of the people will be done."

"That is a sound point."

"That is my point, and if the will of the great majority is not done by law, it will be done some other way. That is all."

"Do you not know, Mr. Reed, that the use of the word 'revolution' in the ordinary meaning carries the idea of force, arms and conflict?"

"Well, as a matter of fact, unfortunately, all these profound social changes have been accompanied by force. There is not one that has not."

"Your mental agility is, I confess, too much for me."

A *New York Times* editorial, commenting the next day on Louise's testimony, noted her admission that she had been sent to jail for burning Wilson in effigy and that she had gone on a hunger strike, and added: "There may be some who will regret that she was not permitted to test that strike to its fullest limit, like so many of the victims of the Bolshevism of which she approves."

The *Tribune,* on the other hand, gave Reed its somewhat grudging admiration. In a signed editorial written a month after Reed's appearance before the Overman Committee, Stanley Frost described Reed:

"A soldier of fortune, adventurous, restless and more than a little reckless, keen to brilliancy, and with a physique that sheds trouble or privation with equal ease, but a man to whom clever phrases are an intoxication and patient study utterly impossible—such is John Reed, wanderer, war correspondent, ex-friend of Mexican bandits, facile writer and just now Bolshevist propagandist."

Observing that Reed had obviously enjoyed his own testimony, Frost said that "his lips kept trying to twitch into grins and his eyes twinkled. He revelled in his own dialectic skill, and he found pleasure in the atmosphere of opposition. It was all good sport, and he is a good sportsman."

On February 26, Reed went to Philadelphia to be tried for "inciting to riot" on the day he had delivered his sidewalk speech. The man who had come to his defense, William Kogerman, was also in the courtroom, charged with having tried to bite a policeman. After deliberating three hours on the following day, the jury acquitted both men.

Assistant District Attorney Charles E. Fox, who prosecuted the case, stopped Reed's lawyer, David Wallerstein, in the street about a month after the trial. Wallerstein wrote to Reed about their conversation. "The verdict in your case was, in Fox's judgment, the most disastrous verdict that had been rendered in Philadelphia since his connection with the District Attorney's office. . . . [Fox said] I would live to regret my share in it. He then promptly deprived me of all share in it by telling me that the Jury had brought in a verdict of acquittal because they were scared out of their wits for fear that the Socialists would do something to them if they convicted you and Kogerman.

"My only answer to that was that this view ought to be a great salve to Fox's own opinion of himself as it robbed me of all credit and acquitted him of all blame. This view of it seemed to be new to him. At any rate, he shut up and walked off."

In April the last of the charges under which Reed stood indicted—his "seditious" speech in the Bronx in September 1918—was dropped; all prosecutions under the Espionage Act begun during the war were under review by the Department of Justice, and Reed's case was among hundreds that were dismissed during this period.

Reed could breathe freely again—for the moment.

Chapter Thirteen

In late February 1919, Reed and Louise once again said goodbye. There was a fateful rhythm to their separations that would continue to their final parting. It was only three years since they had met and fallen in love and during this short period they had separated four times because of illness, misunderstanding, or professional commitments. Except for Reed's one-month hospital stay, it had always been Louise who left—for two months, in a jealous frenzy, to Paris; for three months, on a mixed mission to establish her journalistic reputation and to reclaim O'Neill. And now it was Louise, again, who left—this time for an exhilarating but exhausting lecture tour.

The length of their separations was never planned. Hounded by ill health, political difficulties, and financial need, their lives had acquired a rootlessness they had not foreseen and were beginning to resent.

This new separation, like their previous ones, had the effect of drawing them closer in sympathy and love; absence sharpened their need for each other. As always, when apart, they began a long exchange of letters filled with a mixture of politics, domestic minutiae, and yearning.

During most of the time Louise was away, Reed stayed in Croton. Devoting himself almost exclusively to propaganda, he struggled briefly with a conflicting desire to return to "poetry"—not necessarily the writing of poems, but literature in general.

He wrote a short, satirical piece, in dialogue, called "The Peace that Passeth Understanding, A Cartoon," that the Provincetown Players nervously presented in March. The actors wore masks representing Wilson, Clemenceau, Lloyd George, Orlando, and the Japanese delegate, and were not identified in the program, for fear of personal reprisals. Reed was, of course, satirizing the Versailles peace conference. His stage directions included such devices as a clock on the mantlepiece that was "fifty years slow," and having each of the delegates speak in his own language—presumably understood by few, if any, of the others. It caused less of a stir than had been anticipated. But it put Reed back into touch with the Provincetown Players and all their creative ferment. He was momentarily wistful about the alternative path he had chosen. His mood was heightened one evening when he allowed himself, perhaps somewhat masochistically, to fall under the spell of Edna St. Vincent Millay. The twenty-seven-year-old poet had acted a little with the Provincetowners—in a couple of plays by Floyd Dell and in one of her own (she was to write her provocative *Aria da Capo* by the end of the year.)

The gifted young woman, who had already made something of a reputation, symbolized for many of the emerging artists all that was gallant and romantic and idealistic in their thrust for self-expression. Floyd Dell, in his autobiography, *Homecoming*, described the evening he spent with Reed and Edna Millay whimsically riding back and forth on the Staten Island ferry in a dense fog.

"He was telling her his most thrilling adventures as a war correspondent and Communist conspirator," Dell wrote, "and she said, like Desdemona, 'I love you for the dangers you have passed!'"

Max Eastman, during this same period, asked Reed how his political work was going. "It's all right," Reed told Eastman. "You know this class struggle plays hell with your poetry!" Eastman interpreted this to mean that Reed "was not settled. He was doing a job because things had so shaped themselves that it was up to him to do it."

Reed resisted the temptation to return to poetry and the company of poets. Resolutely, he made a short trip to speak in the Middle West, then returned east to prepare for a debate with Henry Slobodin, an ex-Socialist, on the subject, "Bolshevism—Promise or Peril?" The debate was sponsored by a news syndicate, the Press Forum, and Reed was promised a substantial fee. About halfway through the series, the project was called off for lack of an audience, but Reed had already been paid several hundred dollars.

"My sweet old Big," Louise wrote to Reed from Detroit, her first stop. (She and Reed had fallen into the habit of addressing each other as "Big" and "Small.") Louise had barely begun her trip, and already wished it was over. "I will be so glad when I finish this job," she said, "sleeping on trains certainly isn't awfully nice or restful. And I miss my Big—and I am tired." She told him playfully not to plan to run away himself as soon as she got back. "I want a nice visit with you in the country," she said, adding a warning not to fall out of the trees putting up bird boxes.

From Chicago Louise wrote of her successful speech in Detroit, saying she had been "overwhelmed with affection" by the Russians in her audience. The substance of Louise's lecture was essentially the same as the one she had delivered in Washington, D.C., earlier that month: descriptions of the Bolshevik leaders and their idealistic aims for Russia, denials of Russia's secret collaboration with Germany, praise for the schools.

One of her most effective crowd-pleasing bits was this little story, aimed at reinforcing her denial of the charge of Russia's complicity:

"Lies are constantly told about the poor Bolshevist Government. For instance, Trotsky's daughter is said to take large quantities of money out of Russia. The little girl is only six years old, and she is a very precocious child, but I am sure she is not able to do that."

An anonymous writer for *The New York Times*, signing himself "One Who Was Present," wrote a lengthy analysis of Louise's lecture in Washington. While he was totally unsympathetic to her views, he could not help being captivated by her.

"Miss Bryant appears a demure and pretty girl, with a large hat, a stylish suit and gray stockings. Her voice is high, but it has a plaintive note to it. She amuses the crowd, because, with the air of an ingenue, she hurls darts at Government departments, holds people up to ridicule, and with a fearful voice appeals to American fair play to be just to a beneficent Bolshevist Government and give it a chance. . . . In the burst of applause the demure little speaker sits down."

In Chicago, Louise stayed for the day at Hull House, visiting with Jane Addams. She would leave late that night for Minneapolis, she wrote to Reed, speak there at eight the next evening, then go to St. Louis to speak there the following evening. Even more exhausting than sleeping on trains, she said, was the constant talking she had to do between formal speeches at the dinners and receptions being given in her honor. "Oh, Darl, how I'd love to be in the country! I don't want to *think* at all. I just want to walk around out there and sleep."

In Minneapolis, Louise wrote, the turnout to hear her had been enormous. Sinclair Lewis had brought "a flock of newspapermen" to see her, and "the Socialist bunch" clamored to meet and talk with her. Her voice was still all right, she said, but her throat was a little sore, probably because of the bad weather. "Old honey, I wonder what you are doing? I will be glad to start back."

From Croton on March 16, Reed informed Louise that he had just arrived in the country with his friend, Fred Boyd, who was helping him to research the newspaper debate with Slobodin. Boyd was an Englishman who had joined the IWW. He had been arrested during the Paterson silk strike and sentenced to a six-year jail term. He was released after a year and was still on parole. Just a year earlier he had made newspaper headlines by refusing to rise at the playing of the National Anthem in the popular New York restaurant, Rectors.

"[The debate] is going to be a terrible job," Reed wrote, "but I think I shall be able to pull it off, and so get in hand a little money so that we can have some leisure." He said he had found the house in disorder; a convalescent friend had borrowed it for the weekend and decided to stay on without letting Reed know. "Such a mess— Jesus! It made me sick," Reed wrote. Rats had pulled most of their books off the shelves and eaten the covers, and their kitchen staples were scattered all over the house. Reed's "guest" had made little effort to clean anything up. But Reed and their old housekeeper, Caroline, were putting the house back in order.

"I am so proud and pleased that my honey is getting a fine reception," Reed continued. "Why shouldn't she? She is a good Small. I am, as you know, always unreservedly happy at my honey's successes." He told her not to send him any money, which she had offered to do. "I will soon be flush. And if you want any cash, just wire your Big." He had put up two bird houses without accidents, he said, and planned to stay in Croton with her when she returned. Louise had asked his advice on what she should say to a group of farmers she was going to address.

"You might point out that the banks and the Big Business control of transportation are driving the little farmers in America to become tenants and farm hands, just as the Czar's government did in Russia," Reed wrote. "By joining with the workers to seize control of the banks and transportation system in Russia, the Russian peasants abolished all private property in land, and assured each farmer the free right to operate his own land without interference from any source—since the Government owned the land, and the farmers and workers *were* the Government. That is all I can add that might interest the farmers. They of course object to anything which takes the ownership of their land away from them; but they should understand that private property in land is just a means of being secure in possession of it, which public ownership under Bolshevism makes them automatically."

On the same day that Reed was writing to Louise from Croton, Louise caught a severe cold that developed into a fever. Not sure that Reed was in Croton, she wired a close friend, Norman Watson, that she had gone to bed in the hotel in Spokane. "If fever continues go to hospital tomorrow. If broken will leave for Seattle. Tell Jack not to worry. Excellent care. Lonesome. Love to everybody." The next day Watson received another wire from Louise:

"Could not break fever. Developed influenza. Tell Jack don't come. Not time. . . . Have good doctor."

Reed obeyed her instructions, but was very concerned. "I presume, now that you're so near Seattle, that you'll go there if you're well enough. But as for the rest, honey dear, for God's sake don't tempt fate after the 'flu'; stop speaking and come home. . . . I am so worried I don't know what to do. I hope you didn't lie to me about your condition. You know if it is serious I *must* come at any cost."

Reed went on to warn her, if she insisted on continuing her speaking tour, to cut down on her dates and go slow; He added that his work was going well and went on to describe the beauty of their country cottage in the early spring weather:

"All the birds are back, and are going around from bird house to bird house and asking what the rent is. The crocuses are up all around. . . .

"I'm thinking seriously of getting me a dog. You get a kitty."

Reed asked Louise to "please smooth mother down" when she reached Portland; his mother had been quarreling with him by mail over his radical activities and was "evidently in a fearful state of mind."

A few days later Louise was able to wire Reed that she was recovering, but she could not resist phrasing her news dramatically: "Absolutely out of danger. It was a stiff fight. Most double cases fatal." She promised to "go slow." She would speak in Seattle and Portland, then spend a few days in San Francisco visiting her own mother, and then "hurry home to Big."

But she found, within a day or two, that the people who were arranging her speaking tour were beseiged with requests from radical groups to have her appear, and she could not bring herself to disappoint them. On March 21 she wrote to Reed from Seattle, "My schedule frightens me!" Her illness, she explained, had put her

back a week. She was engaged to speak at thirteen meetings between March 22 and April 13, ending in San
Diego, California. "If I speak on the way back, *Heavens!*
I'll never get home. I have only been away half a month
and I am homesick as a boarding school student." Only a
few of the dates were definite, she said; but she did not
say positively that she would cancel any of them. She
complained about the parties and receptions that were
being given for her. "Everybody sits right near my elbow
'so they won't miss anything *interesting!*' I'm afraid lioniz-
ing is too nauseating for me to bear." But clearly she was
enjoying being lionized. Nevertheless, her tug toward
Croton and Reed was genuine.

"I walked out in the garden [at the house of one of
her Seattle hosts] and spring flowers are opening delicate
faces. I saw a bluebird and could have wept. I want to
dig in my *own* garden. . . . Just do anything you want in
the garden before I come. . . . But *please* promise not to
plan to run away to town as soon as I come home. *I do so
much want to visit you!* And it would be wonderful to
work together, *even a week,* in the garden. Leave anything you can, dear, for us to do together." She had been
very disappointed to find no letter from Reed in Seattle,
she said.

Reed was writing regularly, but it was difficult to time
his letters to reach her. He was, in fact, writing to her on
the same day she wrote to him, also complaining about
not hearing from her; he had wired her at Spokane, miss-
ing her by a day.

"I have been awfully worried about you . . . Please
hurry home here as quickly as possible . . . The country
is absolutely heavenly. I have been pruning the fruit trees
and the grape vine today."

Their housekeeper, Caroline, was providing him with

adequate meals, he said, but her habits of personal clean-
liness were a little distressing. "As the bathtub is still out
of commission I cannot make her scrub her old bones."
To amuse Louise, he reported Caroline's idiosyncracies:
She had conceived a dislike for Fred Boyd ("I suppose
he'll turn up with some chippy pretty soon," she had
gloomily predicted); and she had given Reed fifty cents to
buy her a pair of ladies' drawers—"the largest size."

"I cannot get her to wind a watch, or turn out the
lamps," Reed continued. "When she answers the telephone, she just shouts, 'Mr. Reed will be back at eight
o'clock' and then flees from the thing as if it were going
to bite her."

On a more serious note, Reed asked Louise if she had
read in the papers that President Wilson had sent Lincoln
Steffens, William Bullitt, "and two or three of that sort"
to Russia to investigate the Soviets. He made no further
comment, but it was plain that he was disappointed by
Steffens's continuing sympathy with Wilson's policies.

In a wistful mood, Louise wrote to Reed on March 23,
"How hard it is to be away from you in the spring! . . .
The softness of the air, the fragrance of the flowers,
makes me dizzy. I toss about restlessly all night and fall
asleep only to wake from little troubled dreams of desire."

On March 24, in response to an earlier letter of Reed's
that had finally reached her, Louise told her husband that
she was glad he was going to get a dog; she had been
thinking about bringing one home for him, but was afraid
she would pick "the wrong kind." She would do her best
to find a kitten to bring home. She had cancelled some
proposed speaking dates in Canada, she said, because it
was illegal to enter that country without swearing to the
purpose of the visit. Her manager had suggested she say
she was visiting friends. "I flatly refused," wrote Louise

indignantly. "I'm not going to lie! I was going there to speak on Russia and against Intervention! What a mess I'd get into by trying to evade the facts."

She would be coming home with very little money, she said. Apparently her expenses (with her hospital stay and doctor's fees) were proving too high for her income. But she didn't care. "You say you will be rich! I don't believe it. I think we will always be dead broke—from now on. Well, if I'm with my honey, and we are well, I'm sure I don't care."

She assured Reed that she would, of course, visit his mother when she arrived in Portland. She planned to stay at the Multnomah Hotel, where Mrs. Reed was then living—and where Louise's tearful confession of her love for Reed had been made to Sara Field just over three years ago. "It gives me cold shivers to think of even *being* in Portland," Louise said. "But I guess I just have to see it through."

She was so anxious to be home with him, Louise said. The tour was taking twice as long as she had planned, because she was taking it easy, pausing to rest a day or two between most speeches.

Louise was upset that she and Reed were not receiving all the letters each was writing. She hinted darkly that their letters were being intercepted by "them." But if the Reeds' mail was being censored at this point, it was being done very haphazardly; it is more likely that letters were simply going astray because of Louise's crowded itinerary. One cheerful note was that Louise's book was selling well; copies were on sale at all her meetings and the supply could not meet the demand.

"I'm so glad yours is out," she wrote. "I'll see that it is announced *at every single meeting!*"

That night Louise addressed a huge crowd in Seattle's

Longshoreman's Hall. "It is right near the docks and the roughest, finest most wonderful audience!" she exulted. "I stopped at 10:30 and I could not get to the doors until 12! How many great rough paws have engulfed my 'bird's fingers' (as my honey calls them). I feel moved in a strange manner. I feel, my dear, the same kind of emotion that I feel when I look suddenly at the purple blueness of these great mountains of the west."

Characteristically continuing to mix sentiment with politics, she ended: "I look out of my window at the stars, and the winds of spring fan my hot face. It is wonderful —all this, my lover, all this new awakening—all over the earth. And this *other awakening* [revolutionary rumblings in Hungary]. I can hear the feet of that great army across the world. It will lull me to sleep."

A day later Reed wrote again of his concern for Louise's health, and urged her once again to drop her speaking tour and come home. To entice her, he wrote of the idyllic life they would have together in Croton:

"I have set out four new little trees—fruit trees—and am going to get a hive of honey-bees to make goo for breakfast." Max Eastman was just back from the West Coast, Reed said, and had told him Louise was very popular. He had finished the fifth article of his debate with Slobodin. "He doesn't know anything at all," Reed said. "It won't be very difficult for me to lick him, I think."

"Oh, my old dear, I feel as if I had been away from you for months and years," Louise wrote at the end of March. If she started home right after her scheduled speech in San Francisco, and eliminated speeches in Los Angeles and San Diego, she would be with him in two weeks, she said. What did he think she should do?

On the same day Reed wrote to Louise explaining his mother's situation in Portland. She was having a difficult time, financially. Reed's younger brother, Harry, recently out of the army, could not seem to earn a living. His wife, Polly, was pregnant. Harry was trying to sell some property for his mother, but was evidently mishandling the deal out of inexperience. The whole family situation in Portland was bleak, and Reed had been obliged to send some money to his mother to tide her over.

There had been a sudden sleet and snow storm yesterday, Reed reported, and he was worried about the new trees he had planted. The debate with Slobodin was going well: "Up to date he has said absolutely nothing, and I have him whipped to a frazzle."

Louise arrived in Portland on March 31. Her meeting with Reed's mother was less of an ordeal than she had anticipated.

"I'm *much* relieved!" she wrote Reed. "Your mother seemed quite calm and the reporters met me and spoke of me as a 'celebrity,' had me photographed and gave me sympathetic interviews. So I guess it will all go well. So much for the return of the prodigal daughter. . . . I'll have a long talk with your mother [this evening] and try to put her in a good humor."

Louise said she had been disappointed not to be able to buy a kitten in Seattle, but she had been promised her pick of the next litter by a cat breeder she knew there. She enclosed a snapshot of the kind of cat she would get.

Her speech in Portland's Public Auditorium on April 2 was well received by an audience of 4,000. *The Oregonian* reported the event chattily:

"That American troops should be withdrawn at once from Russia, and that the soviet government should be left to establish order in that distraught country was the 'burden' of Louise Bryant's plea last night at the auditorium. . . .

234

"Despite her exposure to the Russian revolution, Louise has changed little. . . . Aside from the George Sand haircut, she is the same little radicalist and vigorous performer that left Portland three years ago."

"Harry and your mother went and were quite impressed," Louise wrote to Reed. "I seem to stand high with the family at the present moment." She had visited Harry and his wife, and liked Harry, she said. About Polly she was unflattering: "My old honey would go mad if he had to talk to her," she said. To the childless Louise, Polly's attitude toward her advanced pregnancy was particularly offensive. "She's loose jointed and ungraceful and ashamed to have anyone know she's about to have a child."

Mrs. Reed, Louise thought, was in much better shape than her and Harry's letters to Reed seemed to imply; her quarters at the Multnomah were comfortable and she seemed to be managing nicely.

Harry's report to Reed about his meeting with Louise had a note of restraint; he seemed to be trying to like her. "She looked very pretty and attractive and Poll liked her very much but our visit was so short that it was quite unsatisfactory and I was particularly sorry not to have a chance to have a talk with her alone. She told us a lot about you and the trials and the situation in general and I think mother feels better about you and will not be so worried." He and their mother had listened attentively to Louise's speech the night before, and were very proud of her, he said.

He was less sanguine about their mother than Louise. While he thought the financial situation would straighten itself out eventually, she was "tired out and very nervous." But he told Reed not to worry or to let the situation depress him.

Louise's next stop was San Francisco, where she was to meet her own mother, whom she had not seen in several years. She reported breathlessly to Reed on April 5 about her speech. "It was a marvelous meeting! . . . I never *saw* such enthusiasm—and they sent me roses and violets and carnations and tulips to the platform. . . . My mother is absolutely *bewildered*. She isn't sure whether I am a Bolshevik or a patriot or what it is all about. But she likes to hear me get an ovation."

She was speaking "500 times better" than the last time Reed heard her, Louise assured him. She was now being begged to speak in Denver, Salt Lake City, and Butte, before returning home.

"What *shall* I *do?* I want my dearest old honey—and I ought to speak I suppose. But anyway—I'll be home ten days after you get this letter."

On April 16 Louise wrote exultantly, "I am on my way home!" She would stop to speak in Salt Lake City, Chicago, and Detroit—"*Then home*, darling! How long it seems."

Chapter Fourteen

UPTON SINCLAIR labelled Reed "the playboy of the social revolution" and Reed was offended. Sinclair tried to apologize in a letter to Reed on May 14, 1919.

"Louise told me [when she lectured in California in April] that you were irritated with me, because of my phrase 'the playboy of the social revolution.' I explained to her that I meant this in the way of playfulness, and I hope she passed this on to you. It did not occur to me that the phrase was one that could do any hurt. I have a vivid recollection of the zest with which you went through the job of the Paterson pageant, and also your camping out with Mexican bandits—an experience which would not have brought me a particle of enjoyment, I am sure!"

The phrase was catchy and it clung, but it was, like many witty labels, more clever than true. Reed's espousal of socialism had nothing of the dilettante in it. He was so deeply devoted to the cause that he was willing to work for it to the point of exhaustion, and even illness. Capable of earning a very good income as a journalist, he was willing to subsist on token payments as a propagandist. He accepted harassment by his government, snubs from his friends, and the distress of his family, as unfortunate but necessary sacrifices.

He saw no possibility of turning back. While he could not foresee that he was embarking on a course that shortly would crush him, he did see quite clearly that it held great peril. He had no illusion that he was playing a game.

Before plunging into the war that was brewing in the Socialist Party and that would soon split it apart, Reed let Louise persuade him to take a couple of weeks' rest in Truro, the sparsely populated town adjoining Provincetown. Unlike Provincetown, whose summer colony was thickly clustered along Cape Cod Bay, Truro's population perched on the green hills or nestled in the sandy valleys spread over a wide expanse between bay and ocean. While Provincetown had a cozy, fishing-village charm, Truro had a more rugged, elemental atmosphere. Its houses were more isolated in scenic beauty and it was more conducive to peace and contemplation than bustling Provincetown. It was also cheaper, but even to afford Truro's rustic comforts, Reed had to pawn his watch. He and Louise had run out of money. Yet in spite of their financial difficulties, Louise returned a check for fifteen dollars sent to her by the publication, *Soviet Russia*.

"I have never taken a cent for any work I have ever done to help Soviet Russia and to prevent my country from continuing in its criminal efforts to destroy the Russian revolution," she wrote the magazine's editor, Jacob Hartman, from Truro on July 19. (Evidently she discounted her lecture fees, since they had barely covered her traveling expenses.) "I will make my living," she continued, with what proved to be groundless optimism "by fiction and the movies." She added that she would be happy to contribute other articles to the magazine, also without pay, when she returned to New York from Truro. She explained that she had come to Cape Cod with Reed because he was not well and had "no idea how to take a vacation near New York." In Truro, she said, "he cannot even hear the rumblings of battle."

The Reeds were joined in Truro by their Portland friends, Carl and Helen Walters, and spent a restful time swimming and sunning. While Reed knew this was just an interlude, knew what his commitment was, and showed no sign of regretting it, he continued to have a wistful moment now and then. One day he walked to Provincetown to visit Jig Cook and Susan Glaspell. Cook was taking a year off from running the Playwrights Theater, having turned it over to a group of younger members for the 1919–20 season. His wife was working on a long play. The three strolled over to the house, now empty, that Reed and Louise had lived in during their first summer together, and sat down under a big tree that grew in the yard.

"I wish I could stay here," Reed told the Cooks. "Maybe it will surprise you, but what I really want is to write poetry."

Susan Glaspell answered that it didn't surprise them. "Why don't you?"

"He shook his head," she later wrote, "at once troubled, saying he had 'promised too many people.'" It was the last time the Cooks saw him.

Returning to New York at the end of July, Reed took up his political mission and Louise tried to concentrate on writing magazine fiction in the hope of earning some money. She never had much success selling her short stories, but she did, eventually, manage to support herself by free-lance journalism. Louise spent much of the next two months working in Croton, while Reed, who tried to join her there as often as possible, moved into a small apartment on the top floor of a red brick house on Patchin Place, a narrow Greenwich Village alley.

Sometimes, when Reed wanted an extra day of rest in the country, and Louise had to come to New York to see an editor, they would exchange places. On one such occasion in August, when their schedules conflicted, Louise wrote Reed a frustrated little note: "Please forgive me for not being out in the country with you. I am sitting in our room [in Patchin Place] savagely writing and rewriting this fiction story. I am not going to leave this place until it is finished if it takes me until next January." She added that Reed's dog, which they called simply Puppy, needed a bath and that she hoped he had the energy to give him one. Weren't the flowers wonderful, she asked, and didn't the house look nice? "I wanted everything to be that way when you arrived," she said, urging him to please rest, and sending him all her love.

But Reed's days of rest in Croton were rare. During most of August and September he was in the thick of the battle being fought by the right and left wing factions of the American Socialist Party. The right wing, which had supported the war and which was accused by the left wing of betraying the working class, expelled the entire membership of the left wing on August 31. The left wing members, themselves split in ideology, regrouped into two new parties: The foreign-dominated faction, led by Louis Fraina, formed the Communist Party on September 1. The Italian-born Fraina, at twenty-seven, was elected secretary and international secretary.

On September 2, the minority faction, led by Reed and other native-born radicals, formed the rival Communist Labor Party. Benjamin Gitlow, a fellow founder of the Communist Labor Party, spent a great deal of time with Reed during this period. A twenty-eight-year-old native of New Jersey, he had joined the Socialist Party at sixteen and advanced to leadership in the left wing after the Bolshevik revolution. (Gitlow ultimately turned against the Communist Party and became one of its bitter opponents.)

In his book, *The Whole of Their Lives*, Gitlow has described Reed's exhausting hours of labor devoted to the communist cause:

"After a long day of conferences, mass meetings, organizational duties and hours at the typewriter, Reed would drag his tired feet to One Patchin Place and climb wearily up the three flights of stairs to the dingy, dirty apartment on the top floor. . . .

"Strewn all over Reed's living room were newspapers, pamphlets, letters, torn envelopes, manuscripts and books. Ashes obscured the base of the little wood-burning fireplace. Heaps of dust covered newspapers, and printed matter lay piled high in utter confusion on the large flat-top desk. Its drawers were open, each packed with printed rubbish and paper. On a little table stood a dirty, smudged enameled coffee pot, an ashtray full of cigarette butts and a couple of unwashed cups and saucers. The cot against the wall of the small room directly across from the fireplace was always mussed, with a few pillows scattered on its untidy surface.

"Reed on entering the apartment usually threw himself upon the large stuffed chair, pressed his temples between the palms of his hands, stretched out his legs in their full length, and sat motionless for a few minutes. One hardly knew whether he was relaxing or thinking. Then he would get up from the chair with a jump, grab some newspapers from the desk, and toss them into the fireplace. Lighting the papers, he hurled kindling wood and large chunks of coal after them. Throwing off his jacket he picked up the coffee pot, rinsed it superficially, filled it with water and coffee and set it to boil on a greasy, black castiron two-burner gas stove. Lighting a cigarette he would sit down and talk. And when he talked, he rambled over the universe, never confining

241

himself for a long time to one subject. He talked about his experiences as a reporter in Germany during the war, about Mexico, about the West, about his family tree and about anything else that came into his mind."

Drinking cup after cup of coffee and chain smoking, Reed would wax poetic. "I like this place, the building hidden away in an alley, in the center of the metropolis and the heart-soothing fireplace when the coals burn and the blue flames shimmer in the soft red glow of the embers."

Louise, according to Gitlow, tidied the apartment "a little" when she was in town. "Usually she sat perched upon the couch, her shoulders against the wall, a miniature of well-shaped daintiness and charm, with large dreamy eyes that looked straight at you. Jack seldom talked about Louise, but Louise always talked about Jack."

Louise confided in Gitlow. She was concerned because Reed had given up his writing—"what he can do best"—in order to work full time for the Communist cause; she said that he knew what he was doing, but that he also knew he was doing it at a great personal sacrifice.

Reed spent a good deal of time at the Connolly Club, on Twenty-ninth Street near Broadway, which housed two Communist publications—*Revolutionary Age,* edited by Louis Fraina, and *Voice of Labor,* edited by Reed. While he took his political and editorial duties seriously, Reed could still be playful at times. He enjoyed puncturing a solemn argument and stirring up a controversy, and would invent long, abstruse quotations from Marx to prove his point, then rush back to his typewriter and leave his opponents groping for refutation.

But when he discussed Communism seriously with Gitlow, he did not quote from Marx, whom he had never taken time to study. He told Gitlow that the kind of Communist movement he believed in for America was a movement that came directly from the working class, not one dominated by politicians. According to Gitlow's later, sober evaluation, Reed was unaware how little his idealistic conception had in common with Bolshevism. "He thought he could build a Bolshevik organization by simple frank discussion without political pressure and regimentation," Gitlow wrote, "thus displaying his ignorance of the essence of Bolshevik organization. He had been too busy watching the stirring events of the Bolshevik Revolution and had no time left to study the form of Bolshevik organization and how it works. When he did learn how ignorant he had been it was too late. Essentially an artist, Reed refused to reduce life to the mechanistic theoretical equations of the Marxists. His heart beat in unison with the heartbeats and aspirations of humanity and he saw and felt with compassion the suffering of the hungry and lowly of the earth."

The emergence of the two Communist parties had a predictably alarming effect on the government. It was not long before both parties were officially outlawed. Wholesale arrests of Communists and suspected Communists were made and dozens were sent to jail. The parties went underground, and Reed began making plans to return to Russia. He had been elected by the Communist Labor Party to be its representative to the Congress of the Communist International. According to Gitlow, Reed explained the situation to his party's Central Executive Committee thus: "Comrades, we are in the unfortunate position of having two communist parties in the United States. One we control. The other the Russian-Slavic bloc controls. That Communist party will survive which gets the endorsement of the Bolsheviks. It is therefore most important that I get to Moscow before Fraina does. I propose that I leave for Moscow as soon as arrangements for my departure can be made."

Chapter Fifteen

THERE WAS NO LEGAL WAY for Reed to leave the country. In fact, he was in danger of arrest at any moment. But while various associates got to work on the problem of smuggling him out, he took no particular pains to conceal himself. The writer Don Marquis was surprised to spot Reed in the street from the top of a double-decker Fifth Avenue bus one day in early September. He got off to greet him and asked him what he was doing. As Marquis later reported to the biographer and critic, Granville Hicks, "Reed laughed and said he was in hiding."

"This is the dickens of a place to hide," remarked Marquis.

"None better," Reed said, "and besides, the red-hunters never catch anybody."

It was James Larkin, the Irish labor leader, who worked out the method for smuggling Reed out of the country. Larkin was a tall, sharp-featured, raffish rabble-rouser, who was in the United States collecting arms for an Irish uprising. He naturally gravitated to the radical movement in New York, and set up a ramshackle headquarters in a little alley behind Reed's apartment in Patchin Place. Sophisticated in smuggling techniques, he had little difficulty in obtaining forged seaman's papers for Reed (in the name of James Gromley) and getting him a berth as a stoker on a Swedish freighter.

Reed and Louise were dismayed at the prospect of another separation, although neither was fully aware of how dangerous and irrevocable this adventure could turn out to be. They knew that a certain amount of risk and a good deal of hardship was attached to the journey itself. Reed could not masquerade as a coal stoker without doing his share of heavy work. Then there was the tricky problem of getting through the hostile armies of Finland into Russia. And life in Russia, now in the throes of civil war and blockaded by the Allies, was going to be grim. But they agreed that the effort was worth making, and they were both confident that Reed would accomplish his mission and get back to America within a few months.

Having said goodbye to Louise, Reed, accompanied by a few of his close associates in the Communist Labor Party, made his way on a night in late September to the Hudson River docks. Gitlow was among those who saw him off: "Dressed . . . in coarse trousers and a flannel multicolored shirt, a cap cocked rakishly on his head, false seaman's paper in his pockets, a two-weeks' stubble on his chin, Reed bade his friends goodbye. In the company of a couple of Irish dockers . . . he scrambled aboard in the darkness of the night."

The voyage itself was uneventful, and Reed managed to jump ship at Bergen, on Norway's western coast, without detection. Foreign Communists were being arrested every day and anyone without papers was liable to imprisonment. But in Norway, as well as in Sweden and Finland, through which he would have to make his way, an underground network of Socialist and Communist agents had been alerted to help him on to Russia. Reed made the sixty-odd mile trip from Bergen to Christiania safely.

On October 21, from Christiania, he wrote a long letter to Louise, entrusting it to a courier. "At present I am in a safe place and this [letter] goes forward by a safe man," he said. "Tomorrow I must get across the Swedish frontier on foot by night. . . . If I were caught nothing could be done to me except to deport me to the U.S., where I cannot be punished for naturally I have my papers in a safe place and shall not be caught with them on me." While the Scandinavian countries were being much more actively policed than during his last visit, Reed said, he thought his chances of getting safely to Stockholm were good, and from there he would plan to get into Russia.

He wrote at length about the "frightfully mixed up" political situation in Russia which had been conveyed to him by local observers and which he found "heartrending." The White Army was advancing on Petrograd, arms and money were being furnished by the allies. "It is," Reed wrote, "a last desperate attempt to crush Russia, and may succeed. Something appears to be wrong internally."

Interspersed in his almost hysterical preoccupation with recent political events, were messages of endearment. "From now on it seems to me that we must never again be separated. . . . Goodnight, my dearest. . . . Write me very seldom. Inform mother that I am well. Back before Christmas I hope."

Reed crossed into Sweden and made his way to Stockholm without mishap. The next leg of his trip had to be made by ship across the Baltic Sea to Abo, on Finland's northwestern coast. In Finland, where hostility to the Bolsheviks was intense, Reed would be in greater danger than at any point in his journey. While waiting for the arrangements to be made he allowed himself to relax a bit. He dined one evening in a cafe with two prominent Swedish radicals. One of them, as he later wrote to

Louise, had just read her book. "It is the best and cleverest book on Russia which I have read," he told Reed. His companion knew of the book, too, and Reed proudly told them that Louise was his wife.

"I gave one [of them] your picture, which is to be printed in a magazine in Sweden which has a large influence, together with extracts from your book," he said. "I have also told everybody about how my honey broke the Overman blockade, and shall tell at headquarters [Reed's euphemism for the Kremlin]."

Reed left Stockholm as a stowaway. He endured the unpleasant trip, hidden in a pile of greasy rags, happy to be almost within reach of Russia. Sneaking off the ship at Abo he had a moment of panic when he missed the contact he had been promised would await him at the dock. He spent several tense hours mingling with the crowd, trying to be inconspicuous, and was finally picked up by the agent who had earlier failed to spot him, and led to the home of a woman writer who had secret communist sympathies. After a day's rest he was safely conducted to Helsinki, arriving there on October 30.

Again sheltered in a private home, he planned to leave at once for Vyborg (then a Finnish city on the Russian border, now part of Russia). But, as he wrote to Louise from Helsinki on November 9, "Suddenly there were terrible police raids at Vyborg. All our organization there was broken up, and the people we counted on were arrested. If I had gone there when I expected I should now be in the jug, instead of in the comfortable house where I now fret and fume at my delay."

He had been in Helsinki for over ten days, he said, "thinking about my honey and wanting her." He should have been at "headquarters" long since, he said, but now could go neither forward nor back.

But in spite of the frustrating delay he was in good health and spirits and still expected to be home before Christmas. He was confident that his business in Moscow would be settled within a couple of weeks, once he got there. Concerned, as always, about Louise's financial situation, he said that she must ask for help, if she needed it, from the Communist Labor Party. Since he was traveling "on urgent business" in their behalf, they were obliged to look after her in his absence.

He missed her terribly and longed for her, he said, but cautioned her not to think of joining him. "It would be ghastly for you now," he said. Perhaps as a subterfuge, but more likely out of whimsey, he signed his letter with the name on his forged seaman's papers: "Your loving Jim [Gromley]."

The letter did not reach Louise for several weeks, since all of Reed's messages were hand-carried by various couriers making their devious and often illegal way to the United States. But on November 10, the day after Reed wrote the letter, Louise had the dubious pleasure of seeing Reed's name in the newspaper headlines. Seventy-one Communist Party and Communist Labor Party headquarters in New York City had been raided by police two nights before, and Reed's illegal absence from the country had been discovered and indignantly announced.

After the letter from Helsinki Louise had no further word from Reed. Christmas came and went. January and February brought no news. Louise could only assume that Reed's business in Russia was keeping him longer than he had expected, and that messages he sent were intercepted.

When Reed finally did reach Moscow sometime in December, he was cordially welcomed by Lenin and the other top-ranking government officials. Reed immediately

249

presented his case for recognition of the American Communist Labor Party. Grigori Zinoviev, chairman of the Comintern, countered with a request that Reed submit a written report, fully detailing the political and economic situation in the United States. Zinoviev, though he was one of Lenin's closest associates, did not always see eye to eye with him. The impression was conveyed that a decision would not be arrived at without lengthy deliberation.

Reed realized that he had been overly optimistic, but he was not discouraged. The spell that Russia had cast on him before enthralled him again. If he had not missed Louise, his enthusiasm at being able to spend another extended period in Russia would have been unalloyed. He set to work on the report and surrendered himself to the Russian mystique.

Since Reed had always been adaptable to physical hardship, the grim conditions of daily living in Russia bothered him very little. Not many men could have remained cheerful and unruffled under the circumstances. The winter of 1919–20 was one of the cruelest in Russia's history. "It was horrible beyond imagination," Reed later wrote in a two-part article for the *Liberator*. "Transport at times almost ceased. . . . There was, and is, grain enough in the provincial storehouses to feed the whole country well for two years, but it cannot be transported. For weeks together Petrograd was without bread. So with fuel—so with raw materials. . . . In some houses [in Petrograd and Moscow] there was no heat at all the whole winter. People froze to death in their rooms. . . .

"Ghastly things happened. Trains full of people traveling in remote provinces broke down between stations and the passengers starved and froze to death."

Because of the lack of hot water and the scarcity of

soap, sanitary conditions were appalling. Disease spread quickly and typhus alone caused more than two million deaths that year. Hospitals operated under primitive conditions, often without heat and rarely with adequate medicine. For the ordinary worker in Moscow, survival was a daily problem.

Yet Reed, offered comfortable living quarters with access to decent meals and other amenities provided for distinguished visitors, turned the offer down. He preferred to experience the life of the proletariat and took a room in a working class neighborhood, where he cooked his meals on a small iron stove. He was not a man to pay lip service to ideology. He had the truly extraordinary capacity to put the innocence of his belief into practice.

Reed's innocence, however, was the quality that ultimately undid him. He was doomed from the moment he set foot in Russia. On the surface, his relationship with the Bolshevik leaders was cordial and mutually respectful. Lenin was particularly warm and receptive, spent many hours talking with him, commended his choice of living quarters, expressed concern for his health, and encouraged him to learn Russian. Unlike Trotsky, Lenin spoke foreign languages execrably. In spite of his years of exile, during which he had learned to read English, he had difficulty making himself understood in that language. But by the use of a kind of polyglot, and with the help of an interpreter, Lenin and Reed managed to communicate. Lenin praised *Ten Days that Shook the World* and handwrote the introduction that was used in the 1922 printing of the book.

Reed was permitted to travel freely and took advantage of this privilege to explore as far as the Volga, which was frozen over. Stopping at towns and villages along the way, he found that "The Soviet order had bitten deep into the life of the people, that the new society was already an old-established and accustomed thing." What he saw of the workers' and peasants' living conditions during this trip did nothing to shake his belief in the rightness of the revolution. The factory workers were enthusiastic about the new government and peasants' living conditions appeared to Reed better than before the revolution. Improvement was coming slowly, but in Reed's view it was, inevitably, coming.

On his return to Moscow, Reed was informed by the Comintern Executive Committee that their decision was for unification of the two American Communist parties. Whatever his private reservations may have been, Reed accepted the decision. There was nothing now to keep him in Russia except his affinity for the Russian people, and his eagerness to see Louise would probably have impelled him homeward at this point. But while he hesitated, considering the possibility of Louise's joining him in Russia, events at home made the decision for him.

On January 2, 1920, police raids were again made on Communist meeting places, this time nationwide, under the direction of Attorney General A. Mitchell Palmer. Ten thousand persons were arrested and 123 members of the two Communist parties were indicted. Reed was one of them. When this news reached Moscow late in January, Reed, characteristically, decided that he must return at once to face the charges, even if it meant imprisonment, which it almost certainly did. He applied for permission to leave. His application appears to have been neither refused nor endorsed.

Benjamin Gitlow, who, as a key figure in the Communist Labor Party, probably had as good sources as anyone from which to reconstruct the facts, has written that Zinoviev "requested" that Reed remain in Russia, and that other Bolshevik leaders echoed this request. Presumably they felt Reed would be more useful to them in Russia than he would be in an American jail. Reed evidently took the "request" at face value and felt free to decline. His reasons for optimism were supported by the fact that he was given a substantial sum of money and some diamonds to take back, in addition to all the propaganda literature he could pack. He decided to make his way out of Russia at once, by way of Latvia instead of Finland.

Before leaving, he went to see Emma Goldman, who had been deported from the United States and had recently arrived in Moscow. She was able to tell Reed that Louise was well; Reed had received no word from Louise since leaving America. Emma Goldman wrote of the meeting in her autobiography, *Living My Life*, with typical flamboyance, attributing to Reed a highflown conversational style that was probably more her own than his:

"John Reed had burst into my room like a sudden ray of light, the old buoyant, adventurous Jack that I used to know in the States. He was about to return to America. . . . Rather a hazardous journey, he said, but he would take even greater risks to bring the inspiring message of Soviet Russia to his native land.

" 'Wonderful, marvelous, isn't it, E.G.?' he exclaimed. 'Your dream of years now realized in Russia, your dream scorned and persecuted in my country, but made real by the magic wand of Lenin and his band of despised Bolsheviks. Did you ever expect such a thing to happen in the country ruled by the czars for centuries?' "

When Emma Goldman ventured to criticize a recent mass execution of counter-revolutionaries by the Bolsheviks, Reed was "surprised" that she should be agitated "over the death of a few plotters."

"I must be crazy, Jack, or else I never understood the meaning of revolution. I certainly never believed that it would signify callous indifference to human life and suffering, or that it would have no other method of solving its problems than by wholesale slaughter. Five hundred lives snuffed out . . . ! I call it a dastardly crime, the worst counter-revolutionary outrage committed in the name of the Revolution."

Reed tried to calm her. "You are a little confused by the Revolution in action," he said, "because you have dealt with it only in theory. You'll get over that, clear-sighted rebel that you are, and you'll come to see in its true light everything that seems so puzzling now."

Reed's first attempt to leave Russia was thwarted. Part way through Latvia he found that railroad travel had come to a halt. The reason the trains were no longer running, he was told, was because the Red Army was retreating and all communications had broken down. He tried to cross the border elsewhere and again was forced to turn back.

He described his experiences during one of these attempts, in an article he sent to the *Liberator* in July: "Down on the western front, behind the Red Army retreating before the offensive of the Lettish White troops, I had to change trains at a junction. Of course the train I wanted did not come at all, but after waiting a night and a day I managed to climb into the box car of an empty military train going east, together with two soldiers, a railroad worker going home on a visit . . . and an old peasant woman who carried a cage with a dead parrot in it. We built a fire on the floor of the car and, except for the smoke, were quite comfortable until the bottom of the car burnt out.

"But in the meanwhile I had to wait at the junction

all day and all night. It was nothing but a dilapidated railway station with a large village—no town—about five miles away. It was frightfully cold—the awful cold driven by a high east wind over the Russian plain—the cold that smashed Napoleon's Grand Army to pieces.

"Now, Russians can stand more cold than anyone else in the world. But all through the day came peasants' sleighs driven out of the west, carrying what I first took to be logs of wood, but which turned out to be the stiff bodies of Red soldiers, frozen when they had grown too tired to walk any longer. Three hundred of them, piled like cordwood on the station platform.

"The windows in the station waiting-room were broken. The water pipes had burst and the floor was coated with ice. Upon this and on tables, benches, everywhere, lay soldiers, uncountable gray heaps of them, tossing and muttering in the delirium of typhus.

"The other waiting-room was in the same condition, but in one corner stood a stage brightly decorated with red banners and revolutionary posters, with a dim kerosene lamp burning on a table, before which stood a young fellow in uniform making a speech to the dun mass of soldiers who crowded the place, lifting to him their flat, bearded faces with an expression of strained attention. He was agitating for the Communist Party, pleading with the soldiers to join it, and to contribute to the party press. . . . And they cheered, those half-frozen skeletons, waving their hats, their sunken eyes shining."

According to Gitlow, Reed was merely puzzled by his two failures to get out of Russia. "Each time," Gitlow wrote, "he blamed himself and concluded that he was slipping in his technique of crossing hostile borders. Never did he suspect that perhaps Zinoviev and the Comintern shared some of the responsibility for his failure. He did not stop to question why the proficient Comintern apparatus for smuggling persons and revolutionary propaganda and contraband out of Russia had fallen down in his case."

It was late in February before Reed could devise another plan to leave Russia. Much as he would have liked to avoid Finland, that seemed to be the only route by which he could hope to get out. He reached Abo safely and was smuggled aboard a Finnish ship bound for Sweden. But there his luck ended. On March 15, before the ship could sail, a search party boarded and Reed was discovered and arrested. He later found out, according to Gitlow, that a Russian sailor, selected by Zinoviev as Reed's ostensible guide and protector, had betrayed him. Zinoviev apparently preferred to have Reed temporarily detained in Finland, rather than jailed indefinitely in the United States. Max Eastman, who later met Zinoviev in Moscow, described him as "a vain and fluid thing of shifty mind and tongue. His record of switched allegiances, of turning and doubling on his tracks, of squirming and belly-crawling and sleekly gliding in and out, in the conflict between Stalin and Trotsky, would look like acrobatics to a water snake. Moreover, he was laughless, feminine and of a sad complaisance. And his handshake was like receiving the present of a flattened-out banana. No one could more perfectly personify the thing in Bolshevism that Jack Reed could not tolerate than Zinoviev."

The Finnish authorities were fully aware of Reed's political activities—they could not fail to be, after examining the contents of his trunk—but, for diplomatic reasons, preferred not to charge him on those grounds. Instead, they charged him with smuggling jewelry and money.

He was placed in solitary confinement in Abo's police

station. He managed to get word of his arrest to Aino Malmberg, the Finnish pacifist, suffragist, and author, and she sent him a lawyer, who immediately tried to contact the American consul in Helsinki, but without success. Reed himself was allowed to communicate with no one. But Aino Malmberg, who, as official translator of George Bernard Shaw's works into Finnish, had many British contacts, told a British reporter of Reed's arrest. The news, dispatched first to London, reached the United States on March 18.

It was Louise's first inkling in over three months of Reed's whereabouts and welfare, and it was not reassuring. She began making inquiries in Washington, but the State Department said it had no information about Reed. Her dismay was heightened when, three weeks later, the newspapers printed what they called "unconfirmed reports" from Finland that Reed had been "executed" there. But a few days later, on April 15, the State Department finally admitted officially that word had been received from the Finnish Government that Reed was being held by them.

Louise immediately got in touch with the State Department and asked that arrangements be made with the American consul in Helsinki to provide Reed with legal help. On April 22 the Secretary of State wired Louise that the State Department would arrange this at her expense, but cautioned her that neither the American Legation nor the State Department could assume responsibility for the reliability of the attorney they would furnish. If the State Department had been motivated orthodoxly, it would, presumably, have been eager to have Reed released and returned to the United States to stand trial under the conspiracy charge. The inertia that ensued indicates that this was not the case. Possibly the State Department was just as happy to allow Reed to be dealt with by the Finnish Government on its own terms.

Louise cabled Reed in Abo, telling him what she had arranged, and followed with a letter a few days later. Having done all she could, she steeled herself to await the outcome. She was overwhelmed by anxiety and love for Reed. Now, when it dawned on her that there was a very real possibility she might lose him for good, she was fully aware of how much she really loved and needed him. Briefly, she found release for her emotions by turning to poetry.

We have seen life together,
We have seen death
And the thread of our love
Is unbroken.
Now the seas lie between us
And more than the seas.
Is it spring where you are, darling;
Spring, with the music of the melting snow? . . .

When I think of seeing you again
It is as if I saw the snow in Moscow
For the first time
Or heard a skylark
Singing to the sun . . .

I can think of only one prayer.
One more time before I die
I want to see you.

Reed continued in solitary confinement all through April. But at the beginning of May he was, at last, permitted to write letters. He could not know if any of them would be delivered, for they were, of course, censored. But jail guards could be bribed, and various strings could be pulled. In the corrupt and confused situation that existed in Finland, nothing was accomplished in a straightforward manner. His first letter to Louise, written May 3, did reach her. He told her he had received her cable and been relieved to learn that she knew of his arrest. He had been very upset at the thought that she knew nothing of his whereabouts.

"I have heard absolutely not a word from you since I left here—except news of you from Emma and the other exiles, which proved that at any rate you were alive. I have been so fearfully worried—about your health, about whether you had anything to do, enough to eat—whether you were well or ill."

He had been waiting nearly eight weeks for the Finnish authorities to decide what to do with him, he said. The case against him—that of smuggling—had been tried, the diamonds confiscated, and he had been fined three hundred dollars. But he was still being held in prison while the Finns decided whether or not to charge him with treason. "It appears that there are 'diplomatic negotiations' going on between the Finnish government and the United States government. Why, I do not know."

He did not want Louise to intercede in any way for help for him from the American government, he said, adding, "I wish this case to be decided entirely on its merits." He did not elaborate on his reasons. He was in good health, "and almost all the time cheerful enough."

"But the thought of you drags at me sometimes," he went on, "until my imagination plays tricks, and than I almost go crazy. *Please,* please, write me about everything. Don't send any money—I have plenty. And *don't worry*—there's not the slightest danger."

Reed asked Louise to let his mother know of his situation, and to redeem his pawned watch if she possibly could; the watch, on which they had been borrowing money on and off for several years, was very precious to him.

"I hope it won't be long before we see each other again," he wrote. "Anyway, I'll be saving everything for you, as I have ever since October. Spring is coming here and I long for Croton. Your loving Jack."

On May 13 he wrote again, having just received Louise's letter of April 23.

"I am not yet free . . . but on the other hand I am also not accused of anything." He had been informed, he said, that the American Government had demanded that he be surrendered to the American authorities in Finland, but could not understand this. He did not think the Finns would surrender him without first trying him on a treason charge. He did not say what his sources of information were, and seemed somewhat confused. "It is impossible to say what a bourgeois government cannot do," he said, not specifying whether he meant the Finnish or the American government, and forgetting, for the moment, some of the things he had seen a communist government do.

The terms of Reed's confinement were peculiar, by the standards of any government. After weeks of solitary imprisonment, living on a diet of dried fish, all of his possessions—including his clothing—confiscated, he now was able to send Louise three hundred dollars; he did not explain where it came from. Also, he was receiving messages. He had heard from someone that Louise was planning to try to join him in Finland. "If it is for the sake of helping me, I beg you not to do so," he wrote to her. "But if it is because you want to come abroad, and possibly to be with me in case I am delayed—and, of course, if you can find the money—do it by all means. But wait for a cable from me before you actually sail."

Reed went on to assure Louise that he was still very

well. He had given up smoking, he said. He was allowed to walk in the yard every day, and was well-treated. "The Police Master here has really been most friendly and generous to me," he added.

"As for the American authorities, they have of course not been near me, or sent me any word all the time I have been here. But I am thankful for that. I do not want any help from the authorities as regards myself. I think I understand thoroughly the situation at home, and will know what to do." Evidently Reed felt that he was accumulating evidence against the American government that would help him publicize the crimes of a capitalist system, as opposed to the virtues of a communist system; he seemed still to believe that he would soon return to America.

"I am all right, dearest," he assured Louise, "and except for the nervousness of doing nothing and being all alone week after week, and worrying about my honey, I am able to stand it indefinitely." He ended with a message to his publisher, Horace Liveright: "The big chief [Lenin] thinks my book the best."

Two days later, Reed wrote to Louise that as far as he could learn, there was "not the slightest chance" of his being freed.

"The Finnish Government has absolutely no case against me," he said. "It dares not bring me to trial. It does not want to set me free. And so it keeps me here, shut up, day and night and growing steadily more and more nervous."

It is difficult to gauge how serious an effect Reed's confinement was beginning to have on his nerves. At this point, he sounded illogical, and even slightly (and understandably) paranoid. Having told Louise earlier that he wanted no help from his government, he now said that he had written to the United States Minister in Helsinki. "That was two weeks ago, and he has not even answered."

"It will surprise you," he said, "to hear that *I am informed by the Finns that I am kept in prison at the request of the United States Government!*

"The U.S. minister in Helsinki has *done not one thing for me*, except about a month ago to inquire from my lawyer how the case was getting on. Moreover, he knew that I was arrested one week afterward, yet from that time to this not one representative of the U.S. Government has ever been near me or come to the prison. This is, I believe, a record—for they usually send somebody even when a sailor gets locked up."

He had just about decided, if all else failed, to try a hunger strike, he said. A few days later, he did threaten a hunger strike, and it worked.

On May 19, Reed finally had more cheerful news to send Louise. "Today I learned that the Finnish Government will not try me in court—lack of evidence. I am to be freed!" But the Finns were making conditions: They would ask the American minister to give Reed a passport. If it was refused, they would notify Reed that he must leave the country within forty-eight hours, on the theory that Reed would head for Sweden, and not having a passport, would be deported to America.

But Reed, who was sure he would be refused the American passport, did not intend to allow himself to be deported. He was going to ask the Estonian government for a visa, and then return to Russia for a brief period. From Russia, he would again try to find a way to get to America, or, failing that, he would send for Louise to join him in Russia.

He wrote Louise, reassuringly, that he was still very

well. But his health was, in fact, not good. The physical confinement and the diet of salt fish week after week had worn him down. He was showing signs of malnutrition and vitamin deficiency; his legs and arms were swollen. And because he had been living and sleeping in the same clothes, without being able to undress at night, for ten weeks, he had sores all over his body. But for Louise's sake, he continued to be optimistic. "It won't be long now, my dearest—that is, in comparison with what has gone. My only object now is to see you again as soon as possible."

When he and Louise finally were reunited, he told her more candidly about his experiences in jail. "He told me of his cell, damp and cold and wet," Louise later recalled. "Sometimes he was delirious and imagined me dead. Sometimes he expected to die himself, so he wrote on books and everywhere a little verse:

> Thinking and dreaming
> Day and night and day
> Yet cannot think one bitter thought away—
> That we have lost each other
> You and I."

The motives and maneuverings of both the Finnish and the American Governments continued to be obscure. The passport was refused by the American consul, and May 30 found Reed still in jail. Again, he turned to poetry.

> White and slim my lover
> Birch-tree in the shade
> Mountain pools her fearless eyes
> Innocent, all-answering . . .
> All my weak endeavor
> Lay I at her feet

> Like a moth from oversea
> Let my longing lightly rest
> On her flower-petal breast
> Till the red dawn set me free
> To be with my sweet
> Ever and forever.

Reed had asked Aino Malmberg, his only friend in Finland, to help him get an Estonian visa, having decided he had no choice but to go back to Russia. "I am given to understand that . . . the permission will be granted me," he wrote to Louise, "but for some strange reason no answer comes, although it is now *ten days* since I requested permission. And still I sit here, in the bright June weather, spending most of my time worrying about my honey and longing for her."

As soon as he reached Russia he would cable her specific instructions about joining him, he said; she must come first to Stockholm, where he had contacts who would help her.

Reed left his letter unsealed, hoping to be able to send Louise news of his release; he seemed to anticipate a long stay in Russia for both of them, for each day he added a new instruction to Louise:

"Don't forget the interest on Croton due August 1, and on Truro September 26. Don't forget my watch!

"Monday, May 31—Still no word from Estonia.

"Tuesday, June 1—Still no word. It seems to me as if I shall never get out. The worst is to keep on *expecting* release, day after day. My mind is getting just dull. Honey, the house ought to be rented.

"Wednesday, June 2—Still not a whisper. . . . I have nothing to read, nothing to do. I can only sleep about five hours, and so am awake, penned in a little cage, for nineteen hours a day. This is my thirteenth week. . . .

"8 P.M.—Just this minute *word came!* I am to go to Reval [in Estonia] on Saturday's boat from Helsinki—or maybe I must wait until Tuesday. Anyway, *I'm going!* This is the last letter to my honey from this place. Wait for news from me, dearest."

The letter did not reach Louise for several weeks, and by the beginning of June she was again growing anxious. She inquired about Reed at the State Department, but before she could get a reply, she received a cable from Reed in Reval on June 7 saying he was "temporarily returning headquarters," and asking her to "come if possible." Two days later a note came to her from the Second Assistant Secretary of State confirming Reed's release from jail and his departure for Reval.

Louise at once began making arrangements to leave. It seemed not to have occurred either to Reed or to her that she would have any difficulty getting her passport renewed. But on June 18 she was officially informed by the State Department that her passport application was refused. Determined to join Reed at any cost, she began casting about for a way to leave illegally, as Reed had done.

Reed, having reached Moscow in early June, but having received no word from Louise, began sending her cautious messages, advising her to delay her trip. On June 16 he sent her a note by a member of the British delegation who was leaving Moscow. He said that he must stay in Moscow until after the International Congress, scheduled to open in mid-July. "My plans from then on are all arranged," he said, "but I cannot tell you them in this note."

They would be together before the end of summer, he assured her, but she must make no plans to leave "until a friend comes with a note from me telling you what to do." Everything would be all right, if she would trust him and "hang on until I send." He enclosed one hundred dollars for her. (The source of this money was as mysterious as that of the larger sum he had sent her from Finland. It may have been a loan from a sympathetic friend.)

Freedom of movement, the warm weather, and a diet that seemed luxurious after the weeks of dried fish, helped Reed partially to recover his health during the next few weeks.

"Just now it is a beautiful moment in Soviet Russia," he wrote for the *Liberator*. "Clear, sunny day follows clear sunny day. The fields are gorgeous with hundreds of varieties of wild-flowers. Wherever you go by train every inch of the rich country seems to be planted. From bankrupt, speculator-ridden Estonia, where the fields lie unplowed and the factory chimneys stand smokeless, where the ragged people run beside the train begging, to cross the frontier into Soviet Russia seems like entering a rich, well-ordered land.

"Everywhere the green crops are growing, occasionally a wood-burning factory sends up smoke; but more significant is the look of the people—none well-dressed, but none in rags; none overfed, but none who look as if they were suffering. . . .

"In Moscow the public gardens are ablaze with flowers. In Petrograd bands play in the afternoon in all the parks. Thousands of people in variegated, but not ragged summer clothes stroll up and down, or drink glasses of tea and coffee . . . and, if they can afford it, buy lumps of sugar from surrepitious speculators. . . .

"Petrograd is clean; the streets are carefully swept; the Nevsky—that is to say, October 25th Prospekt—is being new-paved, a thing which has not happened since 1915. The militia girls wear flowers in their rifles. . . .

"The summer gardens and the outdoor summer theaters are open and crowded—although most of them, being private enterprises, charge horrible prices for admission. We heard Chaliapin in 'Faust' last week at the Hermitage in Moscow.

"The blockade is at last weakening. Long trains full of agricultural implements and machinery parts trickle slowly through from Reval."

Nothing Reed wrote during this period gives any indication that his enthusiasm and support for the Communists were diminished. Being a guest of the Russian government and with no place else he could safely go, Reed would have been extremely foolhardy to express openly any feelings of disenchantment.

Benjamin Gitlow, however, has written that Reed began to be disillusioned about the Bolshevik regime on his return to Moscow. His discovery of Zinoviev's treachery in Finland, even if the motive seemed justified, was one point that gave him pause. And as the months went by, he found himself more and more often up against examples of didacticism and flagrant double-dealing. While he was prepared to make great allowances for what he called a "temporary dictatorship," for the sake of future benevolence, some of the effects of this dictatorship were becoming difficult to stomach. A faint suspicion that the dictatorship might not be temporary—that, in fact, some of the men in power had never regarded it as temporary —was beginning to gnaw at Reed.

Angelica Balabanoff, who had been appointed secretary of the International, and who was having difficulties in her dealings with the party leaders, was one of the people—according to her, the only one—in whom Reed confided. He felt he could talk freely with her because he knew she shared his misgivings. Balabanoff had openly

defied what she regarded as a high-handed and unjusti-
fied order from Zinoviev to attend a meeting in Turkestan, rather than to take her place at the International.

Reed told her he believed Zinoviev's order was motivated by a fear that she would talk too honestly and
openly to her friends among the Italian Socialist Party
who were coming to attend the International. Balabanoff's flat refusal to go to Turkestan resulted in her
dismissal as secretary. As she later pointed out, this rela-
tively mild punishment was due to the fact that the Soviet leaders were still responsive to working-class opinion
abroad. "In the 1930s," she wrote, "a similar breach of
discipline would probably have resulted in my imprisonment or worse.

"It was John Reed who put into words that which I
had already begun to suspect," Balabanoff wrote. "We
had been meeting frequently since his return to Russia
. . . drawn together by our common disillusionment and
growing despair. . . . I do not think that any foreigner
who came to Russia in those early years ever saw or came
to know so much about the conditions of the people as
did Reed in the spring and summer of 1920. He was becoming more and more depressed by the suffering, disor-
ganization and inefficiency to be found everywhere. . . .
He was particularly discouraged when he saw his own efforts and those of the other friends of the Revolution defeated by indifference and inefficiency. Sensitive to any
kind of inequality and injustice, he would return from
each of his trips around the Russian countryside with stories that were heartbreaking to both of us."

He conveyed no hint of his misgivings in his next few
letters to Louise, however. On June 23, 1920, he wrote to
inform her that she would be visited within one and a
half months by "a friend," who would have instructions

and money for her. About his own plans he said only that he must stay in Moscow until the end of July, but he assured her that they would not be separated another winter.

"It is beautiful here now, and everything is going so well. Great events are expected. I can say no more now, except that I love you and want you all the time."

He followed this with a note three days later, urging her to "just hold out," and they would soon be together "all right and safe."

The opening session of the International, which took place in Petrograd on July 19, did seem to promise the "great things" of Reed's expectations. Largely ceremonial, the session was addressed by Zinoviev and Lenin, who spoke in generalities, heralding the great new era that was to come. Reed was enthusiastic.

"In Russia are now gathering the revolutionary leaders of the entire world," he wrote in the *Liberator*. "Already there are delegates from America, France, Germany, England, Italy, Switzerland, Bulgaria, Rumania, Hungary, Austria, Mexico, Australia, Argentina, Persia, India, Afghanistan, China, Korea, Japan, South Africa, Turkey, Armenia, Holland. . . . Reviews of the Red Army, parades of the cadets of the officers' schools, in their smart uniforms of blue and red, their khaki caps trimmed with silver—the Petrograd cavalry officers' school all mounted on bay horses headed by their silver cavalry band. Red carnations are given to the delegates as they leave the trains, to the cheering and singing of immense throngs of people with their tall red banners. The 'International,' the hymn of the Russian Soviet Republic, is played incessantly, while everyone rises to his feet and sings and the Red Army soldiers stand at salute."

The congress moved to Moscow after the first session,

where the real work was to begin on July 29. Almost at once, Reed encountered opposition. He proposed that the question of trade unions, which he considered the most vital one with regard to revolutionizing the United States, take precedence over other matters. His proposal was voted down. He asked that English be made one of the official languages of the congress, in view of the large number of representatives from Great Britain and America. This proposal was also defeated. Annoyed, but not yet discouraged, Reed accepted his appointment to two commissions—the commission on national minorities and the commission on trade union activities.

Reed's report and recommendations regarding minorities seem to have gone down well enough with the other members of his commission. It is noteworthy mainly for its prophetic liberalism with regard to the oppression of Negroes in the United States.

His efforts to persuade the commission on trade union activities to his point of view met with blank opposition. Reed maintained that the American Federation of Labor was a reactionary organization, could not possibly be used as a revolutionary tool, and should be smashed, not infiltrated, as the Bolsheviks proposed. Lenin, with whom Reed had a private talk on the subject, believed that the reactionary leaders of the A.F. of L. should be destroyed, but did not want to smash the organization. When the question was brought to a vote in the congress Lenin's view, not surprisingly, prevailed.

According to Gitlow, Louis Fraina, who had arrived in Moscow as a representative of the American Communist Party, had been instructed by his own organization to take the same stand on trade unions as Reed. But Fraina's approach was as devious as Reed's was straightforward. He fell in with the conspiratorial spirit and behind-the-scenes maneuvering of the congress, and took particular pains to ingratiate himself with Zinoviev, who, since Reed's return to Russia, had grown openly hostile to Reed. (Fraina later turned anti-Communist, changed his name to Lewis Corey, returned to the United States, and became a successful writer on social and political subjects.)

"Reed took his defeat [on the trade union question] badly," Gitlow wrote, "not because he lost, but because of the methods employed against him." Despite his defeat and despite Zinoviev's hostility, Reed was elected to the Executive Committee of the Comintern, where, for another three weeks, he continued, unsuccessfully, to press his views of the trade union question.

Growing steadily more discouraged, his health deteriorating from the long, exhausting hours of debate, Reed sustained himself with the knowledge that Louise was finally on her way to Russia.

Chapter Sixteen

REED'S MESSENGER REACHED LOUISE in New York at the beginning of August 1920, with instructions and money for her trip to Russia. Plans had been made for her to leave in the same way and follow much the same underground route as Reed. The journey she faced would have terrified any but the most courageous woman.

Louise wrote briefly of her trip in a letter to Max Eastman that he published in the *Liberator* several months after her arrival in Russia. Her account, though sketchy, indicates the horror of the journey.

She disguised herself as a sailor and, like Reed, left New York with forged seaman's papers.

"I had to skirt Finland," she wrote, "sail twelve days in the Arctic ocean, hide in a fisherman's shack four days to avoid the police, with a Finnish officer and a German, both under sentence of death in their own countries."

Reed got word of her arrival in Stockholm near the end of August. He had planned to meet her in Petrograd and return with her to Moscow. But their reunion, after eleven months' separation, had to be put off a little longer. He had been asked, presumably because of his eloquence in the cause of national minorities, to attend the Congress of Oriental Nations at Baku in the Caucasus. He was exhausted and barely had the strength to make the journey, and he resented this new delay in meeting Louise.

On August 25, the day before he was to leave, he invited Angelica Balabanoff to visit him. "I have a little wood and I still have some potatoes. I shall bake them for you," he told her.

She had not seen Reed for several weeks, and found him looking ill and depressed. "It seemed to me that he had aged ten years in the past few weeks. I understood what a blow the Congress had been to him."

"And now comes the farce of Baku," he told her. "Zinoviev has ordered me to leave tomorrow. I will not go. I will tell Zinoviev I can't do it."

Balabanoff knew that Louise was on her way to Russia, but she did not believe that was the reason Reed was reluctant to go to Baku. "Baku would be a repetition, on a smaller scale, of the Moscow Congress," she wrote, "and he had already made up his mind that he had nothing in common with the Comintern."

But Reed decided he would go. "He knew," according to Balabanoff, "that Zinoviev and [Karl] Radek [the Bolshevik's leading propagandist] would stop at nothing to discredit him, and he would not give them the excuse of attacking him on the basis of indiscipline."

Reed left a note for Louise, explaining what had happened.

"I am so disappointed not to be able to meet you when you enter Russia," he said. "But yesterday I was informed that I must go to Baku . . . to attend the Oriental Congress. To this I thought my honey would love to go. I asked for permission to stay here and come later with you. But they refused. Then I asked that you be sent after me. That also cannot be done, because there is a civil war going on down South, and we are going in an armored train. . . . We go tonight. I think the whole trip will take ten days—I hope less."

273

He told her he had been getting all her notes telling him of the progress of her journey and had been eagerly waiting. The Commissariat of Foreign Affairs had sent wires to all the points of her journey, he said, "to see that you had fine treatment and were sent on here at top speed."

He instructed her to see the commandant of the Dielovoy Dvor Hotel when she reached Moscow, and he would provide a room for her. He also gave her the names of other Russians and several Americans who would be awaiting her arrival.

"I am longing to see my honey more than I can tell," he said. "It seems years. . . ." But there was one thing that was worrying him greatly. He must soon try to return to America, and it was going to be difficult for him to get out of Russia—especially so, if accompanied by a woman. "I tried to get word to you to wait for me outside," he said. "But as soon as I found out that you were coming, I was so glad that I was to see my honey sooner."

Reed's trip to Baku—over a thousand miles across the Caucasus Mountains to the Caspian Sea—left him with very mixed emotions. His address to the Oriental Congress was in typical radical-evangelist style.

"I represent the revolutionary workers of one of the greatest imperialist powers—the United States of America," he said. "You know and hate the English, French, and Italian imperialists, but you probably think that 'free America' will rule better, will liberate the colonial peoples, will feed and protect them. But the workers and peasants of the Philippines, the peoples of Central America and of the islands in the Caribbean Sea—they know the meaning of the domination of 'free America.' . . . Don't trust American capitalists. There is but one road to freedom. Unite with the Russian workers and peasants, who overthrew their capitalists, and whose Red Army conquers the troops of the foreign imperialists. Follow the red star of the Communist International!"

Reed was greatly impressed with the colorful sight of 2,000 Turks, Persians, and Armenians, and made it a point to talk personally to as many of them as he could. But the style of the trip to Baku had shocked and sickened him. The armored train, passing through towns and villages whose inhabitants were starving, was supplied with an ostentatious display of rich food and rare wines. When the train entered the Caucasus, it was boarded by beautiful young prostitutes, bought by the Bolshevik leaders for an unabashed orgy. Reed was appalled, not by the flagrant lust displayed by his traveling companions, but by their cynical and hypocritical employment of the capitalist system of barter.

Weary and confused, Reed returned to Moscow. The trip had taken much longer than the ten days he had anticipated. It was mid-September when he got back, and he found Louise waiting. She had arrived two days after his departure for Baku, and had been spending part of nearly every day with Angelica Balabanoff. Even though forewarned by her of Reed's condition, Louise was barely prepared to find him so altered, both in health and spirit.

"On the morning of September 15, he ran shouting into my room," Louise wrote to Max Eastman. "We were terribly happy to find each other. I found him older and sadder and grown strangely gentle and ascetic. His clothes were just rags. He was so impressed with the suffering around him that he would take nothing for himself. I felt shocked and almost unable to reach the pinnacle of fervor he had attained. The effects of the terrible experience in the Finnish jail were all too apparent."

Reed's joy at seeing Louise had a brief, revitalizing effect on him. "Walking in the park, under the white birch trees and talking through brief, happy nights, death and separation seemed very far away," Louise wrote. "We visited together Lenin, Trotsky, Kamenev, we saw the ballet and 'Prince Igor' and the new and old galleries."

To Reed's mother, Louise later wrote, "For one brief, happy week we walked about the city and talked and lived through a second honeymoon.

"I felt how tired and ill he was—how near a breakdown and tried to persuade him to rest. The Russians told me that he often worked twenty hours a day. I asked him to promise me that he would rest before going home, since it only meant going to prison. I felt prison would be too much for him. He looked at me in a strange way and said, 'My dear little Honey, I would do anything I could for you, but don't ask me to be a coward.' I had not meant it so. I felt so hurt that I burst into tears and said he could go and I would go with him anywhere by the next train, to any death or any suffering. He smiled so happily then."

Reed also talked to Louise of his disenchantment; indeed, he no longer bothered to conceal his anger and disappointment, even from the Russian leaders. "Jack noticed how power and the lust for power affected the Bolshevik leaders," Louise later told Benjamin Gitlow. "After his return from Baku he spent a lot of time talking about his experiences and disappointments. He was terribly afraid of having made a serious mistake in his interpretation of an historical event for which he would be held accountable before the judgment of history. He lacked confidence in himself; was not sure of the ground on which he stood. He blamed himself for becoming a politician; he was not cut out for one.

"I tried to argue with him, to bolster up his morale.

'Pull yourself together, Jack,' I pleaded. 'When you get back to the States you can do the things you set your heart on doing.' But he kept looking at me through his saddened eyes and ended up by saying, 'Honey, it's no use.'"

Reed and Louise went together to visit Angelica Balabanoff toward the end of September. "Both of them looked unhappy and tired, and we made no effort to hide from each other what was in our minds. Jack spoke bitterly of the demagogy and display which had characterized the Baku Congress and the manner in which the native population and the Far Eastern delegates had been treated."

While biding his time before making the effort to get himself and Louise back to America, Reed continued to go through the motions of a party delegate, and to at least one foreign visitor in Moscow that fall, he epitomized Communist zeal. She was Clare Sheridan, a British sculptor, whose path Reed crossed briefly, but vividly.

Clare Sheridan was a first cousin of Winston Churchill. She had lived the pampered life of a well-born, well-bred Englishwoman until her husband was killed in the World War. Freed by his death to pursue her latent feminist ideas, she arranged to have her children looked after by relatives and applied herself to a career as a portrait sculptor. To the dismay of her proper family, she demonstrated a remarkable facility for her profession and quickly established herself as a popular portraitist and a liberated woman.

Though politically ignorant, and no Communist, she was fascinated by the romance of the Bolshevik revolution. When Leo Kamenev visited London as his government's emissary in the summer of 1920, she managed to meet him, beguile him, and persuade him to take her back to Russia for the express purpose of doing heads of Lenin and Trotsky. To everyone's surprise but her own, the mission was a success. The two leaders not only found time to sit for her, they chatted with her at some length, and she returned to England after three months, with the busts and a diary, in which she recorded her clear-eyed impressions of the Bolsheviks and of life in Moscow.

Reed amazed her. She described him in her diary as "a well-built, good-looking young man, who has given up everything at home, to throw his heart and life into work here."

"I understand the Russian spirit," she went on, "but what strange force impels an apparently normal young man from the United States? I am told by the Russians that his book, *Ten Days that Shook the World*, is the best book on the Revolution, and that it has become a National classic and is taught in the schools." She was grateful for Reed's advice on how to get started on her promised, but as yet unscheduled, sittings with the Bolshevik leaders. Happening to meet him on September 23, she complained to him that the people Kamenev had delegated to find her a studio and order her clay seemed to be utterly inefficient. "Reed told me that I never would begin work unless I arranged everything for myself, and depended on no one here."

On September 28, Reed complained of dizziness and headaches, and Louise insisted that he go to bed.

"I got a doctor almost at once but [Jack] did not get better," Louise wrote to Reed's mother. "His fever was high. . . . I was told that he had influenza but as the days went by and he got worse and the symptoms were not those of influenza I asked for a consultation and other doctors came. Five days after he went to bed they de-

cided that he had typhus and he was taken to the hospital. I got permission to stay with him although it is by no
means customary to allow any one but doctors and nurses
to remain with a patient. From that time on I did not
leave him. The last five days I did not even take off my
shoes at night but stayed by his bed. . . . Typhus is a
dreadful disease and an epidemic rages in the South now.
He fought so hard for his life—never giving in—trying
and trying to smile and to breathe . . . his right side became paralyzed and they told me it would have probably
been permanent—but even then I prayed that he might
live. He was not able to speak after the stroke but he held
me tightly by the hand through the hardest hours and at
2 o'clock on the night of October 17 he died.

"And an hour after that they pulled me away. He was
quite cold but I could not leave."

Reed's mind, as he lay dying, was "full of stories and
poems and beautiful thoughts," Louise later wrote. "He
would say: 'You know how it is when you go to Venice.
You ask people—Is this Venice?—just for the pleasure of
hearing the reply.' He would tell me that the water he
drank was full of little songs."

To Eastman, Louise wrote, "He would have died days
before but for the fight he made. The old peasant nurses
used to slip out to the Chapel and pray for him and burn
a candle for his life. Even they were touched and they
see men die in agony every hour. Spotted typhus is beyond description. The patient wastes to nothing under
your eyes.

"He was never delirious in the hideous way most typhus patients are. He related, like a child, wonderful experiences we had together and in which we were very
brave. . . . I have a feeling now that I have no right to be
alive."

Reed would have been thirty-three on October 20. On that day, he lay in state in the Labor Temple in Moscow, guarded by fourteen soldiers. The funeral was to take place on the following Sunday, October 24, in order, as Louise wrote to Reed's mother, that all the workers could attend.

To Eastman she wrote: "Many times I went [to the Labor Temple] and saw the soldiers standing stiffly, their bayonets gleaming under the lights and the red star of Communism on their military caps. Jack lay in a long silver coffin banked with flowers and streaming banners. Once the soldiers uncovered it for me so I might touch the high white forehead with my lips for the last time."

Reed was to be buried "in the most honored spot in Russia beside all the great heroes in the Kremlin," Louise wrote to Reed's mother. She said that she had applied for permission to bring Reed's body home, but because of the blockade and the fact that he had died of typhus, she did not think the request would be granted. "But, darling Muz," she added, "you know how honored he is here—and how all foreigners will visit his grave for all time here."

Her own life, Louise said, was "nothing" anymore. She wanted just to do one thing—come home and get Reed's papers in order.

"I do not want anything he has written to be lost. . . . The only plan I have in the world now is to do as well as I can this last service for Jack. . . . I haven't the courage to think what it is going to be like [without him]. I have never really loved any one else in the whole world but Jack, and we were terribly close to each other. . . . I shall work very, very hard and hope Fate will be kind to me and not make my life long. No one has ever been so alone as I am. I have lost everything now. . . . I never had any children because our life was so troubled. . . . I did not want to hold him back and so I gave everything to keep him safe—and I could not think of children. . . . But when I met him here this time he told me he thought we ought to have one child anyway no matter what the circumstances might be and I agreed and we were very happy thinking of all this. But now I shall never, never be a mother—and I can never be happy again. . . .

"Sometimes when I am most unhappy I am a little consoled by the thought that I managed to get here as I did. It was so difficult and yet if I had not done so I would never have seen him again and he would have died all alone. . . .

"You know, dear Muz, that I would rather have died a thousand times than have had anything happen to Jack. But it was not possible for him to survive such a disease with only one kidney. . . . Be brave, dear little mother. Jack was a beautiful and wonderful person and his memory demands that at least of us."

With his death, Reed became almost immediately a mythic figure and the center of a controversy: Did he die a committed Communist, or was he disillusioned with the Bolshevik experiment, and ready to break with Communism? The fact that the Russians buried him at the foot of the Kremlin wall (and have not since written him out of their history) is proof only that it has suited their purpose to regard him as a staunch Communist to the end.

Reed's friends and admirers in America were and still are less united in their view. Those of his colleagues who remained members of the American Communist Party, following the hard party line dictated by the Kremlin, maintained long after his death that Reed was, and would have continued to be, one of them. Others, like Benjamin

Gitlow and Max Eastman, themselves disillusioned with the Bolshevik experiment, maintained that Reed was ready to cut away from Communism just before he died, and would certainly not have remained a party member, had he returned to America.

Reed's actions—apart from the opinions he expressed to Louise and Angelica Balabanoff—in the months before he died, tend to support the latter view. He openly opposed the Comintern leadership, let Zinoviev know unequivocally of his hatred for him, and even, at one point, attempted to resign from the Executive Committee. According to Granville Hicks, Reed was persuaded to withdraw this offer.

According to Max Eastman, the question of Reed's resignation and reinstatement was never satisfactorily explained. Drawing on his memory (twenty-two years after Reed's death), Eastman quoted Louise's account to him of what had happened:

"Zinoviev and Radek got him aside, and Zinoviev said to him: 'Reed, you can't afford to do this—we'll destroy you. You can't fight the organization. We'll destroy you, Reed. You're with us and you've got to stay with us.'

"And Jack said: 'It hasn't worried me when American capitalists threatened to destroy me, and I'm not afraid of you either—go ahead and do your worst.'

"He just came home, hot and angry and tragically discouraged and lay down on the bed and turned his face to the wall, and would hardly speak. And all during his illness none of the Russian leaders came to see him or paid any attention to him until I went to see Lenin, and he gave orders that the best physicians and the best care available in Moscow should be provided."

Emma Goldman also wrote a brief account of Reed's death in her autobiography, published in 1931. Her facts are so garbled that it is impossible to assess the truth of any of it. She said that Reed was stricken with typhus in Baku, that Louise told her he had finally been turned over, in Moscow, to "an incompetent doctor" and that he had not, in his last days, "even been aware of the presence of his beloved." Emma Goldman had a tendency to color the behavior and feelings of her friends with her own powerful emotions, and what she attributed to Louise was probably at least fifty percent Emma.

She said that she asked Louise, before the funeral, "Didn't he speak at all?" And Louise answered, "I could not understand what he meant, but he kept on repeating all the time: 'Caught in a trap, caught in a trap.' Just that."

"Did Jack really use that term?" Emma Goldman said she cried in amazement.

"Why do you ask?" Louise demanded, gripping her hand.

"Because," Emma Goldman replied, "that is exactly how I have been feeling since I looked beneath the surface. Caught in a trap. Exactly that."

At his death, Reed was technically still a Communist. But there is little doubt that he was disillusioned. To a humanist like Reed, dedicated above everything to the alleviation of human misery, it was bitterly apparent that applied Communism was not going to provide the answer.

Communist or not, Reed surely would have approved of the ceremony that accompanied his burial. It had the pageantry and drama to which he was always responsive. And it was attended by throngs of the Russian workingmen and soldiers with whom he had so profoundly identified.

Clare Sheridan was among those who attended Reed's

funeral on October 24. "It is the first funeral without a religious service that I have ever seen," she wrote. "It did not seem to strike any one else as peculiar, but it was to me. His coffin stood for some days in the Trades Union Hall [or Labor Temple], the walls of which are covered with huge revolutionary cartoons in marvelously bright decorative coloring. We all assembled in that hall. The coffin stood on a dais and was covered with flowers. As a bit of staging it was very effective, but I saw when they were being carried out that most of the wreaths were made of tin flowers painted. I suppose they did service for each Revolutionary burial.

"There was a great crowd, but people talked very low. . . . I followed the procession to the grave, accompanied by a band playing a funeral march that I had never heard before. Whenever that funeral march struck up . . . everyone uncovered—it seemed to be the only thing they uncovered for. . . . He was buried under the Kremlin wall next to all the Revolutionaries, his comrades. As a background to his grave was a large red banner nailed upon the wall with the letters in gold, 'The leaders die, but the cause lives on.'

"When I was first told this was the burying ground of the Revolutionaries I looked in vain for graves—and I saw only a quarter of a mile or so of green grassy bank. There was not a memorial, a headstone or a sign, not even an individual mound. . . .

"A large crowd assembled for Reed's burial and the occasion was one for speeches. . . . There were speeches in English, French, German and Russian. It took a very long time, and a mixture of rain and snow was falling. Although the poor widow fainted, her friends did not take her away. It was extremely painful to see this white-faced unconscious woman lying back on the supporting arm of

284

a Foreign Office official, more interested in the speeches than in the human agony. . . . I could not go to her, as I was outside the ring of soldiers who stood guard nearly shoulder to shoulder."

Louise's account of the funeral, sent in a letter to Eastman, is a nightmare of personal anguish. "On the day of the funeral," she wrote, "we gathered in the great hall where he lay. I have very few impressions of that day. It was cold and the sky dark, snow fell as we began to march. I was conscious of how people cried and of how the banners floated and how the wailing heart-breaking Revolutionary funeral hymn, played by a military band, went on forever and ever.

"The Russians let me take my grief in my own way, since they felt I had thrown all caution to the winds in going to the hospital. On that day I felt very proud and even strong. I wished to walk according to the Russian custom, quite by myself after the hearse. And in the Red Square I tried to stand facing the speakers with a brave face. But I was not brave at all and fell on the ground and could not speak or cry.

"I do not remember the speeches. I remember more the broken notes of the speakers' voices. I was aware that after a long time they ceased and the banners began to dip back and forth in salute. I heard the first shovel of earth go rolling down and then something snapped in my brain. After an eternity I woke up in my own bed. Emma Goldman was standing there, and two doctors and a tall young officer from the Red Army. They were whispering and so I went to sleep again.

"But I have been in the Red Square since then—since that day all those people came to bury in all honor our dear Jack Reed. I have been there in the busy afternoon when all Russia hurries by, horses and sleighs and bells and peasants carrying bundles, soldiers singing on their way to the front. Once some of the soldiers came over to the grave. They took off their hats and spoke very reverently. 'What a good fellow he was!' said one. 'He came all the way across the world for us.' 'He was one of ours—' In another moment they shouldered their guns and went on again.

"I have been there under the stars with a great longing to lie down beside the frozen flowers and the metallic wreaths and not wake up. How easy it would be!"

Epilogue

LOUISE WAS CRUSHED BY Reed's death. "Jack's death and my strenuous underground trip to Russia and the weeks of horror in the typhus hospital have quite broken me," she wrote to Max Eastman. "At the funeral I suffered a very severe heart attack which by the merest scratch I survived. Specialists have agreed that I have strained my heart because of the long days and nights I watched beside Jack's bed and that it is enlarged and may not ever get well again. . . . I have to take stimulants and I am not in a bit of pain. I think I have better recuperative powers than they believe."

Louise did recover physically, and emerged from the state of stunned grief into which Reed's death had plunged her. She went on to a brief period of success as a journalist, re-married, and even became a mother. But Reed's memory continued to haunt her, and gave her no peace.

A poem she wrote soon after her return to America illustrates the melancholia that gripped her and held her until her own death.

> Now you are gone—and past our garden hedge
> Walk strangers . . . little knowing
> How brave and fine a soul
> Has loved those clapboard walls,
> That scraggling lilac or yonder spreading elm.
> The young fruit trees remember yet, perhaps,

How gently with your hands
You smoothed their roots in planting . . .
No lesser than a poet could feel
How shrubs and flowers shrink from rougher touch.
Oh, ever-dear and honored love,
I go my lonely way
Far from our garden's sweetly smiling roses.
Yet always does their fragrance
Reach me and enfold me—
Even as now my fancy brings you close
And you're more real to me than all the living.
For nightly do I walk with you
The moonlit roads of home
And there we mingle laughter with caresses
And stories of adventure without end.
What matter if I wake in tears at cock-crow?
I'll have the dreams again at night . . .
And after many dreams the long dream
From which I'll wake not
And no spell of stars be broken.

To a friend, she wrote: "It has been terrible to come back, more terrible than I ever dreamed. I want to finish all these things I have to do so I can go away and not come back."

Three years after Reed's death, Louise married William Bullitt. Bullitt had been in Russia briefly in 1919 on a secret mission to Lenin for Woodrow Wilson, but Louise had left by then and when she met Bullitt in Paris in 1922, it was the first time the two had seen each other since their casual acquaintance in Washington in 1916.

Bullitt, at the time of their meeting, was living in self-styled "exile" from government service. He had quarreled with Wilson after his secret mission to Moscow, and was not to re-enter the diplomatic field until his close friend, Franklin D. Roosevelt, appointed him ambassador to

Moscow in 1933. Louise, in the three years following Reed's death, had been reporting for the Hearst papers from Russia, Turkey, and western Europe. She produced another book, *Mirrors of Moscow*. Her great journalistic coup was an exclusive interview with Mussolini in 1922—the first he had granted to an American.

The courtship of Bullitt and Louise was the sensation of European society. Bullitt was then thirty-one, four years younger than Louise (but Louise, at this point, admitted to being only thirty). He was married to a beautiful Philadelphia woman named Ernesta Drinker, and they maintained lavish establishments in New York and Paris. Many of their friends were shocked when the Bullitts were divorced in 1923 and when, later that year, he married Louise.

Lincoln Steffens's second wife, Ella Winter, wrote about their marriage when Louise was pregnant. "Billy hovered over her like a mother hen," she said, "and when one night he returned to find Stef reading aloud from Joyce's *Ulysses*, he was furious. 'Think of the baby,' he shouted, 'our child—what will it turn out to be if it hears language like that?'" The baby, a girl, was born in 1924; she was named Anne Moen (an elision of Louise's family name, Mohan).

The marriage was not successful. Bullitt, though convivial in society, was a cold man. Louise began drinking heavily. Bullitt divorced her in 1930, charging "personal indignities," and six-year-old Anne Moen stayed with her father.

Louise returned to live for a time in Greenwich Village. As if deliberately to shut herself up with Reed's ghost, she moved into the last apartment she had shared with him in Patchin Place. She tried again, as she had tried many times before, to organize the material she had collected into a book about Reed. The need to write the book was obsessive, but the need to forget her pain was more so. She continued to drink destructively and her drinking led her into ugly little public episodes that embarrassed her and her friends.

Less than two years after her divorce she was involved in the sort of minor, shabby incident that was typical of the life she was living.

It was January 18, 1932, a cold, foggy day. Louise was waiting in the old Jefferson Market Courthouse at Sixth Avenue and Tenth Street to testify in a case she had set in motion, but in which she had already lost interest. She was dressed fashionably, but not quite tidily. Her figure, at forty-four, was still slender, but the delicate lines of her heart-shaped face were blurred. Her large, blue-gray eyes had lost their candor and her chin its jaunty tilt.

A few days earlier she had reported a theft to the police of the Charles Street Station—the theft of a Spanish comb. The man she had accused of taking the comb—he, too, was waiting in the courtroom—was a thin, unshaven, thirty-year-old clerk named Julius Mack. The comb was a valuable antique, but that was not why Louise had brought her charge.

Mack had been her lover for a year. During that time he had helped himself to a number of Louise's possessions. She had until now excused this petty thieving. But she had discovered that Mack had given the stolen Spanish comb to another woman, the flamboyant owner of a famous Village restaurant, and a self-styled clairvoyant, known as Romany Marie. Wounded to the depth of her tattered vanity, Louise had made this pitiful gesture of assertiveness. But now she wavered.

Called before the judge, she summoned the shreds of her dignity and declared that she had decided not to press charges against Mack. "It would be injurious to my reputation," she told the judge.

The court reporter for the *Herald Tribune* had recognized Louise's name, listened with interest to the brief proceedings, and cornered her as she left the courtroom. For an instant, Louise's eyes flashed with their old defiance. "It just happened, that's all, and I'm very sorry and have nothing to say," she told the reporter. But the reporter, who had followed Louise's career and knew her background, managed to get up a full column that ran in the next day's newspaper.

Louise had very little money. Bullitt must have made some sort of financial settlement, but it was not, evidently, a generous one. (He had been so humiliated by Louise's behavior that he had insisted that the papers in the divorce case be sealed.)

The misery of Louise's life in Greenwich Village finally became more than she could bear. She scrounged the money for a steamship ticket and, early in 1935, sailed for Paris. She still had vanity enough to lie about her age. On her passport renewal application she gave the year of her birth as 1894, this time taking off seven years. But it was a pitiful deception. She was forty-eight, pretending to be forty-one, and by now she looked a dissipated fifty.

Living in a shabby hotel on the Left Bank, she continued to drag out her life. She began taking drugs in addition to drinking and became so ill that she had to spend some time in a sanitarium. Released, she went back to drugs and drinking.

Angelica Balabanoff, having broken with the Bolsheviks, was now living in Europe, and when she visited Paris she was told by a mutual friend that Louise was not likely to live much longer. She soon had an opportunity to judge for herself.

"I scarcely recognized her," she wrote. "I would not have believed that anyone could change so, not only in appearance, but in her manner of speaking, her voice and tone. Only at intervals when I continued to see her was she the old Louise I had known with Jack. Whenever we met, she spoke of him with deep sadness, of his disappointment in Russia, his illness and death.

"'Oh, Angelica,' she would say in these moments of lucidity and confidence, 'don't leave me, I feel so lonely. Why did I have to lose Jack? Why did we both have to lose our faith?'"

During this time, Art Young also heard from Louise. He had been told by friends of her condition and concluded, accurately, that she was, "committing slow suicide."

"I suppose in the end life gets all of us," Louise wrote to Young. "It nearly has got me now—getting myself and my friends out of jail—living under curious conditions—but never minding much. . . . Know always I send my love to you across the stars. If you get there before I do . . . tell Jack Reed I love him.

Janet Flanner, the writer, knew Louise during her marriage to Bullitt and saw her when she returned to France. Louise's drinking, Miss Flanner said, had been a terrible embarrassment to Bullitt. He had tried to have her committed to a nursing home. She felt persecuted by him and developed a bitter hatred for him, which made her behave even worse.

"Her life was a maelstrom," Miss Flanner said. "When she came back to Paris she was in the lowest stage of degradation. One of the last times I saw her was on a rainy night when I was walking along Rue Vavin in Montparnasse. Literally out of the gutter rose a terrifying creature. Her face was so warped, I didn't recognize her. She held up her hand. 'Don't you recognize this?' she asked, showing me a sapphire ring." Miss Flanner recognized it as a ring Bullitt had given her. Still, she could scarcely believe it was Louise.

Louise died on January 6, 1936. She was forty-nine. The newspaper accounts said that her death was caused by a cerebral hemorrhage. She had collapsed while climbing the stairs to her room in the Hotel Liberia, and had died in a nearby hospital shortly afterward.

But Louise had died in spirit sixteen years earlier. She had merely been going through the motions since the day Reed's coffin was lowered into its grave beside the Kremlin wall.

I AM GREATLY INDEBTED to Granville Hicks, whose book *John Reed, the Making of a Revolutionary* (The Macmillan Co., 1936) has been an invaluable source of material. Mr. Hicks also was very helpful in providing me with additional material based on his correspondence and personal recollections of the Reed era and in guiding me to friends and acquaintances of Reed.

The Harvard University Library was the chief source for letters, photographs, and other memorabilia. Additional information came from the Yale University Library, the California State Library, Syracuse University Manuscript Collection, Henry E. Huntington Library and Art Gallery, the University of Oregon, and the University of Nevada.

My very warm thanks to Leonard Harris, whose expertise as an editor and publisher and whose devotion as a friend were of great help during various stages of the preparation of this book.

Most of the persons interviewed for their recollections of John Reed and Louise Bryant are acknowledged in the text. I thank them, again, for their help and cooperation.

I want also to thank the following persons who helped me on one aspect or another of my research and writing: Wayne Thompson, Lou Rasmussen, Nona Parkin, Horace W. Robinson, Robert E. Ericson, Katherine Caldwell, Brenda Ueland, Alan R. Ottley, Rita Semel, Robert O. Anthony, Jack Shirley, Gertrude Ruhnka, Marvin Kalb, Joseph Vecchione, Alma Brackett, Alden Whitman, and Jon Rosenthal.

INDEX

Adams, Franklin P., 83
Addams, Jane, 226
American Federation of Labor, 270
American Magazine:
    writing by Louise Bryant, 136
    writing by John Reed, 45–47, 51, 55
Anderson, Sherwood, 53
Astor, Vincent, 129

Balabanoff, Angelica, 193, 267–68, 291
    and Louise Bryant, 275, 277, 291–92
    My Life as a Rebel, 193–94
    and John Reed, 193–94, 267, 268, 273, 277, 282
Barnes, Djuna, 127
Barnes, Earl, 200, 207, 208
Beatty, Bessie, 168, 171
Bell Syndicate:
    writing by Louise Bryant, 123, 144
Benchley, Robert, 111–12
Berkman, Alexander, 127, 136
Boardman, Sally, 156
Bodenheim, Maxwell, 76
Boissevan, Eugen, 145, 196
Bolatov, Colonel, 74
Boni and Liveright, 212, 213, 261
Boulton, Agnes, 185
    and Eugene O'Neill, 185–89 *passim*
        marriage and divorce, 96, 189–91
    Part of a Long Story, 186, 187–88
Boyce, Neith:
    Trifles, 89
Boyd, Fred, 227, 231
Bradhurst, Maunsell, 123
Breshkovsky, Katherine, 171–73
Brisbane, Arthur, 133
Broun, Heywood, 136
Bryan, William Jennings, 80–81
Bryant, Louise (Anna Louise Mohan):
    age, lies about, 9, 13, 289, 291

arrest in Washington, 215, 217, 221
and Angelica Balabanoff, 275, 277, 291–92
and Earl Barnes:
    correspondence, 207
birth and early life, 11, 35, 36–37
and William C. Bullitt:
    marriage and divorce, 288, 289, 291, 292
daughter, Anne Moen Bullitt, 289
death of, 293
descriptions of, 9–10, 12, 35, 42, 79, 105, 106, 122, 184, 242, 290, 292–93
and Mrs. Mabel Dodge, 79–80
and Max Eastman, 79
    correspondence, 272, 275, 279, 285–86, 287
education, 35, 37–39
and Sara Bard Field, 18, 42, 232
    correspondence, 18
and Benjamin Gitlow, 276–77
and Emma Goldman, 79, 253, 285
health, 108, 112–16 *passim,* 228, 229, 287
    drinking and drugs, 289, 290, 291, 292
journalism, *see* writing and journalism
lectures, *see* Russia, lectures and speeches on
and Nikolai Lenin, 180–81, 276, 282
love affairs of, 11, 12, 80, 81
    Julius Mack, 290–91
    see also and Eugene O'Neill
in New York (1930–35), 289–91
and Eugene O'Neill, 84, 86, 90, 91, 93, 94, 95
    correspondence, 184, 186–90 *passim*
    love affair, 95, 96, 97, 101, 102, 103, 105, 106, 108, 110, 122, 125, 184–91 *passim,* 196, 223
in Paris:
    in 1917, 123–41 *passim*
    in 1935–36, 291–93

297